WITHD

CREATE
YOUR OWN
RELIGION

CREATE

YOUR OWN

RELIGION

A HOW-TO BOOK WITHOUT INSTRUCTIONS

DANIELE BOLELLI

disinformation®

Published by Disinformation Books
An imprint of Red Wheel/Weiser, LLC
With offices at
665 Third Street, Suite 400
San Francisco, CA 94107
www.redwheelweiser.com

ISBN: 978-1-938875-02-1

Library of Congress Cataloging-in-Publication data available upon request

Cover design by Jim Warner
Interior design by Dutton & Sherman
Typeset in Adobe Garamond Pro and Univers LT Std

Printed in the United States of America
TS

10 9 8 7 6 5 4 3 2 1

CONTENTS

CHAPTER 1

A CALL TO ARMS: CREATE YOUR OWN RELIGION

What you are holding in your hands is not another angry, organized religion-bashing atheist book; it is not a New Age self-help book revealing the deep secret that positive thinking is better than negative thinking; and it most certainly is not an academic dissertation on the world's religious traditions.

It is true that a strange twist of fate has pushed me into an academic career teaching university courses on the history of religion as well as a few other subjects. It is also true that in these pages you will find references to individuals and practices from many religious traditions that may not exactly be common knowledge to those readers who have better things to do than pore through impossibly thick volumes on the topic. But make no mistake about it—this is not an academic work. Most scholars love spending their time devising new ways to dissect knowledge into tiny compartments and making it completely irrelevant to anyone's life—dusty creatures who forgot that real life takes place outside of the library. The game is being played in front of their eyes, but rather than joining it, they prefer to sit on the sidelines and observe. No, this book is about real life, and as such, it dwells outside the boundaries of academic knowledge.

Since I have spent quite a few lines telling you what this book is not, now may be a good time to begin telling you what this book is. What you are holding in your hands is a call to arms. It is an open invitation to tackle the key questions at the root of all religious traditions and, for that matter, of life itself. It is an invitation to question all the values, all the beliefs, all the worldviews that humanity has so far held as sacred in order to find the answers we need to the very practical problems facing us. The goal is nothing short of reexamining what it means to be human and bringing a better way of life into existence.

If this seems like a daunting, overly ambitious goal, you are probably right. Timidity was never my strong point. This is not a task for small-minded people. We are on a quest to shake off the dust from the theoretical building blocks on which modern civilization rests. Our worldviews are in desperate need of some housecleaning. We enter the twenty-first century still carrying on our backs the prejudices and ways of thinking of countless past generations. What worked for them may or may not still be of use, so it is our job to save the tools that are still relevant and let go of the dead weight.

I am inviting you to embark on an adventure with a double purpose. The first is purely personal. On an individual level, one of the healthiest things we can do is question everything we have ever been taught. This is not motivated by disrespect or some adolescent desire to be rebellious. It is simply what becoming an adult is all about. Once we are old enough to figure things out for ourselves, we can look back at the beliefs we were taught to live by and decide what works for us and what doesn't. Any parent who is not a psychotic control freak would be proud to see his or her kids grow up to think for themselves. Most people, however, go through existence in a state of perpetual psychological infancy. They hold on to certain beliefs because that's what they were taught. They internalize some values as kids and never stop to think about whether those values are actually healthy or not. Like trained poodles, they will simply live their lives according to the rules that were passed on to them. They never become individuals, never psychologically grow up and choose their own values—they are mere machines replicating a program that was downloaded in their brains.

What this book proposes to do is to look at many religions' answers to the key questions of human existence and, on the basis of this knowledge, come up with our own answers. In some cases, what resonates as true to you may be identical to an answer that already exists within a certain religious tradition; in other cases, it may come from mixing answers from different traditions; and in yet other cases, you may end up rejecting everything that has been proposed so far and create new answers that satisfy you better.

This book is not going to try to sell you on a particular ideology. Obviously, I will be answering these questions from my particular perspective, but the goal here is not to turn readers into Bolelli-clones going around spouting my ideas. I am not inviting you to trade a prepackaged ideology for a new one. I don't want to make anyone my follower, and I certainly don't want to be anyone's follower. Life is too short to spend it living according to somebody else's dogma. This is simply a blueprint to give you ideas and stimulate you to come up with your own worldview.

Moving beyond the individual level, the second purpose of this book is much more global in scale. Humanity today finds itself at the proverbial crossroad. On one side, we have the technological skills to dramatically improve life on the planet in very meaningful ways. Never in human history have we had so much power at our fingertips. For the first time, people across the globe can communicate with each other at astonishing speed, and many are beginning to look at life from a global perspective rather than from the narrowly provincial one that has characterized human life so far. On the other side, the beginning of the twenty-first century finds us flirting dangerously with self-destruction. Whereas some technologies can help solve our global crisis, others have the power to annihilate us. Our beliefs, values, and ideas are what determine how our increasing power will be employed. If it was perhaps excusable for human beings to hold on to crude and potentially dangerous beliefs when our capacities did not exceed those of glorified baboons, we can no longer afford plain, old-fashioned stupidity—not when we have the ability to wipe each other out and take the natural world along with us. There hasn't been a better time for a dramatic shift in human consciousness than now. Our very survival is at stake. What we need is a new way to face life that will increase our chances of tilting toward happiness and wonder rather than misery and species-suicide. As good old Albert Einstein put it, "We shall require a substantial new manner of thinking if humanity is to survive."[1] And this is exactly what this book is for. A better world needs to start somewhere, and there is no easier place to begin the work than in our hearts and minds.

I hold no naïve expectation that humanity is going to achieve collective enlightenment any time soon. There is a thin line between idealism and self-delusion. If our hopes rested on a global awakening, we would be in serious trouble. Betting on gloom and doom would be much more logical. However, if a strong enough minority of people changed positively in their thought and capacity for action, and if most other people at least switched to less destructive beliefs, it would be more than enough to give cause for celebration.

Religion Is Here to Stay

So how does religion enter the picture? After all, wasn't religion supposed to become obsolete in the modern world? Scholars, journalists, and various pundits have been proclaiming for over a century that the popularity of religion would steadily decline. In an age in which science, reason, and separation of church and state are becoming the bedrocks of modernity, many expected it would just be a matter of time before religions would fade away.

If there were a prize for the least successful prophecy in recorded history, this would be a top contender. Forget fading away. Flying in the face of what the experts predicted, religion remains as important today to billions of people around the world as it ever was. The only place religion has declined in popularity is Western Europe, where mostly secular outlooks dominate, and overcrowding is never an issue in church. Put your finger anywhere else on the map and you will run into a very different story. With the end of the Cold War, more wars are waged now because of religion than for any other ideological reason. Religious doctrines affect the laws and policies of most countries on earth, including those that are theoretically based on separation of church and state. The clash between religious conservatives and those arguing for more individual freedoms that for several decades has characterized the political discourse in the United States is becoming a global phenomenon.

The reasons why all the predictions about the demise of religion have failed miserably are fairly obvious. No matter how much scientific knowledge continues to grow, as long as human beings don't find answers to certain questions (Is there any meaning in life? Where do we come from? What happens after we die?), they will continue to turn to religion. Science is simply too dry to fill the void left by leaving those questions unanswered. For better or worse, religion is central to how most human beings perceive themselves and the world around them. Thus, it is plain stupid to assume that religion is irrelevant to finding a solution to the problems facing us: religion is both part of the problem and part of the solution.

Religion or Philosophy?

Before leading you on too far, let's set the record straight about how I will use the word "religion" throughout this book. I don't need psychic powers to foresee that quite a few readers will have problems with it. Many will be puzzled when they find out that what I argue does not require believing in the afterlife or in the existence of God and is not in any way based on faith.

How does what you advocate fit the definition of religion? they will ask. In an effort to avoid leaving you stranded in ambiguity, let's deal with this issue right here, right now. Once, during the course of a lecture, an audience member asked renowned quantum physicist David Bohm, "Professor Bohm, this is all very interesting philosophy. But what does it have to do with physics?" Bohm replied, "I do not make that distinction."[2]

No clue where I am going with this? Let me try with another example. In 1492, when Christopher Columbus began shoplifting the American continent from its indigenous peoples, he wrote back home that "Indians could easily be made Christians because it seems to me that they have no religion of their own."[3] Following in Columbus' footsteps, many European colonists thought that American

Indians practiced no religion because they never saw them going to church or performing actions that the colonists could identify as distinctly "religious." In an odd way, you could say they were right. Among the hundreds of American Indian languages that existed, we would be hard-pressed to find a single word that could be translated as "religion." If by "religion" we intend a special set of beliefs and practices that are separated from day-to-day activities, Columbus was dead on. Native peoples had no religion. But the truth was that religion pervaded every aspect of their lives. As a Dineh tribal member stated, "We don't have a religion, but we do have a 'way.'"[4] The "way" referred to here is what exists before religion is formalized into a set of theological dogmas and rituals. It's what writer Peter Matthiessen calls "religion before religion."[5] From this perspective, the entire spectrum of a healthy way of life is religion. The rest is a bunch of useless theology.

If we restrict our definition of religion to the belief in a god or gods, strict rules of behavior, and an emphasis on faith and the afterlife, then early Buddhism, much of Taoism, Confucianism, and Shinto, along with many different Animistic traditions, would not fit the bill; rather, they would be considered philosophies. The traditions just mentioned are more than pure philosophical systems because they focus on nonrational experiences such as meditation and rituals. Yet they are not religions in the classic sense, either. Personally, I am not incredibly interested in debating the subtle differences between religion and philosophy. The ideas we will discuss in this book can appeal to people who believe in the existence of one or multiple gods as well as to people who don't. Does this make this book more philosophical or religious? If I may steal Clark Gable's famous line, "Frankly, my dear, I don't give a damn." We have too many important things on our plate to waste time arguing about semantics. To the readers who feel that the dictionary police are on their side: I suggest you close the book, cross the word "religion" from the cover, and write "philosophy" or whatever else you prefer in its place. I have no quarrel with you calling it whatever you want to call it in order to feel better (although simply removing that giant, very stiff dictionary from your butt and relaxing a little may provide the relief needed). Ultimately, regardless of which name we attach to it, the quest here remains to search outside of existing dogma for ways to connect with ourselves and the universe, and walk through life in a healthy way.

Knock, Knock . . . The Inquisition Is at the Door (a.k.a. Everyone Already Creates Their Own Religion — Some People Just Don't Lie About It)

Shaking the semantic Nazis off our trail was just a warm-up, however. Once we get to the essence of what this book is arguing, things may get considerably more heated. In many times and places, a call inviting people to create their own religion would be enough to send the villagers into a frenzy, convincing them to dust off their pitchforks and light their torches. The whole notion of creating one's own religion goes against the claim made by many religions that they alone possess the Only Truth revealed to them by the deity of their choosing. In their eyes, religion is to be followed by human beings, but is never created by them. Countless people have been burned at the stake for simply urging others to challenge religious dogma and question beliefs. While this injunction is no longer followed literally, Jewish scriptures sanction the murder of anyone inviting us to change religious outlook. The Inquisition, which lasted over 600 years, fills the history of Christianity with plenty of mass killings of people whose only crime was holding unconventional opinions in matters of religion. Still today, in some Muslim countries, any Muslim who decides to abandon Islam faces the death penalty for apostasy.

Why such venom and brutality? Because many of those claiming to be speaking for God have little patience for people who want to figure out for themselves what life is about. What is so terrible about it? Because *you* should not search for what is wise and good. You should listen to what *we* tell you is wise and good.

In light of these attitudes, it should become clear why a call to "create your own religion" is by its very nature quite radical. But it doesn't have to be that way. OK, since you are a most pleasant reader, I'll share a secret with you. Lean toward me so that I may whisper it in your ear. . . . Everyone already creates their own religion. Some people just don't lie about it.

Did I say something offensive or shocking? It's a dirty job, but somebody's got to do it. At the risk of raising the blood pressure of some modern wannabe inquisitors, let's look at the ugly truth for what it is. Despite their professed devotion to a text or a teacher or a path, even members of established religions don't observe literally the dictates of their religion of choice. Many believers claim to be strict followers of their traditions, and some actually believe they are. But the reality is that they all are engaged to some degree in a selective reading of their sacred texts, adopting what suits them and rejecting the rest. It's a simple process, really. Pick up the sacred books of your religion, look for passages supporting your values, and adapt them a little to your liking. Then highlight their importance in the overall balance of the religion, and conveniently forget all those other unsavory passages that either downright contradict your values or support behaviors and attitudes that don't fit with your inclinations. Rather than having the guts to admit what they are doing and openly defend their right to pick and choose the passages they want to live their lives by, most people prefer hiding under the fable that their particular take on religion is the only correct one. All other people who put the accent on different messages and values contained in the same scriptures, they claim, are heretics who are twisting the essence of the religion. If this strikes you as intellectually dishonest, it's because it is.

Hey Bolelli, are you really accusing billions of orthodox believers worldwide of being consummate liars? Not necessarily. Some don't lie consciously. They just happen to be masters at self-delusion, so skilled at lying to themselves that they can do it without ever becoming aware of it. Why would they do this? you may ask. Because it would be too scary to take responsibility for choosing which values, among so many, to live by. It's much more reassuring to go on pretending that one's values are the only true eternal ones that enjoy God's stamp of approval.

Other believers, on the other hand, don't lie at all—not even subconsciously. What shields them from facing the contradictions that exist in every religious tradition, including their own, is plain old ignorance. As is the case with many faithful followers, their actual knowledge just doesn't match their religious passion. Great numbers of Christians have never read the Bible cover to cover. Many Muslims only know the Koran through the passages their preachers decide to share with them. The same goes for the adherents of most religions. In the absence of direct knowledge, most people end up espousing some simplistic fairy tale version of what they believe their religion is about, never bothering to find out that reality is quite a bit more complicated. They are too lazy and unwilling to deal with complexity to want to dig a little deeper. It is easy to avoid facing contradictions if you don't know about them. And the dealers of second-hand religious fairy tales are very careful to feed their audience only coherent, simple stories that will not require them to ask questions and think for themselves. Still mad about the day when they were told that there is no Santa, masses of people swallow up these stories and gladly ask for more.

Even if ignorance were not so widespread, things would not be much simpler. If you care to lean toward me again, I'll share with you one more secret: most sacred books revered by various religions are filled with internal contradictions. Since the contradictory character of most scriptures leads believers to pick and choose which passages to follow and which to ignore, it should come as no surprise that the very same sacred books have been used to support drastically opposite ideas. During the American Civil War, Abraham Lincoln noted that, "Both [Southern and Northern soldiers] read the same Bible, and pray to the same God; and each invokes his aid against the other."[6] It was in this same time period, after all, that Christians used the Bible to argue for the abolition of slavery while just as many Christians found in the Bible the ideological ammunition to support slavery as a divinely ordained institution.

Other time periods tell the same tale. Early Christians were as divided then as modern Christians are today. For example, Saint Paul advocated celibacy and held a very negative view of any type of physical pleasure, whereas second century CE Christian teacher Carpocrates stirred his followers toward juicy sexual orgies. Martin Luther King Jr. was a Christian and so were the members of the Ku Klux Klan. Protestants and Catholics have slaughtered each other for a couple of hundred years all in the name of Jesus. Even today, you can find Christians who are gay and Christians who consider homosexuality to be the most horrid of sins; Christian feminists and Christians who abhor feminism; anticapitalist Christians who view the accumulation of wealth as a sin, and Christians who believe wealth to be a sign of divine blessing; Christians who are very liberal, and Christians who are very conservative. Naturally, they all believe God supports their point of view.

This same story could be repeated about pretty much any other religion. Each denomination is usually firmly convinced that it is the only one that is faithful to the original message of its tradition and accuse all others of having strayed away. The simple fact that every religion always gives rise to multiple variations (Christianity, for example, has over 30,000 different denominations) is enough to tell us that Truth with a capital *t* is not exactly self-evident.

Trying to figure out who is right is a hopeless undertaking. We are too far removed from the origins of most religions to establish with any degree of certainty what the founders really meant. Most established religions, in fact, are based on shaky sources. Divine revelations seem to indulge in the very annoying habit of popping up in semiliterate corners of the world at a point in human history long before accurate, modern means of recording information were invented. What results, then, is an endless chain of revelations being told and retold over decades until somebody finally writes them down. Clearly, this is a process that leaves much room for error.

Did you ever play the game "Telephone" as a kid? Yeah, the game in which you whisper something in someone's ear who then whispers it in somebody else's ear, and so on down the line until the last person says out loud what he heard and everyone laughs because it usually has nothing to do with the original message. Imagine doing this for a few decades with a few thousand individuals before writing the results down. Then, let a few more decades/centuries go by before a council of "authorities" gets to vote on which versions are accurate and which ones need to be destroyed. As weird as it may sound, this is exactly how the modern versions of most sacred texts were produced. No wonder these texts are littered with contradictions. And it is on the authority of these very dubious, very old documents that followers then fight among themselves regarding the essence of the original message.

Far from being an obstacle, this confusion is a gift that most members of organized religions actually cherish. The fact that their prophets are long dead and little information is known about them makes it easier for followers to project their own ideas, values, and expectations onto their favorite authority figure—something that many believe gives more legitimacy to an ideology. This allows people to create their own religion within a respected, established tradition while keeping the appearance of following the "official" version.

In the midst of these endless arguments, the founders' original intention is clouded beyond recognition. Organized religions end up killing the insights of the prophets/gods they supposedly revere. Like demented kids hugging a puppy too tight and crushing him to death out of "love," followers destroy their founders' teachings with blind devotion. The freshness, beauty, and vital energy of the original message dies a miserable death when the message is turned into dogma. And what followers are left to worship is the dried-up, mummified corpse of what was maybe once a wonderful idea.

What this book invites you to do is to take responsibility for your ideas and, without slavish devotion to dogma, create your own religion. Rather than groping the past to find justification for your values in centuries-old texts, and using revered corpses as a source of authority, it is time to grow the heart and guts to follow your own insights and defend them on their own worth. Don't believe something because Buddha said it, or Jesus said it, or Muhammad said it. Don't believe it because I say it. (OK, don't listen to this last sentence. I just threw it in there to look democratic. Of course if I say it, you should blindly believe it.) Better yet, don't believe anything at all that is not born out of your own experience. Belief is the habit of those too lazy or too scared to trust in themselves. Let's try a more courageous path: find out for yourself. If we want to stop wiping each other out over religious dogma, this is the healthiest step we can take.

If rejecting dogma and nourishing the courage and creativity required to make our own choices is a good idea in all times and places, it is a talent that is becoming even more essential in today's world. This, after all, is the age of globalization, choice, and syncretism. More people on earth have access to more information now than at any other point in human history. We know more about each other than ever before; ideas circle the globe at a speed our ancestors never even imagined. The most learned intellectual from just a couple of centuries ago had access to far less information than anyone alive today who happens to have Internet access. Being exposed to different stimuli and ideas coming to us from every corner of the world means we have more material to play with. It is only natural then that greater numbers of people are mixing the ingredients, making new connections, and revolutionizing traditions.

This explosion in creativity can be seen everywhere. For example, just about any song born today comes from the union of musical traditions that just a few decades ago had never been introduced to each other. "Fusion" seems to be the operative word at the root of everything, from the types of food we eat to the movies we watch—even the diverse ethnic makeup of many people alive here and now.

With every facet of human culture being touched by this rapid exchange of information, it only makes sense that religion would be affected as well. In the days before our globalized, interconnected world, people practiced whatever religion happened to be the dominant one in the country of their birth. Thankfully, the stupidity of the belief that by random luck one is born in the one true religious tradition, while the rest of the world needs to be shown the light, is beginning to become progressively more evident. In the face of increased knowledge and choices, traditional forms of authority are collapsing. Rigid identities—be they national, ideological, or religious—are becoming more obsolete. Prepackaged answers satisfy fewer and fewer people. Solutions and ideas that appeal to a particular place and time reveal themselves to be painfully narrow-minded in a global world. Many of the answers people still turn to were born in a world where one couldn't see beyond the confines of one's village—where what existed in the next valley was foreign, exciting, and mysterious. But this will no longer do. Nostalgically holding on to the past is not going to help us face a reality that's changing at breakneck pace.

Damn, it's an exciting time to be alive. We are just a few steps away from self-destruction, but we are also a few steps away from creating a better world that could exceed the imagination of the most optimistic prophets from our past. We are dancing on a tightrope stretched on the abyss, the destiny of the world in our hands. The weapons we take into battle are heart, vision, and creativity. What we need are new solutions that reflect the greater degree of knowledge and the radically different experiences that characterize the modern world.

The availability of a much wider range of choices is transforming the face of religion today. Many individuals belonging to several mainstream religions have responded by dramatically reshaping some of their core beliefs. Increasing numbers of people are opening new paths outside of the confines of mainstream religions altogether. Most traditional religions, in fact, change only under duress; otherwise, they resist change and any challenge to their authority with tooth and nail.

The most conservative, fundamentalist branches see the global world as a threat. To them, more choices mean more opportunity to fall in error and stray from the One True Way. In their worldview, choice is the Devil's tool to lead us away from the truth. Confronted with a world offering greater chances for choosing one's own way, their answer is to dig deeper trenches and become even more radically rigid. The more freedoms human history offers us, the more fundamentalists will fight them. Despite their mutual hatred for one another, Jerry Falwell and the Taliban are twins separated at birth— modernity makes both of them recoil in horror.

I see the global world as the greatest opportunity humanity has ever had. In my view, it is healthy for traditions to be challenged. If traditional values lose popularity, it's either because they are poorly communicated or because they are not relevant anymore. No healthy solution was ever born from whining about the good old days. As Nietzsche puts it, "[The sage] does not acknowledge custom or tradition, but only new questions from life and new answers."[7] While it is not necessarily true that newer is always better, it is certainly true that any theory, religion, or philosophy that was born in the midst of intellectual poverty can only be improved upon today. Whatever was good in it will endure, and whatever fails will do so because it belongs to a darker, more ignorant world.

What we will do here then is take aim at all the central questions debated by different religions in order to see what gifts of wisdom the past has to offer us, and how we can use that to come up with our own answers.

CHAPTER 2

A CALL TO ARMS: THE SEQUEL

Nothing to Lose

Countless peoples have an irrational fear of questioning what they hold most sacred. Because they think that certain beliefs are desirable, they come up with contorted rationalizations to justify them against any possible attack, rather than taking an honest look at them. They are terrified by the thought that if they begin doubting their certainties or looking at them with a critical eye, the entire castle of values upon which they have based their lives will come tumbling down. For this reason, they try their hardest to avoid facing any facts that would force them to revise their ideals. Taking this course of action (actually non-action) may feel safe and reassuring; however, indulging in this paranoid phobia can only hurt us in the long run. Testing our most sacred values against different options will only strengthen us. We really have nothing to lose by being open-minded. It's a win-win situation.

Let's look at it this way. If we test our most sacred values against all kinds of different options, two things can happen. In one case, we find out that all the other alternatives are not as effective as what we already believed in the first place. This is clearly a win, since it will increase our self-confidence by reinforcing the feeling that we are on the right track. Moreover, when we engage in discussions with others who swear by different ideas, our arguments will be stronger and more effective because we have already explored all possible counter-arguments and discovered their weaknesses.

If instead we find out that our ideals were not as good as we thought they were, and there are better alternatives available, this is just as good a result. We win again because we have a chance to correct our mistakes, stop living according to flawed ideas, and discover a better path. In either scenario, we can only gain by testing and questioning. We truly have nothing to lose but our prejudices.

Untested beliefs are not a treasure to conserve but rather a cage to escape. They keep us prisoners of our opinions and prevent us from facing reality for what it is. As Nietzsche puts it, "[I am] a man who wishes nothing more than daily to lose some reassuring belief, who seeks and finds his happiness in this daily greater liberation of the mind."[8]

Here we reverse the traditional attitude. Instead of thinking, "It *must* be good because I believe it," we can switch to "I believe it because it is good." Whatever conclusion we end up embracing will not be born from fear of change, excessive attachment to one's preconceived opinions, or a scarcity of alternate viewpoints. It will be the result of testing what works and what doesn't, and picking the best option among many at our disposal.

Only those who are scared of the truth are hostile to questioning. No one would refuse evidence if it confirms and gives greater credibility to their ideas. The centuries-long persecution of science by religious authorities cannot be explained unless religious authorities already knew they were frauds and were afraid of somebody exposing them. Unless you are a liar or are pathologically attached to your opinions, you should not be afraid of the truth.

Heretic and Proud

Although I have tried to be reassuring and nonthreatening in the preceding paragraphs, I have no illusions. This book is a declaration of war against all those traditions that want to limit our choices, stifle our growth, and restrict our freedom. This is a battle between the heaviness of tradition and the daring to create, between the conforming crowd and the individual shaping his/her own destiny. Most, but not all, forms of organized religions stand firmly on the conformity side of the battle line. They don't want you to think for yourself, or they would go out of business. Their clergy is always threatened by direct individual experience because it makes them obsolete and takes away their source of authority. Dogma is safe only when individuals give away their power to religious institutions, stop questioning the world around them, and gladly accept pre-packaged answers. Thomas Paine saw this clearly when he wrote:

> I do not believe in the creed professed by the Jewish church, by the Roman church, by the Greek church, by the Turkish church, by the Protestant church, nor by any church that I know of. My own mind is my own church. All national institutions of churches . . . appear to me no other than human inventions set up to terrify and enslave mankind, and monopolize power and profit.[9]

What we are engaged in here is, by its very nature, a heretical project. Forget the virgin-sacrificing, devil-worshipping, religion-destroying image that centuries of inquisitions and authoritarian brainwashing have attached to the word "heresy." What we mean here goes back to the original Greek meaning of the word, which is translated literally as "to choose," or "to go one's own way." This meaning points to the sacred word at the roots of this enterprise: choice. The choice to go one's own way; the courage to explore life's mysteries for oneself rather than accepting second-hand answers; and the refusal to bow to the dogma of existing dominant theories—these are the things that make this quest a heretical one. In the eyes of many established religions, in fact, choosing your own way rather than blindly following theirs is a horrendous crime and grounds for persecution. The history of both Christianity and Islam is stained with the blood of those tortured and killed because they committed the unforgivable sin of questioning the answers provided by religious authorities.

What is bizarre in all of this is that many of the religions that try to squash independent inquiry today were founded by supposed heretics and dangerous outlaws: Jesus was crucified for blasphemy, and Muhammad was chased out of Mecca by assassins. Think of the irony. These men were all about questioning tradition and established forms of authority, which is exactly what the fundamentalists claiming to follow them hate. All religions were born because someone departed from an existing tradition and created their own. But instead of honoring their example, most of their followers turn their insights into one more dried-up dogma used to repress individual freedom.

This book, on the other hand, invites you to honor their pioneering spirit by doing exactly what they did: create your own path. As William Blake beautifully said, "I must invent my own systems or else be enslaved by other men's."[10] If we are successful, things may turn out the way Walt Whitman predicted, "There will soon be no more priests. Their work is done . . . A new order shall arise . . . and every man shall be his own priest."[11]

Some hardcore atheists, in an effort to attack anything that goes under the heading of "religion," lump together all religious traditions as equally evil. In doing so, they completely miss the fact that within every religion, even the ones with a long history of intolerance, there are branches that are more than willing to make room for individual exploration.

In yet other religions, in fact, respect for independent inquiry is not present only in some heretical faction, but is at the very foundation of their ideas. While plenty of things about Buddhism turn me off, here is a tradition that allows and encourages freedom. Consider this. Lin Chi, a Chinese Buddhist teacher, once said, "If you encounter the Buddha, kill him."[12] Kill the Buddha?!? Buddhists certainly seem to have a weird way to revere their founder. What's this crazy Chinese talking about? Far from being a blasphemous statement, Lin Chi's words are a metaphorical rejection of the dogmatism that inevitably results once we've put our teacher on a pedestal. Precisely because Lin Chi loved Buddha, he warned people against turning him into an object of worship (a warning that has gone unheeded by many Buddhists throughout history). Can you imagine a Christian inviting people to "kill Jesus," or a Muslim to "kill Muhammad"? No matter how well intended the metaphor, the odds are that whoever spoke the words would have to run far and fast to escape being lynched. In Buddhism, on the other hand, this kind of iconoclastic statement would hardly raise an eyebrow. This is why Lin Chi could say what he said, or why the Japanese Zen monk Ikkyū could write

Without a bridge
Clouds climb effortlessly

To heaven;
No need to rely on
Anything Gotama Buddha taught.[13]

Buddha himself argued that his teachings were but a means to an end. On his deathbed, Buddha told his followers, "Do not accept what you hear by report, do not accept tradition, do not accept a statement because it is found in our books, nor because it is in accord with your belief, nor because it is the saying of your teacher . . . Be lamps onto yourselves. . . ."[14]

In a similar vein, one of the pillars of Taoism, Chuang Tzu, wrote, "The torch of chaos and doubt—this is what the sage steers by."[15] Here we are 180 degrees away from what you hear from many other religious leaders who threaten hellish punishments unless we obey their every command. Fixed certitudes, comfy reassurances, never-changing rules; the entire baggage usually fed as religious dogma . . . Chuang Tzu will give you none of that. Instead, what he brings forth to light the path is doubt—what Alan Watts called "the wisdom of insecurity"—the force that invites us to constantly test our most cherished ideas. This is a clear example that not all religious traditions shove dogma down our throats. Rather, some encourage us to embrace doubt, question all conclusions we are offered, and experiment on our own.

Epistemological Anarchism, Bruce Lee, and the Freedom to Be Who We Are

As much as doubt keeps dogma at bay, doubt for doubt's sake can paralyze us, making us too timid and insecure to commit to any ideal. Clearly, this is not the kind of doubt we are talking about. The aim of this book is to provide tools to create your own path and solve very real, very scary problems. I certainly don't intend to confuse you with some relativistic, wishy-washy crap that only leads to weakness and indecision. No, the doubt we are referring to here is a fire lit under our butts to keep us alert; to constantly prod us so we never get so comfortable in our findings that we turn them in absolute laws; to make sure we don't get so enamored with our theories that we lose touch with real life. Both Heraclitus, one of the greatest philosophers in history, and Lao Tzu, the author of the Tao Te Ching, stress over and over again: life is constantly changing. What proved useful yesterday may not work in tomorrow's context. No matter how good something is, it never works 100 percent of the time. No rule, no recipe, no fixed formula can ever capture the flow of existence. When you start believing otherwise, you are on your way toward creating another dried-up tradition that will be kept alive out of inertia rather than because of its effectiveness. Chuang Tzu's brand of doubt is about engaging in a constant process of re-search, continually testing our truths, and keeping the river of our ideas flowing so that they will not turn into the stagnant swamp of dogma. As Bruce Lee said, "How can there be methods and systems to arrive at something that is living? To that which is static, fixed, dead, there can be a way, a definite path, but not to that which is liv-ing. Do not reduce reality to a static thing and then invent methods to reach it."[16] Or, as he puts it here, "Knowledge is fixed in time, whereas, knowing is continual. Knowledge comes from a source, from accumulation, from a conclusion, while knowing is a move-ment."[17]

If you are wondering what Bruce Lee has to do with religion, you have my sympathy. I concede that the connection is not the most obvious, but please indulge me for a little while. I swear there is a point to this. While he may be better known as the star of the kung fu movie genre, Lee was also a brilliant philosopher who successfully applied his insights to the martial arts. What this book intends to do to religion, in fact, is exactly what Bruce Lee did to the martial arts.

At a time when the Confucian reverence for tradition characterized the martial arts world, Lee came along to challenge it all with an antiauthoritarian approach that was unlike anything anybody had ever seen in the West. While the exponents of different martial arts styles argued among themselves about which art was the best, they all agreed on one basic concept: there is such a thing as one perfect art, with a perfect methodology and perfect techniques, which alone embodies the Truth in regards to combat. Naturally, much like the members of many organized religions, each claimed their art was the One. But according to Lee, they were all wrong because the very concept of separate "styles" of martial arts is wrong. He considered styles to be ideological prisons limiting the individual freedom to pursue one's own path. In Lee's view, they all had good ideas and good techniques, but they were all hopelessly deluded if they thought their partial truths were the Only Truth. Not all knowledge can be found in the house of the same teacher. Certainly agreeing with Thomas Paine's idea that "Every person of learning is finally his own teacher," Lee believed individuals needed to be exposed to different methods in order to figure out what works for them.

Long before Lee's time, many great innovators in the history of martial arts had created new styles by mixing ideas and techniques from various systems. Lee took a much more radical step. Following the ideas of Zen Buddhist master Hakuin, Lee coined the motto "Using no way as the way." This cryptic slogan meant it was not enough just to create a new style, with its inevitable rigid methodologies and fixed curriculum. Instead, Lee advocated cross-training, picking and choosing what suits one best from all different styles of martial arts. Lee's revolutionary yet simple approach was broken down into four steps:

1. Research your own experience.

2. Absorb what is useful.

3. Reject what is useless.

4. Add what is specifically your own.[18]

In other words, people should experiment with as many paths as possible and extract the best out of all of them. In doing this, Lee invited martial artists to resist the temptation to crystallize their discoveries into a fixed style. Instead, he invited them to engage in a process of research that would keep their ideas fresh, and would spur them to constantly evolve as fighters and as human beings. As Lee further wrote about his martial arts philosophy, "Jeet Kune Do favors formlessness so that it can assume all forms and since Jeet Kune Do has no style, it can fit with all styles. As a result, Jeet Kune Do utilizes all ways and is bound by none and, likewise, uses any techniques or means which serve its ends."[19] Lee's plan was to be able to use the strengths of any style without being bound to its weaknesses.

Following a method—any method—too closely robs us of the flexibility necessary to face life since, by its very nature, life is vaster than any law or rule. Too many rules suffocate individuality. People are different by talent, taste, and experience. To expect everyone to follow the same formula is a fascist dream that is completely out of touch with the essence of life. As Chuang Tzu puts it,

Water is for fish
And air for men.
Natures differ, and needs with them.

Hence the wise men of old
Did not lay down
One measure for all.[20]

If you have ever seen any great chef at work, you know that they don't follow a recipe. They follow their nose. A recipe may be a good guideline for people who are lost. But if you develop timing, awareness, and sensitivity you no longer need recipes. And this is precisely what Bruce Lee was trying to teach: develop the tools to trust in yourself more than a method.

The Fear of Freedom

To put it mildly, most of the martial arts community didn't respond kindly to Lee's ideas. They were outraged by what they perceived to be an arrogant slap in the face of tradition: Who is this young punk, they wondered, to question the teachings passed down by our masters? It takes a lifetime to learn and perfect the practice of one art, and yet this guy has the audacity to think he can briefly dabble in many arts, and based on that experience extract the best out of them? By abandoning time-honored methods, all he is going to accomplish is to become a stereotypical jack-of-all-trades, and master of none.

This is the same reaction that most anyone rejecting ancient dogmas in favor of exploring new paths has encountered. The idea of "creating your own" (whether it be a martial art, a religion, or anything else) always arouses hostility. Many people object that by merging separate traditions we end up watering down the truths contained in each. These people tell us that any type of syncretic mixing leads to hopeless confusion and spineless relativism. The do-it-yourself approach, they insist, is for people who are looking for an easy way out by custom-making comfy beliefs tailored to their needs; these people lack the discipline and commitment to explore the depths of a single tradition.

If you are an acute observer and you actually still remember the title of this book, you may have noticed that I'm not exactly in agreement with this position. To put it more bluntly, I see this hard-line insistence on absolute values, and on the sanctity of traditions written in stone, as a tough-guy act that stems from insecurity, poor self-confidence, and fear. To argue for a greater possibility of choice is anything but relativistic. Not only is mixing more in tune with the globalized world, it is more in tune with the biological essence of life itself. Mutts are always healthier than purebred dogs. A person who develops the many talents necessary to explore a variety of different sources, discovering their strengths and mixing them together harmoniously, is not showing weakness or lack of discipline. They are making a choice that is born out of very strong convictions—strong enough as to be willing to experiment and change one's mind. This is definitely not the easy way out. If anything, the easy way out is buying into beliefs and adhering to them without question. It takes incredible guts to leave the herd behind, to become your own leader, forging yourself in the fire of unfiltered experience.

Much of the hostility toward "creating your own" comes from a deep fear. Most people are too scared of their own shadow to dare taking full responsibility for their values, actions, and lives. The prospect of having to rely entirely on themselves, without a group to fall back on or a dogma to reassure them, terrifies them to the core. Deep down they know they lack what it takes to live up to the challenge.

Freedom, in fact, is not for everyone. Besides sounding horribly undemocratic, the sentence I just wrote may also seem counterintuitive. Freedom, after all, seems to be everywhere around us. Most people list it as one of their primary values. Hardly any war is fought without at least one side (and usually both) claiming that they are fighting for it. Songs and movies always talk about it. Politicians use the word when they are shopping for votes. Advertisers use it to sell their products. Freedom is the star in plenty of catchy slogans, songs, movies, political rhetoric, advertisements, etc. With such an overabundant use of the word "freedom," and with so much lip service paid to it, it would be easy to be fooled into thinking people actually love freedom. Nothing could be further from the truth.

What people love is the *idea* of freedom. They love to think that they are not slaves. They go to great lengths to convince themselves they are independent, and that no one can boss them around. But reality tells a different story. Most people badly want some parent figure—whether that's a teacher, president, gang leader, pope, guru, God, or Santa Claus—to whom they can delegate their power of choice, for they would much rather trust anyone other than themselves. Having to figure things out on their own and take responsibility for their lives is too scary of a prospect. Following a path is much easier than creating one. This accounts for the popularity of dogma; and this is why, despite all the rhetoric suggesting otherwise, real freedom terrifies people.

What they crave is not freedom but authority figures to give them orders. If I can go on record with another runner-up for the most undemocratic sentence of all times . . . most people seem to be born to obey commands. They probably resent the commands, often complain about them, and occasionally secretly break them only to feel guilty later, but the truth is they would be totally lost without them. If you try to take away their chains, they'll scream and shout because their security, their very identity, is in their chains.

Give them real freedom and they'll run back to their dogmas crying "please mama hold me tight." Dogma is what reassures them and lulls them to sleep at night. "No, dear child—dogma whispers softly in their ears—you don't need to venture alone in that big, scary world. Stay by my side instead, and I will always take care of you. I promise you will never have to make difficult choices all by yourself. I will map out the path for you, and all you'll have to do is follow. You will never be lost again."

Forget freedom as a family value. Real freedom is scary. Real freedom is for people with broad shoulders and big hearts. So, if the thought of refusing to surrender your power to authority and becoming the leader of your own life scares you, I strongly recommend you quit now. The rest of the book is not going to get any easier.

Not So Fast

OK, now that I've had a chance to get off my chest just how deeply I dislike the critics of the "create your own" approach, let me freely admit that sometimes they are right. Exhibit A in their favor is the New Age movement.

If I listen carefully, I can hear my publisher crying somewhere. No, Bolelli, c'mon. You have already pissed off scores of militant atheists. Fundamentalists from different religions are united in gloating at the thought of you burning in hell. At least, be nice to the new agers . . . Do you want to sell books or not?

Sorry, man, but I got to tell it like it is.

The New Age movement bugs me precisely because it takes some beautiful ideas, and turns them into a parody. Don't get me wrong. Plenty of great people with nothing but good intentions are connected with the New Age phenomenon. But the whole thing most often appears so painfully superficial as to give ammunition to those opposing the notion of anyone "creating their own."

Today after yoga, I'll try Tibetan meditation. Tomorrow I'm off to healing with crystals, and then I'll complete my spiritual joy-ride playing with the dreaming techniques of Australian aborigines.

Mixing different elements together is an art. Tossing a bunch of random ingredients together without truly understanding any of them is not. Even though many individuals are genuine—albeit somewhat desperate—seekers, just as many are on an ego-inflating trip taking them from one spiritual fad to the next. Besides making me sick, the pseudo-mystical posing that characterizes plenty of new agers ends up giving a bad name to the very ideas I am advocating, and this is why it bothers me to no end.

Everyone has the right to be free to pick and choose the best from different ideas and practices, thereby creating his or her own path. But clearly, merely rejecting traditional dogmas and creating your own way is no guarantee that you'll come up with something good. Talent and intelligence—unfortunately—are not distributed equally. The abundance of choices is welcome to those who have the skills to choose wisely, but is overwhelming for those who don't. If you combine the right elements together, you can come up with a masterpiece. I worship daily whoever first departed from tradition by deciding to throw in the pan noodles from Asia and tomatoes from the Americas, and came up with Italian pasta. On the other hand, mix the wrong ingredients, and you end up with Alfredo sauce.

This is probably why Benjamin Franklin promoted freethinking in matters of religion for highly educated people like himself or Thomas Jefferson, but at the same time he argued for the necessity to keep the masses anchored to traditional forms of religion. In his opinion, in fact, they lacked the wisdom and self-discipline necessary for a healthy use of freedom.

This same elitist attitude has characterized the history of many philosophical schools of Taoism. They rarely ever tried to recruit people to their ideas. Most often, they tried to discourage them. If, like most people, you are too stupid to play with us—argued the Taoists—you better stick to Confucianism. There, they will give you rules to limit the amount of damage you can do, and feed you fairy tales to comfort you. It's better for you. If you try to play with the big boys, you may get hurt.

In the same spirit, Nietzsche wrote, "And he who is not a bird should not build his nest over abysses."[21] An echo of this is heard in Hermann Hesse's warning at the entrance of the Magic Theater in his famous novel *Steppenwolf*, "MAGIC THEATER—ENTRANCE NOT FOR EVERYBODY."[22]

Call me idealistic, but I see no reason to discourage freedom just because most people use it poorly. Sure, not everyone can create something wonderful, but everyone can and should be pushed to honestly express themselves. Despite all the possible problems, I agree with Bruce Lee. I'll take a daring experiment that fails over a safe, wimpy devotion to dogma any day.

The Evidence Never Lies[23]

The task of weaning people from dogma is challenging in all times and contexts, but Bruce Lee had an advantage in his antiauthoritarian quest. Because of the very physical nature of martial arts, one can go on talking for only so long before he or she is invited to step up and put their theories on the line. Martial arts theory is tested not through flowery debates but combat. At the end of the match, you are either the one left standing or the one on the floor. No arguments there. Fighters can spout the best speeches in the world about the superiority of their art and training methods, but if they keep getting knocked out, they will be forced by reality to revise their ideas.

Because of this wonderfully concrete aspect of martial arts, Lee's inflammatory ideas were eventually tested and vindicated in the early 1990s through the development of the new sport of mixed martial arts. Competitions such as the Ultimate Fighting Championship, in fact, invited fighters to test their skills in contests with as few rules as possible. Traditional martial artists from every corner of the globe stepped up to defend the honor of their systems. This, after all, was their chance to prove in a public forum the superiority of their style. Much buzz was in the air: maybe the debates among martial artists about which art was the best would be finally settled. What resulted shocked everybody. No single art turned out to be "the best." Just as Bruce Lee had predicted, traditional martial artists became easy prey for those fighters who followed Lee's insight by picking the best techniques from several different sources and mixing them together. This was the most indubitable proof that, in the right hands, an eclectic syncretism is far superior to rigidly following a single path.

In case you are wondering, I am not proposing an Ultimate Fighting competition for religions. While I have to admit that the prospect of having a beer in front of pay-per-view matches between Shinto and Judaism, or Islam and Buddhism, seems like lots of fun, I am afraid it wouldn't work. The effectiveness of a religion cannot be measured through objective, physical standards. No concrete testing ground exists to prove beyond a shadow of doubt the superiority of one religion over another.

We can't test objectively the existence of God, or of heaven and hell, but this doesn't mean that we can't test religious theories at all. What we can do is look at the effects that certain religious ideas have had throughout history and continue to have today. It is a much nerdier approach than a knock out, and it certainly doesn't possess its discussion-ending clarity, but it's the next best thing. We can observe the historical consequences of certain beliefs, and decide which ones have had more desirable effects on our lives. Clearly, a subjective element enters the game here. Different people are going to judge the same consequence positively and negatively. But we don't need to fall in a relativistic trap. We are not going to accept some cop-out excuse about how it's all just a matter of opinion. Beliefs that cause people to behave decently toward each other are not just *different* from beliefs leading to widespread warfare, bloodbaths, and misery. Positive beliefs are qualitatively superior much in the same way that health is preferable to sickness. In creating our own religions, we should carefully separate those ideas that have contributed to the amount of violence, conflict, and suffering in the world from those that have helped alleviate or diminish those things.

Our task is going to be complicated by the fact that beliefs have different effects on different people. The same belief can often result in both pleasant and horrific consequences for different people. What we need to figure out is what seems to be the exception and what is the rule. For example, there is plenty of anecdotal evidence suggesting that so-called family values among fundamentalist Christians may have helped thousands of people to lead better lives. However, objective statistics point to much greater rates of social dysfunctions (from divorce to murder) in states where fundamentalism is powerful, compared to states where liberal Christianity and secularism are more popular. This suggests one of two things: in the best case, these "family values" are not very effective at fixing the problems they try to address; worse, they actually may contribute to them. In either case, the evidence tells us that fundamentalist family values could use some serious adjustment.[24]

In choosing the values we want to use to create our own religions, let's always keep an eye on the evidence. Effectiveness is not measured by the complexity of a theological argument, or by how loudly its supporters scream. It is measured in action. Values are only as good as the results they produce.

CHAPTER 3

THE INTANGIBLES: GOD

I have known many gods. He who denies them is as blind as he who trusts them too deeply. I seek not beyond death. It may be the blackness averred by the Nemedian skeptics, or Crom's realm of ice and cloud, or the snowy plains and vaulted halls of the Nordheimer's Valhalla. I know not, nor do I care. Let me live deep while I live; let me know the rich juices of red meat and stinging wine on my palate, the hot embrace of white arms, the mad exultation of battle when the blue blades flame and crimson, and I am content. Let teachers and priests and philosophers brood over questions of reality and illusion. I know this: if life is illusion, then I am no less an illusion, and being thus, the illusion is real to me. I live, I burn with life, I love, I slay, and am content.

—Robert E. Howard, L. Sprague De Camp,
and Lin Carter. *Conan of Cimmeria*

May I have a drum roll, please? Are the cheerleaders ready? Good, because this is it. It's showdown time. The big game is on. While the topics of several other chapters may be more stimulating to me on a personal level, no religious issues are as important and hotly contested as God and the afterlife. They are the two forces at the very core of the religious life of billions of individuals around the world. In addition to the central role they occupy, the Big Two have something else in common. They are completely beyond the realm of tangible, day-to-day experience. We crave knowledge about them but possess not a shred of physical evidence to guarantee us the existence of either. However, the lack of logical or physical proof doesn't diminish our desire to know.

It is precisely for this reason that, while the Big Two steal the spotlight in many religious traditions, they find little or no sympathy in others. Some branches of Taoism, Buddhism, Shinto, Confucianism, and Animism discount to varying degrees the importance of the Big Two in favor of more pragmatic concerns. Buddha, for example, snubbed his disciples' requests to discuss the existence of the gods and the nature of the afterlife; he argued that such things had nothing to do with his central goal—the improvement of the quality of our present lives.

In the minds of most people, God and the afterlife are what religion is all about. I don't agree with this view, but that doesn't mean I believe these issues should be ignored. Everyone on earth will have to take the Big Two's challenge head-on. Whether you end up agreeing with my answers or not, it is crucial to clarify where we stand on these issues. Much depends on the conclusions we reach.

What Are We Talking About?
From Santa to the Tao

God! God! Oh God! Yes! Oh God! The voice of my screaming neighbor makes me painfully aware of several things at once: *(a)* she is either great at faking it or she is having some seriously mind-blowing sex; *(b)* whoever built this house should be shot for making the walls way too thin; and *(c)* I am always uncomfortable when people toss out the word "God" like they know exactly what they are talking about. Most of the time it sounds like they are referring to something that's part of their ordinary experience—something visible, concrete, obvious to anyone—as if God were the guy they hung out with last Saturday, eating ice cream and catching a movie together. Every time I hear the word I can't help but wonder how they know with such seeming certainty what "God" is.

When I dare to ask for more information about their invisible friend, typically I receive answers that leave me even more confused, because they seem to be describing Santa Claus. Being told in all seriousness about a perfect and wise being in the sky who knows everything that happens on earth, keeps tally of who has done good and who has committed evil, then rewards the former and punishes the latter never fails to crack me up. Just add the flying reindeer and the picture is complete.

Now, I enjoy a good fairy tale as much as anyone else, but the most prevalent image of God that is pushed in some religions is too ridiculously anthropomorphic to be taken seriously. Turning the divine mystery into a character from a Disney movie strikes me as not only childish, but as downright disrespectful to the very idea of what God may be. It seems like something you would tell a kid—and not a particularly smart one—to keep him quiet and ease him to sleep. We have taken something that is far beyond our powers of imagination and understanding, that is supposed to exist beyond time and space, that is supposed to be at the very roots of reality, and we have turned it into a reassuring father figure for people with unresolved daddy issues.

Worse yet, so many religious tales depict God as a terribly flawed character in a gory story written by sadists: he is an insecure tribal chieftain with a mean streak; a jealous God who whines about not receiving enough attention by his creatures; a murderous God who guides his chosen people toward genocide; a tyrannical God who punishes horribly anyone who disobeys. Who decided to cast Joseph Stalin as God? These are the qualities of a totalitarian, raging dictator—hopefully that is not what is at the foundation of our universe. In my mind, anyone who accepts this view of God does more damage to religion than the most belligerent atheist.

Despite arguing endlessly about the specific characteristics attributed to God, some religions (for example Christianity, Judaism, and Islam) view God as a personified, conscious being who is responsible for the creation of the world, is active in human affairs, and is able to reveal his will to people.

Others (for example, Hinduism, Shintoism, some branches of Taoism and Buddhism, most tribal religions, ancient Mesopotamian and Greco-Roman religions, and a myriad of other traditions) believe in many divine beings, each one with its own peculiar characteristics. Some of these polytheistic traditions include a supreme creator figure who stands above all, while others do not.

And still other religions (particularly Buddhism, along with the more philosophical schools of Taoism) acknowledge the existence of powerful spirits all around us, but don't attribute much importance to them. According to these traditions, ultimate reality can't be found in any anthropomorphic ideas about God or gods, but rather in an impersonal force that is greater than any particular being.

Do you understand now why I am disturbed when people use the word "God" as if there were a single, crystal-clear meaning for it?

How Do We Know God?

Let's backtrack for a second. In order to avoid getting lost in this jungle of different definitions and ideas attributed to God, we need to start from the beginning. How do these contrasting images of God originate in the first place? How are we to decide which one, if any, is correct? How does anybody know anything about God?

Where Not to Look: Revelation

The most typical way people form their ideas about God is through second-hand revelation. Somebody, preferably in the very distant past, heard the voice of God and went around preaching this message. Later, his followers eventually collected these revelations in the form of a sacred text. This is how the scriptures of Judaism, Christianity, Islam, Hinduism, and a few other religions were created. Everyone else living after this time period is supposed to turn to these books to learn the truth about God. And why should we believe that a certain book truly contains the word of God? Because it says so. Anyone with a double-digit IQ can plainly see that the logic behind this argument is laughable, and yet many individuals who are far from stupid in other areas of their lives surrender their intelligence in order to embrace second-hand revelations.

Sacred books make very poor candidates as possible places for hearing God's voice. First, God's voice has to pass through the very human filters of the people who receive these revelations and the people who later commit them to writing. Even if we assume that a revelation is based on authentic experience, it is unclear how much of a divine message can survive after being processed by human perceptions, memory, and language. Further complicating the puzzle is the problem of translation from the original language in which a sacred text was written into all other languages. Then factor in human error of people copying these manuscripts over the centuries and the intentional alterations sometimes made by theologians and politicians who felt the need to amend the divine messages to their liking.[25] When we stop to consider everything that goes into the making of any religious scripture, it would truly be a miracle if the final product contained anything more than a glimmer of the divine. Any message that has been retouched by so many human hands is hardly credible as "the word of God."

Revelations also pose another problem. How can we trust that someone claiming to be God's spokesperson is not just a skillful manipulator? As Susan B. Anthony wrote, "I distrust those people who know so well what God wants them to do because I notice it always coincides with their own desires."[26] What better way to silence the potential critics of one's message than to attribute the message to God? It doesn't take a Machiavellian genius to figure out that enlisting God to one's cause is a great technique to gain power. Revelation is a handy vehicle for making God say whatever we want him to say. A classic example of this is when the Mormon Church realized that previous revelations about the inferiority of black people lost popularity in the post-Civil Rights era, they conveniently received a new, more politically correct revelation that overruled the older doctrines.[27] In other words, before the 1960s God was a racist, but afterward he changed his mind. Similarly, in many occasions when Muhammad was criticized, God would come to the rescue and deliver a revelation that sanctioned the prophet's behavior.[28]

Even if God's mouthpieces had nothing but the most honorable intentions, how do we know they weren't lunatics? Moses, Abraham, and Muhammad—some of the most influential prophets in Western history—all claimed to have heard voices that either ordered them to kill people or praised them for doing so. Adding blasphemy to injury, they all claimed that the murderous advice came straight from God. If anyone today stated to have received such a message, we would quickly find them a comfy straightjacket, lock them up, and throw away the key. I have no reason to find the revelations of the New Testament any more credible than those of the Old Testament or of the Koran, but at least Jesus had the decency to never claim divine sanction for massacring people.

No, there is too much room for error and abuse inherent in the idea of second-hand revelation. Furthermore, if revelation was indeed the best way for human beings to know God, why wouldn't God reveal him/her/itself to people today? Why rely on ancient revelations made under highly suspicious circumstances? If God is a conscious being, he/she/it could appreciate that anyone born today may not want to rely on centuries-old pieces of hearsay of dubious authenticity that originated among semiliterate people in the desert. Plenty of well-meaning seekers of the truth would be thrilled to hear God's voice and change their agnostic or atheist ways if they only had even a shred of direct evidence. Today, humanity has more capacity than ever to record, communicate, and verify information. If God really has something to say, now would be a good time to say it.

Anyone with a brain should question why would God choose to reveal him/her/itself only to one individual in remote historical times, expecting everyone else to follow this person's guidelines forever afterward? It would seem that a divine intelligence could come up with a better communication strategy.

Now that we know where *not* to look, let's figure out an alternative. Thomas Paine, one of the most brilliant writers of the 1700s, offered this advice, "Do we want to know what God is? Search not the book called the scripture, which any human hand might make, but the scripture called the Creation."[29] As a result of a Christian smear campaign against Paine, many people today mistakenly label him an atheist, but Paine was a Deist. Deists—unlike atheists—believe in the existence of God, but they reject the idea of "revealed" religions. They view sacred books as collections of human hopes and dreams, fears and paranoia projected onto God. According to the Deists, then, organized religions give us nothing but human opinions, conjectures, and wild guesses about God. The reality of God is to be found elsewhere.

Like Taoist thinkers before him, Paine argued that true religion begins with the study of nature. Whereas language can be manipulated by human beings, nature is what it is: an unadulterated, living testimony of whatever power is behind the creation of everything that exists. If you want to learn about the character of a creator, look no further than his creation. Discover the principles of nature and you discover the secrets upon which the universe is founded. In Paine's mind, science and religion can happily go hand in hand. This is precisely what Einstein meant when he wrote, "I do not believe in a personal god . . . If something is in me which can be called religious then it is the unbounded admiration for the structure of the world so far as our science can reveal it."[30]

In some ways, studying nature can turn out to be anything but an uplifting experience. Nature can often be cruel and indifferent to humans and animals alike. Natural selection knows no mercy. The alliterative trio of disease, death, and decay feast on everything that lives. When we stop to consider that about 98 percent of all species that ever roamed the earth have gone extinct, our fuzzy notions of a benevolent Mother Nature and a loving creator fly out the window.

On the other hand, any time I see tomatoes growing in the garden, a glorious sunset, or perfectly natural boobs (if given a choice, I'd take the latter over any tomato or sunset in the world . . .), I feel there must be a good and just God who is responsible for all this sublime beauty. Whatever power created a universe in which I can dip a spoon into a jar of Nutella and partake of this sacrament is worthy of the deepest admiration. If this sounds superficial and frivolous, it's probably because I am. And yet, whether you can relate to my specific examples or not, everyone can see that at times the design of the world seems to point to a higher intelligence. Often, nature seems just too beautiful and amazing to be the product of some random chance. The structure of any living being is too complex to have happened by accident. If nothing else, contemplating nature induces a sense of wonder. We can't help but stand in awe in front of the immensity of the universe. The powers of nature remind us that forces much greater than we can comprehend rule over our lives, and all of our scientific and religious ideas are primitive attempts to come to terms with the mystery beneath it all.

While studying the principles of nature can offer great insights, it certainly doesn't provide the clearest answers as to the existence and nature of God. If we crave more than what the observation of nature can give us, I can't think of a better place to continue our search than our own personal experience.

The clergy in most organized religion will be shaking their fists at anyone emphasizing personal experience as a road to God. The clergy loves second-hand revelation because it gives them a primary role as the interpreters and custodians of God's word. Personal experience, on the other hand, robs them of their power and diminishes their authority. But ultimately, our own experience is the only honest guide we have. Anything else is just hearsay.

So what does my life tell me about God? Everyone else seems to be having such precise ideas about what God is. Their God is clear, accessible, and free of contradictions. But what I hear has nothing to do with what I know. My life, in fact, tells a very different story. I have experienced such diametrically opposite feelings that trying to reduce them to a simple, coherent idea would require some heavy editing of the truth. Either most people have had experiences completely unlike mine, or they are very good at lying to themselves.

In some ways, God is nowhere to be found. I have sent out multiple rescue missions, but my search parties have come back empty-handed. The first problem is shared by millions of people who find themselves falling down a cynical slope. Look in any direction, in any country, at any point in history and you'll find yourself staring into the eyes of forces that will send chills down your spine. Human life is filled with more pain than you could ever wish to see. Horrific suffering is not an anomaly, or an occasional unfortunate event. It is as much a part of existence as oxygen and water. Sooner or later, it visits everything that lives and tries to rip their hearts out. If you want a happy story, where evil is defeated, goodness always triumphs, and compassion and love abound, go rent a Disney movie. The screenwriter who put together Life's script is too mean for that. If there is a God, he/she/it is not in the business of keeping good people from being hurt. Any notion of a moral God who rewards goodness and punishes evil finds no support whatsoever in the experience of life on earth. Only by conjuring up otherworldly rewards and punishments (e.g., karma or heaven and hell) can we still cling to the image of a moral God watching over the universe.

In this world—the only one we know exists for sure—fortune and misfortune indifferently visit the sweetest, most loving human beings on earth just as often as the most evil.

This is the most classic stumbling block to the religious idea that God is a merciful, morally inclined, omnipotent being, with full awareness of everything that happens. It would seem that a merciful, omnipotent God would break the fangs of evil and soften its bite. A conscious, all-powerful being who allows all the horror that exists in the world must not be omnipotent after all. Alternatively, an omnipotent God who allows tragedy to tear apart the lives of millions is a monster.

Throughout human history, many different religions have tried to find an answer to this universal objection. Some simply throw up their arms and argue that there must be a reason for suffering even when we can't see it, and that "God works in mysterious ways." This argument is hardly better than no argument at all, since it asks us to ignore all the evidence and rely on blind faith.

Another very common answer blames the existence of so much pain and evil on the inherent sinfulness of human beings and their misuse of free will. But this "answer" does equally little to solve the problem. An omniscient, benevolent God should know ahead of time that some people will use their free will to cause horrific suffering to innocent individuals. And if God is the creator of everything that exists, he/she/it also created the weakness and stupidity that lead humans to abuse their free will. Which brings us back to where we started. No amount of intellectual contortions and complicated rationalizations can change that.

Poking another hole in this theory is the fact that terrible things often happen naturally, without any help from the supposedly flawed human free will. Try telling the parents of a baby born with a painful, lethal disease that suffering is the result of the misuse of free will. Natural disasters and random accidents are just as likely to open the floodgates of pain. Only someone with an overblown sense of self-importance could think that human beings have a monopoly on the ability to unleash horror.

Let's be clear: this is not an academic debate or an exercise in abstract speculation. This is as real and concrete as it gets. My own experience forces me to face it again and again. A friend of mine—one of the happiest, kindest, most positive individuals I have ever met—literally drowned in her own blood as a result of a freak accident. Another person very close to me—someone who never hurt a fly in her life—has been thrown into the living hell of nearly complete paralysis because of a brain hemorrhage. A wonderful woman I know had her seemingly healthy four-year-old daughter die in her arms because of an undiagnosed genetic defect. Yet another friend had his throat cut by some racist prick who was not too fond of Vietnamese people. And the list goes on. Every one of these experiences left me with a sense of randomness and complete chaos. I felt like a tiny pawn in a game that's unaffected by moral considerations. In my mind, I can't reconcile any of these events with the notion of a moral, benevolent God who oversees human life. This is why any time someone tells me that everything happens for a reason, I have to work really hard to avoid punching them in the face.

In contrast, some religions don't even bother trying to defend the existence of a moral God in a seemingly amoral universe. Buddhism—and to a much greater extent Taoism—doesn't place a loving creator at the root of the world. The most important Taoist book, the Tao Te Ching, states,

Before the Heaven and Earth existed
There was something nebulous:

Silent, isolated,
Standing alone, changing not,
Eternally revolving without fail,
Worthy to be the Mother of All Things.
I do not know its name
And address it as Tao. . . .[31]

According to the Taoists, the Tao is "the mysterious secret of the universe"[32] and the "parent of the gods."[33] Unlike the God of Western religions, the Tao is not a personified being. Powerful spirits and gods are born out of it. But the Tao has no personality. Rather, it is a natural force that is entirely beyond good and evil, and, much like nature itself, it is indifferent to the desires of human beings. When we take into account the incredible amount of suffering that characterizes life on this planet, the idea of an unsentimental, morally neutral power seems much easier to swallow than that of a loving, caring God.

If what I described in the preceding few paragraphs was all I ever experienced, I would have every reason to find my home in the atheist camp, or among the gloomiest of the Taoists. And yet, I have experienced much, much more than this . . .

Many times I have felt an undefined "something" close to me. The best word I can use to describe it is a presence—an almost tangible presence that holds me close, if only for a second. For a moment, it fills the room and lets me now that there is so much more out there than my mind can comprehend. Just a few hours ago, as I was writing some of the harshest, most cynical paragraphs of this chapter, it stopped by for a quick visit and moved me to the core. This presence doesn't negate the sense of chaos and randomness I have felt on so many other occasions, but for a while, chaos and randomness are replaced by a sense of purpose and connectedness.

It whispers in my ear to trust life—despite everything. As much as I'm firmly opposed to any anthropomorphic concept of God, I feel, in some weird way, that I can communicate with this presence as if with a conscious being. I don't hear voices coming out of burning bushes or anything of that sort, but my mind is filled with knowledge I didn't previously have. Sometimes I know exactly what's going to happen before it happens. Sometimes I receive answers to problems I couldn't solve before.

Am I going nuts? Am I delusional? I don't rule it out. After all, I don't know what this is. I don't know how to define it. I don't know how to explain it. I don't know anything about it except that I feel it and it seems very real—or at least as real as anything I have ever known. But I don't experience it all the time. For that matter, I don't even experience it a fraction of the times that I call out to it. Most often, a cold silence is all that answers me. And yet, other times I do feel it's unmistakably there.

Where This Leaves Me

OK, so what? Clearly this kind of experience can't be used to build a nice, coherent theology. It doesn't supply any reassuring, deeply satisfying answer, but this is my experience—nothing more and nothing less. It's all I have to work with. I would very much love to have more precise ideas about the existence and nature of God. But the only way to do it would be to lie to myself and embrace some bullshit rationalization for experience that's beyond ordinary language. And yet, this vague, imprecise experience is what pushes me to skip the atheist camp and the simplest version of agnosticism (if by agnosticism we mean not knowing anything about God because of lack of information). Unlike this type of agnosticism, I feel I do have some direct knowledge; it just happens to be extremely incomplete and very contradictory. This is why I consider myself an agnostic with an asterisk—not the agnostic that is sitting on the fence unsure which side to support, but one who can be simultaneously very atheist and very religious because his experience leads him down both paths at once.

To me, nature appears cold and horrific as much as it seems wonderful beyond words. My own life tells me in no uncertain terms that there is no higher, caring power, and yet I feel something I can't comprehend that is suggesting otherwise. If I were inclined to melodramatic metaphors, I would say it's as if I was pulled by two horses running in opposite directions. If I wake up in a better, mellower mood, I could say life is stretching me to make me more flexible. Things would certainly be simpler if I could convince myself to follow one point of view at the expense of the other. For the sake of consistency, I could just dismiss as delusions those feelings telling me there is something out there, and embrace hardcore atheism. Or I could take the other route and begin reading much more into these feelings, and build a whole cosmology around them to explain everything about God, the universe, and the meaning of life. I could end up with a perfectly consistent theory to do away once and for all with any doubts and ambiguities. I would be free of contradictions. I would be strong in my forceful conclusions. I would feel confident thanks to the clarity of my certainties . . . and I would be a liar.

The only way to come up with a seamless theory would be to ignore all those experiences I can't explain. But that is the coward's way out. It's what people choose to do when they are driven by a curious blend of ego-driven arrogance and tremendous insecurity. Disturbed by not knowing the answer to many of life's secrets, some believers seek comfort in the self-important illusion that they and they alone own the truth about God. With equal dogmatic certainty, hardcore atheists deny the existence of God, no matter how the word may be defined. Unfortunately for believers and atheists alike, certainty in these matters is the enemy of truth and the building block for reassuring lies.

The Nez Percé leader Chief Joseph once remarked, "We don't want churches because they will teach us to quarrel about God."[34] Chief Joseph gets my vote because any organized religion that promises to offer crystal-clear answers about God stops the individual search for God cold in its tracks. On the other hand, I have no problem whatsoever with traditions that don't insist on forcing God to fit into a rigid theology.

The Lakota people use the term *Wakan Tanka* to speak of a divine energy that pervades all things. The most common translation of Wakan Tanka is "Great Mystery." This is probably as close as we get to my idea of God. It's something that you may perceive, something great and powerful, but also mysterious and so far beyond human understanding that trying to conceptualize it would be ridiculous. Similarly, the Taoists refer to the Tao, the power that is at the roots of all things, as a "cosmic mystery."[35] We are very far away from any sense of atheist denial here. Wakan Tanka and the Tao recognize an energy that is as real as it is sacred. And precisely because it is real and sacred, little effort is wasted trying to explain it away.

After all is said and done, what we know is very little. And anyone—believer or atheist alike—offering certain answers does so because he or she is too scared to admit having doubts. Only strong personalities can accept to live with mystery. But let's try to resist the urge to oversimplify reality. Any answer based on incomplete information is at best tentative, a work in progress. No one can know what God is or what he/she/it wants us to do. The search for God is an ongoing quest with no destination in sight. The healthiest step we can take in this search is to remain flexible while striving to do one's best.

CHAPTER 4

THE INTANGIBLES: DEATH AND AFTERLIFE (MAYBE . . .)

Believe in life after death, and you will die. Don't believe in life after death, and you will die. Any way you slice it, you will die. Death laughs at our beliefs and disbeliefs. No one has a clue, and yet everyone has beliefs. All our theories, all our conjectures, all our promises of rewards and punishments. . . . Things must definitely be funny from Death's perspective. Not knowing drives us crazy, and Death loves to tease. Like all good attention-magnets, Death knows that the secret to popularity is mystery. Once people become too familiar with something, they lose interest. But the mystery . . . ah, the mystery is hard to resist. And this why the riddle of death captivates the minds of human beings and never lets go.

The concepts of God and the afterlife are intimately tied. In most religions, those claiming to know God's will promise rewards for following them (e.g., an eternity of bliss in heaven or a much better reincarnation in a future life) and punishments for disobeying (take your pick: burn in hell while being tortured by demons, or be reborn as live bait for a fish).

God and the afterlife are connected in yet another way: there is no irrefutable evidence for the existence of either of them. This is why Buddha strongly resisted indulging in his disciples' curiosity about both God and the afterlife. Why bother with things that are beyond human comprehension and that we have no control over? Buddha suggested in the Parable of the Arrow. Focus instead on what you can do: find a way to eliminate the causes of suffering and improve the quality of your life. Buddha's brutal pragmatism has no patience for idle speculation. His philosophy/religion is driven by a practical purpose, and is not meant to console us or comfort our fears. And this is why Buddhism is an exception among the world's religions, since most religions are built on the twin pillars of God and Death.

But as human beings, we crave solutions to these problems too badly to let a simple lack of evidence stand in the way of some answers. Does life have meaning? Is a benevolent force watching over me? Will I go on existing after my body turns into the main course at a banquet for worms and bacteria? Those who are alive can't discuss the subject based on their experience because they haven't died, whereas the dead have first-hand experience but are usually not too talkative.

I am obviously no different, so my feelings on the topic are nothing but the speculations of a blind man musing about the nature of light. And yet, they are all I have, since I can't turn to more reliable sources, for there is no one alive who has more (or less) experience when it comes to God and the afterlife than I do. Pure logic tells me that the odds of someone having an "afterlife" after their physical body dies seem slim. How could consciousness continue when you no longer have a brain? Those who suffer severe damage to certain areas of their brain may go on living, but the spark of consciousness is gone forever. How, then, could we expect consciousness to survive the complete annihilation of the brain?

Plenty of people like to find support for the reality of an afterlife in tales of near-death experiences. Some of these survivors recount a whole array of fantastic events: white lights at the end of dark tunnels; visions of angels or demons; guest appearances by Jesus, Krishna, or another deity the about-to-be-dead are fond of. Typically, the visions end when the individual is brought back to life. This is the closest that anyone alive has come to experiencing death, so these stories receive much attention from those looking for proof of an afterlife.

Personally, I badly want to believe these stories. They offer hope for something beyond death, and I'm not about to spit on something so desirable. My annoying logical side, however, forces me to cancel my membership in the believers' club and throw my enthusiasm under a cold shower. Near-death experiences, by definition, are not death itself. Science tells us brain activity can continue for several minutes even after somebody is declared dead. In other words, not all of the body dies at the same time. What this means is that the visions of the nearly dead may just be one last big show put on by our very imaginative brains before the lights go out for the last time.

It doesn't surprise me that vast numbers of people choose to abandon logic when it comes to the existence of an afterlife. Life would truly be grim if the only alternatives were between a cold, heartless logic condemning us to a gloom-and-doom vision of the universe and a cowardly delusion filling us with false hopes. But I'm not sold on the idea that these are our only options. Logic and reason are great tools, but they are also very limited because they are only as good as the information available. Imagine putting the most brilliantly logical human beings of a few millennia ago in front of a television. Without any previous familiarity with electricity, they would be at a loss to explain it. All their logic and reason would do little to help them solve the puzzle. When we face the possibility of life after death, we are in a similar situation. We hardly know the first thing about death, so how is logic going to explain it all? Even though logic and reason don't seem to offer support for the idea of life after death, it doesn't necessarily mean much.

In my own life, I have had plenty of experiences that left me in the dust when trying to make sense of them. I have seen perfectly blue skies fill with storm clouds and heavy rain within a few minutes of someone praying for rain. I was told by a medicine man that my urine would turn black right before I would be freed from a spell that had been placed on me: I nearly doubled over laughing since this sounded like the weirdest bullshit I had ever heard . . . until a few weeks later when my urine did turn black. While camping, a friend of mine and I stared at each other when, on a day with no wind, we saw my tent shaking as if someone was moving inside of it. No big deal, we figured. One of our friends must have decided to use it. Except that when we opened the flap no one was inside. While helping cut a tree for a Sun Dance, one of the most important ceremonies of the Lakota people, one of my fingers was broken in three parts and nearly severed when a tree fell on it. I was less than reassured when the old Lakota man running the ceremony told me not to worry because he prayed about it, and the spirits told him they would take care of it. Prayer was not exactly my number one choice as medical treatment for multiple fractures. But I was hours away from the closest hospital and didn't have many other options. Sure enough the old guy could not stop laughing when I undid the bandage to see an extremely swollen finger with much of its skin gone, but otherwise back in one piece. A few weeks later, the skin was fully regrown and you couldn't even see a scar. X-rays showed no signs that any trauma had ever occurred.

I could go on, but I'm sure by now you get the point. Plenty of experiences in my own life seem to violate the normal laws of physics, and yet they happened anyway, right in front of my eyes. I could explain these experiences away with wild theories about spirits, the afterlife, the power of prayer and God, but I would be lying. At the end of the day, I don't know why or how these things happened. I just know they did, and I have no explanation for them. This is why I don't rule out the existence of an afterlife despite the protests of my logic and reason.

The long loop of my personal experiences brings us back to our starting point: we have no certain answers about the afterlife one way or the other. Anyone claiming to know otherwise is trying to sell us something. And yet, death is too big of a topic to ignore. While the nature of death is a mystery, the fear of death is as real and concrete as it gets, so it needs to be addressed. The rest of this section will do precisely that by focusing on the strengths and weaknesses of the various religious approaches toward death in order to fish for something we can use to face the most terrifying force confronting everyone who lives.

Fear, Fear, and More Fear

There is no greater source of anxiety for human beings than the inevitability of death. Death is a demon that sinks its fangs in our soft flesh and tears it apart. It feeds on our very muscles and blood. It consumes our bodies, our identities, our emotions, our memories. It is a vampire that can't be stopped, a hunter who never fails to bring down its prey. Nothing is as scary as knowing that, at this very moment, Death is tracking us down. Sooner or later, it will tire of the chase: it will overtake us and devour everything we have ever been.

Normally, we get mad if anything makes us waste a few hours. We flash with anger if something ruins our day. But our daily problems suddenly seem petty if we weigh them against the immensity of death. We are no longer talking about a few lost hours or days or years. We are talking about eternity here. Clearly, all our other concerns pale in comparison.

This very legitimate fear of death is the engine driving most religions. One of their primary reasons for existing is to help human beings deal with the prospect of physical annihilation. This is the hottest merchandise sold in churches and temples: the promise that they'll help us escape death's sharp teeth.

Religious opposition to secular viewpoints often stems from the fear that if we abandon organized religion, we will abandon the only force standing between us and death. Tom Stewart, a co-prosecutor at the infamous 1925 Scopes trial, opposed Darwin's theory of evolution not because of any evidence, but because accepting evolution would rob him of any hope of defeating death: "Would they have me believe that I was once a worm and writhed in the dust? Will they take from me my hope of hereafter? I want to go beyond this world to where there is eternal happiness."[36] Clearly, Stewart was too terrorized by death to let facts interfere with his hopes.

When grown men so badly need reassurance that after death they will live in eternal happiness with God and all their loved ones, it seems both desperate and pathetic. They use religion the way some infants use pacifiers. Karl Marx used a harsher metaphor when he famously called religion "the opium of the people."[37] Both metaphors may be accurate, but so what? Pacifiers and opium exist because they fulfill a need. If you want someone to quit drugs, you have to offer them an alternative to fulfill that need. Contrary to what Nancy Reagan believed, no one quits drugs because someone tells them drugs are bad. No secular challenge to organized religions will ever succeed unless it offers something to replace what it takes away. Freud correctly argued that religion would never disappear as long as human beings continue to be afraid of death.[38] Most secular movements are doomed to failure because they do nothing to lessen the fear of the unknown. So before we turn to possible alternatives, let's look at how different religions address the fear of death.

From Heaven and Hell to Reincarnation

You can't hush the terror of death with a few vague, fuzzy words. And so most religions come to the rescue with detailed descriptions of the afterlife, and clear-cut maps to get us there safely—bedrocks of certainty to protect us from death's merciless power.

In the entire history of the world's religions, two main models have emerged to reassure us of life after death: One tells us that at death our soul survives to be reincarnated into a new body through an eternal cycle of life after life. This is the option favored by Hinduism, some versions of Taoism, several tribal traditions, and—in a modified format—Buddhism. The other says the soul survives death by going on to live for eternity in either heaven or hell. Among the principal proponents of heaven and hell are Zoroastrianism, Christianity, Islam, and some branches of Buddhism and Taoism. For the sake of fairness, I should mention that whereas many traditions hold their followers to very strict dogmas regarding the nature of the afterlife, a few exceptions (particularly branches of Judaism, Taoism,

Buddhism, and various tribal traditions) allow followers to entertain multiple possibilities. These, however, are not the religions we are focusing on right now, so my moment of fairness is over.

Although they may differ in form, the concepts of reincarnation and heaven and hell fulfill similar functions. Both reassure us that there is life after death. Both argue that—despite massive evidence indicating otherwise—the universe is governed by a moral order. Both console those who suffer in this life with the prospect of finding fortune in the next.

No religion has emphasized the idea of reincarnation as much as Hinduism. In the Hindu version, the individual soul (the Atman) is incarnated into a physical body about to be born. At the death of this particular body, the soul abandons the flesh to jump into a new body about to be born. In a perfect chain of cause and effect, the next incarnation is determined by the soul's karma—the force generated by the sum of all choices, intentions, and actions made in the previous lives. Good karma leads to a favorable reincarnation, while bad karma leads to being reborn as a lower form of life. The soul's options for reincarnation are not limited to human beings. Animals are also fair game since, according to Hinduism, they also possess souls—albeit ones which are inferior to human beings'.

On the surface, the whole notion of karma attracts me. It almost has a scientific ring to it, a spiritual version of the law of cause and effect. Since cause and effect rule every other aspect of life, karma doesn't seem too farfetched a concept. Also, it offers us a great antidote to the endless whining that many human beings love so much. Karma basically tells us that we have total responsibility for everything in our lives. In this worldview, there is no such thing as bad luck, because everything that happens to us is a result of our previous karma. So, rather than complaining about our bad luck, we are better off doing something about it and changing our karma at this very moment. Destiny deals us some cards based on our previous behavior, but it's up to us to decide how to play them in the present.

On the other hand, this seemingly empowering idea can very quickly turn sour and end up smelling of fascism. By suggesting that everything happening to us is a result of our previous behavior, the concept of karma places the blame squarely on the victim. If something horrific happens to you . . . well, that's because you deserve it. A baby dies in childbirth? It's because of his and his parents' karma. While I'm all for emphasizing personal responsibility, karma takes it too far. Extending personal responsibility to actions supposedly taken in previous lives, of which you have no memory and no proof, appears to me as a perversion of personal responsibility. There are too many ifs for my taste, too much desire to rationalize all facets of existence.

Additionally, Hinduism has historically used the concept of karma to justify an extremely hierarchical view of existence, resulting in the stifling social oppression of the caste system. You are poor because you are born into a lower caste? That's because of your previous karma. Be a good boy by fulfilling the duties of your caste (that is to say, by doing menial labor and accepting suffering without complaining) and in the *next* life, you'll have a better birth. For much of Indian history, social immobility has been enforced with the threat of negative karmic consequences for those wanting to change their lives here and now.

Even when the concept of karma is not spoiled by such obvious ploys to defend the socio-political hierarchy, nagging questions still persist. Assuming that reincarnation is real, what exactly is reincarnated? Your physical self dies, and similarly all your memories disappear. In this world, our bodies and our memories determine our personal identity. Without them, how can it still be "I" that goes on to the next life? This is where Hinduism and Buddhism differ in their views of reincarnation. Whereas Hinduism is attached to this single soul that moves from body to body, most schools of Buddhism deny the existence of a permanent self. Rather, they argue that upon death a person's consciousness merges with other energies to give life to a new consciousness, much in the same way that a wave crashing on the sand goes back in the ocean and becomes part of another wave yet to be formed.

If the theory of reincarnation, in all of its possible variations, leaves me unconvinced, the concept of the afterlife popularized in Christianity and Islam downright disturbs me. At least the cyclical nature of reincarnation gives us plenty of opportunities to correct our mistakes and start anew. The linear ideology of Western religions gives human beings one chance and one chance only. Depending on how people behave and on the strength of their faith (different denominations disagree about whether both faith and actions determine our destiny in the afterlife), at death the individual soul will spend *eternity* in either heaven or hell.

This notion of eternal punishment strikes me as one of the most perverse ideas ever devised. Monotheistic religions describe their God as merciful and compassionate, and in the same breath tell us that this merciful and compassionate God will sentence people to eternal torture if they don't believe in his existence, despite a complete lack of objective evidence. Is it just me, or are we looking at a bit of a contradiction? What loving parent would burn his children forever for misbehaving? The idea of hell seems like nothing short of religiously sanctioned sadism. Tertullian, one of the early Church Fathers, makes this abundantly clear when he states that one of the joys of paradise consists in witnessing the unbelievers being tortured in hell.[39] Most scriptures of the heaven-and-hell religions take inordinate joy in detailed descriptions of the gruesome punishments awaiting unbelievers. Sadism oozes out of these pages.

Among my personal favorites is the Zoroastrian punishment for a man who has sex with a woman during her period: he is force-fed menstrual blood for eternity save for brief breaks during which he has to cook and eat his own son.[40] The Old Testament is more moderate in this regard: it simply asks that a man having sex with a menstruating woman be sentenced to death in this life.[41] In comparison, the Muslim and Christian hells in which you are *only* burned for eternity suddenly appear benign by comparison. Zoroastrianism may take the cake for its graphic goriness, but some versions of Christianity win the prize for the most shocking theological argument: those who commit evil actions are not the only ones deserving of hell. Rather, everyone, including newborn babies, deserves to be tortured in hell because of humanity's original sin. Only through repentance and begging for God's forgiveness can anyone be spared this fate.

The emphasis on otherworldly punishments found in the ideas of karma and heaven and hell betrays an attitude that is based on fear rather than understanding. Believers argue that a divinely supervised system of rewards and punishments is useful to teach people how to act in a moral manner. Heaven and hell (or karma, for that matter) are the supernatural equivalent of the carrot and the stick. With no incentive to behave morally, people would act like the selfish bastards that they are at heart. According to this logic, fear is a necessary tool to enforce social rules. But there is plenty of evidence to indicate that many human beings can act decently without being scared into it by boogeyman tales.

The belief in supernatural rewards and punishments may help people overcome their fear of death. After all, the only thing you have to do is declare your faith and follow the rules, and you no longer have to fear death since you are offered an eternity of bliss in heaven or a brand new body in a better reincarnation. But this idea has too many disturbing and horrifying side effects. If the goal is to conquer our fear of death, and we are so desperate as to be willing to embrace beliefs for which there is no evidence, we can surely come up with something better than this.

Heaven and Hell's Cousin: The Apocalypse

Before we start to explore alternatives, it's worth pausing to look at a concept that is very much related to the heaven-and-hell system just discussed. The apocalypse, the end of time, judgment day, Armageddon: it goes by many names, but they all refer to the same thing: a prophecy predicting a global catastrophe that will put an end to the world as we know it.

Several traditions speak of it, but none develop this concept with as much enthusiasm as Western religions. Many scholars believe that this idea of the apocalypse comes to us courtesy of Zoroastrianism, which later passed it on to Judaism, Christianity, and Islam. In Zoroastrianism, in fact, we find the essential elements of Western theology: God and the Devil; heaven and hell; an eternal battle between the forces of good and evil, with angels and demons competing to recruit human beings to their respective sides; the arrival of a Messiah before the last battle, which will destroy the world and banish evil forever; the creation of a new universe after the destruction; and, finally, the resurrection of the dead and a final judgment of the souls.

It doesn't seem to be a coincidence that the same religions that attribute much importance to the idea of heaven and hell also believe in an apocalyptic showdown between good and evil. Both beliefs indicate a craving that evil be punished and good be rewarded. Both point to a bad relationship with reality as it is, and a wish for something to transform it drastically. The only difference is whether setting the record straight will take place in the next world after we die, or if it will occur with the destruction and recreation of this world.

Both beliefs, however, stem from the same frustrations and desires. We shouldn't be surprised, then, to find the idea of the apocalypse thriving among people who feel powerless to change the unpleasant reality facing them. We clearly see this at the origin of Christianity. The first followers of Jesus were Jews whose people had been conquered by the Roman Empire. Life wasn't exactly rosy, particularly for the poorer people in Jewish society. Not only did they resent Rome ruling over them with an iron hand, but they were also locked in a deadly struggle with the Jewish elite who cooperated with the Romans and lived off the labor of lower classes. Add to this mix the incredibly harsh conditions they faced day after day, staying just a few steps ahead of starvation, and you can begin to appreciate just how desperate the world appeared to them. But all was not lost. These, after all, were people who believed that the universe was ruled by a good and just God who regularly intervened in human affairs. Therefore, it was only logical for them to assume that a good and just God would not allow his faithful followers to suffer so horribly for much longer.

This is why preachers like John the Baptist gained huge followings by predicting that God would crush the existing powers of the day, bring the world to an end, and restore justice in a new world. Jesus, following in John the Baptist's footsteps, similarly raised apocalyptic expectations among his followers. Mark 13, for example, quotes Jesus telling them that the end of the world was at hand. Stars would fall from the sky, the sun and moon would stop shining, and massive suffering would sweep through the land before the Second Coming. Emphasizing the immediacy of this prophecy, Jesus declared, "Truly, I say to you this generation will not pass away before all these things take place."[42]

A similar story can be told about some American Indian tribes during the last few years of the 1800s. Much like the lower classes of Jewish society during Jesus' times, American Indians in the late 1800s were witnessing their world falling to pieces. The US government was their Roman empire. By the 1880s, all tribes within the borders of the United States had been conquered. Of a population of several million at the time of first contact, fewer than 300,000 survived. The government was busy trying to wipe out any remaining traces of their cultures. Their political independence was gone, their economy destroyed, their traditional religious ceremonies outlawed. They lived as little more than prisoners of war. Their situation was as bleak and hopeless as it could get.

It's within this context that a Paiute Indian named Wovoka began mixing the Christian theology of the apocalypse he had been taught by missionaries with his own native traditions. Wovoka claimed to have received a vision from God during a solar eclipse: a cataclysm would annihilate white people and cause the resurrection of dead Indians and the return of the buffalo (of which less than 1,000 survived from an initial population of more than forty million). Wovoka said that all American Indians had to do to bring forth this event was to practice a ceremony known as the Ghost Dance. Most Native Americans badly wanted to believe, for it gave them hope at a time when there was none. Just like the first Christians, the Ghost Dancers expected God to fix the intolerable situation they were enduring.

Apparently, in both cases, God was otherwise occupied. Several decades after Jesus' death, the Jewish unrest was repressed in blood by the Romans, and the Ghost Dancers were massacred by the American Army in 1890. The promised apocalypse had not come after all. American Indians, for the most part, reacted by abandoning this belief, whereas early Christians got over the embarrassment of the failed prophesy by simply postponing the apocalypse to a later date.

The theology of the apocalypse is born from despair, among people who suffer horribly, hate the world as it exists, and wish for its destruction. Because they can see nothing but more pain and hopelessness, they are in dire need of the consolation offered by a promise that things are about to change in the near future. This promise gives them a taste of revenge against their oppressors; they can gloat at the prospect of a role reversal when their enemies will burn in hell or be wiped out during the apocalypse. This is perhaps why most descriptions of the apocalypse are filled of rivers of blood and other gory images indicating a frightening level of repressed anger. If we stop to consider the incredibly high numbers of people wishing for their version of the apocalypse to materialize, there are clearly a lot of angry people out there who can't wait for the world to end.

Apocalyptic expectations get on my nerves for the same reason the emphasis on heaven and hell does. Not only are they the mean-spirited, vengeful, sadistic fantasies of those who derive pleasure from the suffering of others, but they are also rooted in resentment toward life in this world, and in a sick relationship with reality. A healthy religion makes no space for these feelings.

Anywhere But Here, Anytime But Now

Let's play a game. It's Religious Trivia 101. Who said "My kingship is not of this world"?[43] How about "As for our own fortune, it is not in this world. And we are not competing with you for this world, because it does not equal in Allah's eyes the wing of a mosquito"?[44] The first is Jesus. The second is Waleed al-Shehri, one of the 9/11 hijackers. Similarly, in 1 John 2:15–16, the Bible gives us this advice, "Love not the world, neither the things that are in the world. If any man loves the world, the love of the Father is not in him. For all that is in the world. . . is not of the Father, but is of the world."[45] In another passage we are told, "This worldly life is no more than vanity and play, while the abode of the Hereafter is the real life, if they only knew."[46] In case I forgot to mention it, this last sentence is not from the Bible, but the Koran, which also tells us, "This worldly life is no more than a temporary illusion."[47] If we didn't already know where these quotes come from, it would be almost impossible to guess since they mirror each other so closely.

All these statements look like contenders in a competition to determine who can most effectively put down life in this world. Christianity and Islam aren't the only competitors: several passages in Hindu and Buddhist scriptures refer to this world as an illusion. The Hindu ideal of Moksha, in particular, means liberation from the cycle of death and rebirth. Worldly existence, in other words, along with the passions that characterize it, needs to be transcended. Contempt for this life and this world seems to be a recurring thread among many branches of most major religions.

I'm allergic to this desire to escape the physical world and the present time. And I sneeze often because this desire is not restricted to the religions described above. Several secular ideologies also preach a faith in pure, abstract ideas that can never be realized in the world as it is. Plato's philosophy is a prime example of this. In his view, the real can never match the ideal; what is earthy is rejected in favor of a "pure" dimension beyond the earth. The ecstasy of being alive in this world is being trampled by those who can't appreciate what's under their feet! I'm allergic to seeing life as a sin, as merely a test to be endured on our way to eternal rewards. I'm allergic to all this because the focus on what is "beyond" is a slap in the face of the here and now. I'm allergic to all those who separate the physical from the spiritual and end up poisoning both.

I worship Life—all of life. The life that burns without shame. The life that dances, smiling, just one step away from the abyss. The life that sips margarita on the beach, surrounded by seagulls. The life that cries tears of blood when it gives everything it can give, but everything is not enough. The life in whose veins flow lightning. The life whose depth hurts. The life moved by the autumn rain and by the summer heat. The life that doesn't wait to continue after the commercial break. The life that sticks its tongue out at Duty. The life that runs in the woods chasing its meal. The life that reveals itself only when you are ready to leave it on the battlefield. Most of all, I worship the life that refuses to regret even one of the days it wasted.

This is why I can't stomach all these gloomy people who can't wait to go to another world. And I'm equally turned off by those salivating at the prospect of destroying this world. Hey! It's my world. Get your hands off it.

But what disturbs me most is that the more you adhere to fundamentalist ideas about the apocalypse and the afterlife, the more likely you are to attribute little value to human life. Life can be more easily sacrificed when you believe you are dying for God's cause and you will later be rewarded for it. It's from this mentality that the cult of martyrdom is born. For this reason, at least on this particular issue, I'm much more comfortable with religions that focus on the here and now, such as some versions of Judaism, Buddhism, Taoism, Shinto, and certain animistic traditions.

Never Underestimate the Power of Fanaticism

Even though I'm clearly not a fan of focusing on the afterlife, I do recognize that this belief carries a very real power: it defeats the fear of death. Antonin Scalia, one of the conservative bulwarks of the US Supreme Court and a Roman Catholic, expressed the connection between certain religious doctrines and a casual attitude toward death with brutal lucidity (I never thought I would write the words "lucidity" and Scalia in the same sentence, but let's move on). The more Christian a country is, Scalia stated, the more it is willing to embrace the death penalty because "for the believing Christian, death is no big deal."[48]

José Millán Astray, the ultra-Catholic and ultra-fascist founder and first commander of the Spanish Foreign Legion, butcher of the Spanish Civil War, and one of dictator Francisco Franco's main henchmen, turned this theological insight into a battle cry: "¡Viva la Muerte!" ("Long live death!"). The survival instinct was seen as cowardly and a symptom of a weak faith, since death was but a doorway to heaven. Their fanatical faith freed Astray's soldiers from fear and allowed them to focus only on slaughtering as many enemies as possible.

This necrophiliac enthusiasm is even more evident today in the ideology of Muslim terrorists. In a tape attributed to al-Qaeda sympathizers claiming responsibility for the 2004 bombing of trains in Madrid that killed almost 200 people, the same concept reappears. "You love life and we love death," they say. In other words, you are attached to life because your faith in the afterlife is not strong enough. We think nothing of dying for our cause because for us, as Scalia would put it, "death is no big deal."

Expanding further on this morbid creed, Chief Palestinian Authority cleric Mufti Sheikh Ikrimeh Sabri said: "We tell them, in as much as you love life, the Muslim loves death and martyrdom. There is a great difference between he who loves the hereafter and he who loves this world. The Muslim loves death and [strives for] martyrdom."[49]

Antonin Scalia and the most extreme Muslim fanatics have probably nothing but contempt for each other, but their attitude about life and death is formed by the same mold.

I'm disgusted by these people, but I'm not quoting them out of moral outrage. Rather, it's to show that their macabre theology can grant a tremendous power. The toughest enemies to fight, after all, are those who are not afraid of dying as long as they can kill you. Their power does come at the very steep price of lessening the importance of this life, but what they achieve is the conquest of the most primal human fear—not a small feat.

How can we tap into the strength of this belief without paying the horrific price it requires? Isn't this chapter about finding alternatives to defeat the fear of death? How about showing these gloomy bastards that loving life is not a weakness?

Hoka Hey

Ever since I can remember I have been terrified of death. One night, when I was four years old, I voiced my fear to my mother. She laughed, patted me on the head, and told me not to worry—it would be a long time before I would have to deal with death. I hate to point this out, Mom, but your answer didn't exactly solve the problem for me. I kept hoping that somehow growing up I would come to terms with death, and the fear would just vanish away, but things didn't turn out that way.

Fear never let go of its hold on me. It has been my constant companion since then, following my every step. It has stared me down time and time again. No matter how far or how fast I run, I carried my own inner demon with me. It injected a pinch of anxiety into even the happiest moments of my life. No accomplishment, no amount of self-esteem, no wonderful experience made me forget that death could take it all away at any second. This thought turned me into a bit of a control freak (OK, maybe more than a bit. . .). My innate devotion to laughter kept me sane, but I still felt I was fighting a losing battle.

And then I arrived at a proverbial crossroad. I reached a point in my life where I saw everything that I worked so hard for fall to pieces before my eyes. For years, I had strained every fiber of my being to bring happiness to the people I love. I had fought tooth and nail to make sure everything and everyone around me would be all right. But things slipped through my grip, despite all my efforts. A sense of powerlessness and desperation overcame me. The control freak in me was frustrated to the core. Staring me in the eyes was the realization that no matter how hard you try, you can't lock your doors enough, you can't prepare enough, you can't defend yourself enough. Ultimately, everything can and will be taken away from us—the people we love, everything we've ever accomplished, even our memories. At the end of it all, we don't control anything in life. No matter how careful or smart we may be, horrible things can still hunt us down. What we love will be ripped away from our arms. As Johnny Cash sang in one of the last songs he recorded, "Everyone

I know goes away in the end." Our hearts will be broken over and over again. Maybe we will be lucky and we can delay the inevitable, maybe not. Either way, it doesn't really matter. We can play our cards well, but we can't choose what happens to us. At the end, we are bound to lose it all.

After all my illusions of control vanished, something snapped inside of me. Desperation gave way to rage. I'm tired of feeling anxiety breathing down my neck, I told myself. I'm tired of my many obsessive-compulsive habits. Most of all, I'm tired of living in fear. None of my efforts can spare me from pain, so screw it. I'll do the only thing I have control over. I can't choose what will come my way. The worst things in the world may happen to me regardless of my wishes, but I can choose how I will face them. And what I choose now is to not let fear boss me around for one more minute.

In that second I experienced more freedom that I had ever known.

Life will hurt me? My heart will break every day? So what. I'll deal with it. The typical reaction in the face of pain is to close up, become more defensive, build a higher wall. The fear of getting hurt pushes plenty of individuals to squash their emotions because their ability to feel makes them vulnerable. In this way, they die before dying and live at less than their full potential—mere shadows of who they could be. The fear of death encourages them to embrace religious fantasies offering them the illusion of control.

Despite my best efforts, I can't lie to myself. So I guess I'll face death without any fables to boost my morale. I'm OK with giving up the illusion of control. Come to terms with this, and the doors to true freedom open up. This is the same discovery that changed Frederick Douglass' life (one of the most famous abolitionists in history). After being terrorized for his entire life as a slave, Douglass one day decided that no matter what punishments he may have to endure, he would not live another day in fear. He wrote, "I had reached the point at which I was *not afraid to die*. This spirit made me a freeman in *fact*, while I remained a slave in *form*."[50] Accepting death is the key that frees us from the prison of fear.

The battle cry of Lakota warriors perfectly captures this idea. "Hoka hey" is usually translated as "today is a good day to die." The same sentiment is found in the war cry of their allies, the Cheyenne: "Only heaven and earth are eternal! I am not!"[51] Unlike the "¡Viva la Muerte!" of Spanish fascists, the Lakota and Cheyenne battle cries don't indicate a death wish or a desire for martyrdom. Rather, as they get ready for battle, the warriors acknowledge that they won't be able to control everything that is going to happen. They can't be sure that death will not strike them down, but they can choose the state of mind in which they'll face whatever is coming their way. They embrace the possibility of death to avoid the fear that paralyzes those who cling to the hope of survival. If, after all is said and done, they end up surviving, so much the better, but they won't head into battle holding on to this hope, because hope breeds attachment, attachment feeds the fire of fear, and fear paradoxically increases the odds of getting killed. "Hoka hey" is about refusing to let any situation—even the prospect of death—rob you of your attitude toward life.

Yamamoto Tsunetomo, author of the Bushido classic known as the Hagakure, calls this mindset the "rainstorm attitude." As he writes,

> When caught in a sudden shower, one may determine not to get drenched, running as fast as one can or trying to thread one's way under the eaves of houses along the way—but one gets wet nonetheless. If from the outset one is mentally prepared

to get wet, one is not in the least discomfited when it actually happens. Such an attitude is beneficial in all situations.[52]

When you accept the fact that—like it or not—you'll lose everything, a strange ecstasy shows up at your door. Being ready to die at any moment gives greater intensity and beauty to all of your actions. The first time I felt it, I understood the euphoria experienced by those who don't fear death. But unlike Scalia, al-Qaeda, and the other religious death-lovers who look forward to the "afterlife," I don't feel the need to put down life in this world. Actually, the opposite is true. Without fear, I am liberated. Without attachment, everything makes me smile and the joy of being alive shines unspoiled by worries, hopes, and expectations.

If it weren't tacky to quote oneself, what I wrote in another book would fit perfectly . . . On second thought, tackiness never stopped me before so here we go: "The fear of failure, the fear of rejection, the fear of opening up to another human being, even the fear of death itself begin to lose their power over you. No longer afraid to be who you are, you face life with no regrets, no self-imposed limitations, free. Armed with the courage to take risks, you don't allow the fear of losing what you value the most hold you back anymore. It's only when you are ready to lose it all that life reveals itself in all of its beauty."[53]

Clearly, there is no recipe to reach this state of consciousness. Mine was desperation and powerlessness. Hopefully yours is more pleasant, but I doubt it since the game is about facing our most terrifying fears, and that is never fun. It's like building strong muscles by lifting weights. Lift too much, and you'll get crushed. Don't lift enough, and you never get strong. Like any other muscle, a fear-defeating muscle is developed by degrees, tackling small fears before moving on to bigger ones. And even after you tame the deepest fears, they will rise back up unless you keep them in check. It's a constant process.

At the heart of it all is a paradox. On one side, we have other-worldly delusions that breed contempt for this world. On the other, we have a love of this life and an attachment to it, with the accompanying fear of death that makes it impossible to live and die beautifully. Do we have to become fearless death-loving freaks or life-lovers whose dreams are haunted by the terror of losing it all? The only way out is to develop the seemingly impossible ability to enjoy every last morsel of life without any attachment to it. But who is capable of the deepest passion without attachment? It's human nature to become attached to what we love. One seems inextricably connected to the other. This is why in trying to free us from attachment, many forms of Buddhism end up driving passion away as well.

A Zen Buddhist story, however, points to a different possibility. It tells of a man hiking in the forest who stumbles into a tiger who is in the mood for lunch. Chased by the tiger, the man reaches a cliff and, in an effort to avoid turning into the tiger's meal, he grabs hold of a vine and swings himself over the cliff. As he is trying to measure the distance to the bottom of the cliff to see if he can jump, he notices another tiger looking up at him. This is definitely not the man's lucky day, for the situation is about to get worse. Since his life was already not complicated enough, two mice decide to begin munching on the vine. With the range of available choices shrinking by the second, the man notices a ripe wild strawberry growing barely out of his reach. It would be reasonable to assume that the two tigers ready to snack on him plus the pesky mice would give the man plenty to think about, but our hero instead decides to let go of the vine with one hand and swing himself within reach of the strawberry. It's just too damn red and juicy to ignore. Never did the man taste such a sweet strawberry.[54]

This is a riddle that can't be solved intellectually but through experience. Sounds difficult? You bet. But solve it and you'll defeat death, and simultaneously escape the clutches of those who offer you the consolation of otherworldly fantasies for the price of renouncing your love for this life.

CHAPTER 5

THE MOTHER OF ALL CHOICES: INCLUSIVE OR EXCLUSIVE RELIGIONS

Moses's Cute Little Death Squad

Understand this story and you'll understand what drives people to fly airplanes into buildings. Understand this story and you'll understand what pushes people to kill and be killed in the name of God. Understand this story and you'll understand the forces at the roots of all the Crusades, 9/11s, Inquisitions, and other religiously motivated forms of violence that have drowned human history in rivers of blood.

It's one of the most meaningful moments of the Old Testament. The Hebrew tribes have just escaped decades of enslavement in Egypt and Moses is the man of the hour. Not only has he led this daring bid for freedom, but when Pharaoh's armies gave chase, he thwarted their efforts by parting the Red Sea. With little time to rest on his success, Moses is now called up Mount Sinai for a face-to-face meeting with the one and only God. As thunder and lightning fill the air, God gives Moses the stone tablets containing the Ten

Commandments—the essential laws forming the moral foundations of Western religions.

This is such a central, climactic episode that even people who have never read the Bible are familiar with it. Less well known, however, but by no means less important, is what happens right after. What follows *after* the delivery of the Ten Commandments, in fact, is at the heart of our story.

While Moses is hanging out with God at the top, at the bottom of the mountain the Hebrew tribes are growing restless. Many days have already passed since Moses left, and no one can be certain whether he is ever coming back. For all they know, he could be dead. Everyone has seen fire and smoke enveloping the summit, so his prolonged disappearance raises several eyebrows. Worn out by the wait, some people, who were less than fully sold on Moses' insistence on monotheism to begin with, decide to kill time by having a ceremonial feast around the statue of a golden calf—a classic symbol of one of the fertility deities worshipped in those days by polytheistic people throughout the Middle East. By the time Moses comes down the mountain, he finds himself in the midst of a full-on orgiastic ritual: wild music, naked bodies of men and women dancing themselves into a frenzy, and perhaps even juicier stuff that biblical authors are too bashful to describe in nitty-gritty detail.

To say that Moses is not pleased would be an understatement. Rather than saying "Hey guys, would you mind keeping the music and the moaning down?" or simply making fun of the worship of a funny looking cow, Moses smashes the tablets with the Ten Commandments and gathers his most loyal followers. "Who is on the Lord's side?" he yells out. "Let him come unto me. Put every man his sword by his side, and go in and out from gate to gate throughout the camp, and slay every man his brother, and every man his companion, and every man his neighbor."[55] Yes, you read right. Moses organizes a religious death squad that will end up massacring 3,000 fellow Jewish tribesmen by hacking them to pieces with swords.

Let's look at it again. "Put every man his sword by his side, and go in and out from gate to gate throughout the camp, and slay every man his brother, and every man his companion, and every man his neighbor." This is Hitler speaking. It is Stalin speaking. It's Mao. It's Pol Pot. It's Torquemada. These are the words of all the self-righteous fanatics in history who ever felt entitled to wipe out anyone daring to think differently from them.

What's going on here?!? God, after all, has just spelled out as an absolute moral law that you should not murder people. Without skipping a beat, Moses feels it's a sacred duty to order the killing of 3,000 of his own. Through this story, the Bible seems to be telling us that if you run into people who don't worship the one God who says murder is bad, then you should murder them.

If you are confused, you are not alone. The rest of this chapter will explore the differences between inclusive and exclusive approaches to religion, and the effects these opposite worldviews have on everything, ranging from religious freedom to "holy" wars, from the possibility of interfaith dialogue to vice laws.

Grandma from Hell

I was reminded of this uplifting story not too long ago. I had just finished teaching a night class and was on my way home. After flipping through a few channels on the radio and finding no good music, I stumbled upon the beginning of a religious broadcast about the difference between "politically correct" and "biblically correct." The voice of the lady lecturing was pleasant. She sounded like some sweet, old Grandma—you know, the type who spoils you with gifts, pinches your cheeks, and bakes you cookies. I was stuck having to drive for an hour anyway, so I figured, why not? Let's check out what Grandma has to say.

In her delicate little voice, she began explaining how nowadays many Christians believe that even if someone belongs to a different religion, as long as they are good people, they are still worthy of respect and may be admitted to heaven. Nothing wrong so far. But, the lady warned, this belief is just a modern fad, some wishy-washy, liberal version of postmodern Christianity. This idea may be politically correct, but it is not "biblically correct."

"You want to know what God thinks of religious diversity?" she asked. "Turn to Exodus, chapter thirty-two." Chills went down my spine. After quoting the Moses death squad story, she continued with another pearl of religious fascism coming from the Old Testament. In Numbers 25, over 24,000 Jews have died in a plague sent by God as punishment. Why? Many Jews have married foreign women and agreed to honor their spouses' deities. In the midst of this crisis, Phinehas, the "hero" of the story and a Moses loyalist, stalks a Jewish man who has gone back to his tent with his Midianite wife and thrusts a spear through both of them while they are having sex. Extremely pleased with this act, God halts the plague and spares the remaining Jews.[56]

Grandma is on a roll now, and nothing can stop her. She tells how the prophet Elijah received divine assistance in having 450 priests of Baal slaughtered.[57] She gloats as she describes how the pagan queen Jezebel was tossed out of a window to be eaten by dogs.[58] And she continues on, quoting one passage after another to reinforce the legitimacy of murdering religious dissidents. "If you truly follow God's word," she finishes, "then you can't tolerate other religions."

Damn . . . I'm not so sure I want your cookies anymore. You are one scary old lady. At the beginning of the twenty-first century, she is regretting the passing of the good old days when we burned people at the stake. Most Christians today—along with most followers of just about every major religion—are probably not inclined to share the lady's cheerful enthusiasm for spilling the blood of unbelievers. The pluralistic notion that we shouldn't persecute followers of a different path has gained ground even among many of the most hardcore religious individuals. But the speech by the grandma from hell offered a sobering reminder that while in some parts of the world chopping people's heads off with swords over religious differences has fallen out of fashion, the ideology justifying religious violence is far from gone. It is right there, in the pages of scriptures, waiting to be dusted off and brought back into the mainstream.

Renowned religious scholar Charles Kimball has argued that religions are innately good vehicles of love and compassion, but they can turn evil when they give in to rigid dogmatism. When this happens, religious violence is just a few steps away. Following this line of thinking, he separates authentic religions that are pluralistic and inclusive from corrupted forms of religion that encourage conflict and hostility toward different ideas.

Even though I like his work, I don't share Kimball's certainty over which religions are "authentic" and which are "corrupted." My concern here is not to establish the authenticity of a certain religious doctrine, since it seems like a hopeless undertaking. After all, many sacred texts contain lines supporting compassionate, friendly interpretations as much as bloody, intolerant ones. This is why, within most religions, you are bound to find very open-minded people willing to consider other points of views as well as people who swear by the exclusivist claim that their way is the Only Way. I don't care to debate which one is true. I only care about the consequences. Certain religious attitudes encourage dialogue and respect for individual inquiry. Others plant the seeds for a harvest of blood. These very concrete, opposite results are the main reason why I embrace the former and oppose the latter.

Inclusive Religions: More Than One Path Can Reach the Top of the Mountain

Since the religious difference between inclusive and exclusive views is quite possibly the most meaningful there is, and since so much depends on this choice, let's see what pushes people to join either camp.

The basic assumption at the roots of an inclusive approach to religion is that no one can ever know the entire truth. No matter how much knowledge we gain, the essence of life can never be caught and neatly explained. For this reason, both Taoists and Lakota people speak of life as a Great Mystery. Divine power may be perceived, but it can never be fully understood. And an individual's search for truth is a work in progress, not something to attain once and for all.

The impossibility to know the truth from A to Z inevitably implies no one can claim its exclusive ownership, for no single method or doctrine is big enough to capture it all. This realization is what prompted the fourth century pagan apologist Symmachus to state, "What does it matter by which wisdom each of us arrives at truth? It is not possible that only one road leads to so sublime a mystery."[59] The same sentiment is echoed by Thomas Paine when he wrote, "The key to heaven is not in the keeping of any sect, nor ought the road to it be obstructed by any."[60]

This doesn't mean there is no truth and everything is relative. It certainly doesn't mean all approaches and conclusions are equally valid. Some paths are going to produce good results, and some won't. But you will not know which is which until you test their effectiveness. No idea is to be rejected without giving it a chance to prove its worth.

If one religion is a good thing, the inclusive approach reasons, then two or three are even better. It's for this reason that polytheistic and animistic religions throughout history rarely had any problems borrowing from other traditions.

Even more importantly, in this way of looking at the world, difference is not perceived as a threat. Maybe a different idea will turn out to be good so we'll use it, and maybe it won't, and so we'll discard it. In either case, just because somebody lives by a different religion, philosophy, or set of priorities doesn't automatically mean they are our enemies. The inclusive approach is not driven by the territorial instinct that pushes a rooster to attack any other male venturing in his coop. Rather than automatically reacting with hostility, the inclusive approach will take a look at the new arrival to decide whether to become friends, fight, or ignore it. Typically, embracing the novelty or ignoring it will be the main options, for the inclusive approach holds that as long as something doesn't directly threaten us, the best policy is to live and let live.

Taoism, Buddhism, and many forms of Animism are all classic examples of inclusive religions encouraging people to think for themselves. The same tendency is also found among the more liberal interpretations of any other religion, including Christianity, Islam, and Judaism. In many ways, in fact, liberal Christians, Muslims, and Jews have more in common with Taoists and Buddhists than they do with very conservative branches of their own religion.

In the same way you can find inclusive currents in just about every religion, it is also possible to find exclusive factions in otherwise inclusive religions. The founder of a branch of Buddhism known as Nichiren, for example, considered most other forms of Buddhism corruptions that should be prohibited, and even hinted that killing heretics may not be such a bad idea. But these slips into the waters of rabid fundamentalism tend to be the exception in traditions like Buddhism, because there's absolutely nothing in their doctrines to support them. They are considerably less rare when the very scriptures of a religious tradition contain exclusive messages such as the lovely golden calf episode mentioned earlier.

Exclusive Religions: "If You Are Not With Me, You Are Against Me"

In order to understand the exclusive way of thinking, consider this story. When the first permanent English colony in North America was established in Jamestown in the early 1600s, the early settlers ran into more trouble than they had expected. Poor planning led them to the edge of starvation. Wintertime found them so hungry and desperate that, in a few cases, they dug up the bodies of their deceased companions to eat them. In the midst of this crisis, the colony was saved by the intervention of the Powhatan, a local tribe that took pity on them by bringing them food and showing them where and when to plant crops.

Logic would dictate the English would be eternally grateful to the Powhatan, since in their moment of greatest need the Powhatan had saved their lives. But no. Here is a diary entry by one of the settlers, offering us a window on the inner workings of the English colonial mind: "If it had not pleased God to put a terror into the savages' heart we would have all perished by those wild and cruel pagans, being in the weak state that we were."[61]

What kind of sick bastard would write this? Complete strangers come to rescue you from certain death, and rather than recognizing their kindness, you still consider them "wild and cruel pagans" who have been momentarily pushed to good actions by God's intervention?!? Some very strange logic is at work here. What, more than saving you, can they do before you acknowledge they are not "wild and cruel," but perhaps nice people after all?

This is the problem. There's absolutely nothing they can do, for the exclusive mind is not going to be convinced by actions or empirical evidence. The religious ideology of the English told them that no matter how nice somebody is, as long as they don't subscribe to your same set of beliefs, they are evil. The fact that someone may behave in a perfectly decent way—and, incidentally, save you from *feeding on your dead companions*—doesn't diminish their evil status, because they still don't belong to the Only True Religion.

In Asia, an inclusive approach in many instances allowed the Chinese to practice Taoism, Buddhism, and Confucianism at the same time, while in the West just the thought of following two religious traditions simultaneously was enough to send the local inquisitor on your trail. Why can't Westerners practice Islam and Christianity at the same time, or whatever other combination they feel like? Because most versions of these religions assume God lays out a single path for human beings to follow. Mixing it with anything else would be diluting the truth with errors. As Jesus said in the Gospel, in one of the lines most loved by fundamentalists, "I am the way and the truth and the life. No one comes to the Father except through me."[62]

Once internalized, this concept has a tremendous impact on how we perceive anything and anyone who doesn't share our same theology. If you firmly believe there's only one way to the truth, a difference of opinion means at least one of us must be wrong. And since the fans of the exclusive approach believe they have a monopoly on Truth, it means whoever disagrees with them is in error.

Exclusive religions also tend to be characterized by a sharp dualism: there is God and the Devil, absolute good and absolute evil, and not a whole lot of room in between. This logic is clearly articulated by Jesus in his statement, "He who is not with me is against me"[63]— a sentiment that has been repeated by plenty of people, from Benito Mussolini (his "either with us or against us" was one of his classic slogans) to George W. Bush ("Either you are with us or you are with the terrorists"[64]). Neutrality is not an option, for this worldview forces you to pick sides.

Since exclusive religions don't allow neutrality and view the whole world as a battlefield between the forces of good and evil, open conflict is inevitable. This mentality, in fact, is rooted in rivalry, direct opposition, and a quest for supremacy. Just like an Old West gunslinger, the exclusive mindset swears "this town ain't big enough for the both of us." Anyone who disagrees with them is not just wrong but—whether they know it or not—is also an agent of evil. And in order for good to triumph, anyone engaging in "wrong" behaviors or harboring "wrong" ideas needs to be stopped.

Not everyone in the exclusive religious camp agrees on the methods to employ in order to stop the agents of evil. The more benign version consists of preaching one's message in the hope of converting other people, and leading them away from their mistakes. This approach is a bit arrogant and self-righteous, but at least it tries to reach out to those who disagree with them, and so I have nothing against it. If nothing else, it is an honest attempt to win hearts and minds by doing your best to convince people.

The other strategies by which the exclusive crusaders try to conquer the world are considerably less benign. Usually, they either try to impose their viewpoint on everyone else through violence or through laws enforcing their own idea of morality. We will return to these themes later in the chapter since they dramatically affect everyone in the world.

In either case, this dogmatic certainty of being the only ones to have access to the truth makes the adherents of the exclusive approach intolerant at heart. Whereas individuals who follow multiple paths have no problem with those who wish to follow only one, the courtesy is usually not returned, since the believers in a single path typically want everyone else to abandon their ideas and embrace theirs. Not only do these guys hate the supporters of an inclusive outlook, but they also hate each other, since the proponents of a single path to the truth other than one's own are competition. Not until the entire world believes what they believe will they feel satisfied. This aggressive tendency marks these people as a threat to anyone who is unwilling to join their ranks.

For this reason, the inclusive and the exclusive approach are not simply different, equally legitimate points of view. This is not a matter of personal taste. In one case, we are faced with a rigid choice precluding all other choices. In the other, we are allowed full freedom of choice as long as we don't infringe on the freedom of others.

Personally, I regularly run into plenty of philosophies and religions I don't like and with whose conclusions I disagree. But this doesn't mean they should be stamped out of existence. Since the truth is not self-evident, I fully believe people should have the freedom to find out for themselves. Independent inquiry is sacred to me. Freedom is the key value that makes everything else possible.

Unfortunately, most exclusive ideologies don't share my enthusiasm for liberty. True freedom, in their mind, is found by following their brand of religious dogma. Freedom of choice, by contrast, is seen as an opportunity for evil to prosper, and as an act of aggression against God's revealed truth. This is what the Puritan John Norton expressed with great clarity when he referred to liberty of worship as "a liberty to seduce others from the true God."[65] More recently, a fundamentalist Muslim preacher said, "secularism is a disgusting form of oppression . . . No Muslim can accept secularism, freedom, and democracy. It is for Allah alone to legislate how society shall be regulated! Muslims wish and long for Allah's law to replace the law of man."[66] In other words, regardless of which particular religion they embrace, fundamentalists are at war with the very idea of freedom, and with anyone who refuses to help them impose their doctrine on every aspect of life.

Fundamentalists Are All Alike

Most fundamentalists deeply resent being compared to fundamentalists from other religions, since they are locked in a fierce competition with them. But their ideological underpinnings are the same. They all promote an exclusive theology, and they all want the whole world to follow their beliefs.

Genuine differences also exist, however. Save for a few exceptions, most Christian fundamentalists today are considerably less prone to violence than their Muslim counterparts. This has less to do with profound religious differences than with historical transformations. If religion was the cause, then it would be logical to expect fundamentalist Christians to have been a peaceful lot throughout the centuries, and this is clearly not the case.

CREATE YOUR OWN RELIGION

The first reason is simple: the growth of secularism in the West and the historical experience of the Enlightenment have hobbled the repressive power of fundamentalist Christian institutions. To put it bluntly, they no longer have the power and the widespread support necessary to squash dissent. As long as they did have it, they were only too happy to use it.

The second reason also has nothing to do with theology: without even realizing it, through living in democratic societies and being exposed to pluralistic cultural influences, modern Christian fundamentalists have internalized at least a few more tolerant values. And this makes them less likely to act on the bloodiest passages in their scriptures. If it weren't for these two accidents of history, there would be nothing preventing some of them from behaving like their witch-burning ancestors.

But in order to avoid the unflattering comparison to Islamic fundamentalists, hardcore conservative Christians like to reinvent a more pleasant history for themselves. As an example of this creative endeavor to rewrite the past, they sometimes argue that the libertarian ideals of the Declaration of Independence are derived not from the Enlightenment, but from Christianity! This sounds great until you consider the nearly 2,000 years of evidence to the contrary. Considering the amount of religious oppression enacted by Jesus' fans for many centuries before the Declaration of Independence, the notion that the freedom-loving ideals stem from Christianity can only be bought by someone who knows nothing about history. If true Christianity does indeed encourage freedom, then the logical conclusion is that only a tiny minority of people through the ages were "true" Christians. The good old days when fundamentalist Christianity was in power, in fact, show us a record as bloody and repressive as that of modern fundamentalist Islam.

Despite the best efforts to clean up the past, the similarity in worldviews between different brands of religious fundamentalism still transpires in some of their comments. Osama bin Laden, for example, believed God made 9/11 possible, and considered secularism a crime deserving punishment. Christian evangelical leaders Pat Robertson and Jerry Falwell interpreted 9/11 as divine retribution for secularism. Consider Jerry Falwell's comments: "We make God mad. I really believe that the pagans, and the abortionists, and the feminists, and the gays and lesbians who are actively trying to make that an alternative lifestyle, the ACLU, People for the American Way—all of them who have tried to secularize America—I point my finger in their face and say 'You helped this happen.'"[67]

And not to be outdone, here is Pat Robertson:

> I believe that the protection, the covering of God that has been on this great land of ours for so may years, had lifted on September 11, and allowed this thing to happen. God apparently had good reasons for exposing the USA to such destruction, given the many sins that Americans have committed ever since the Roe versus Wade court case and the Supreme Court's decision to keep God out of the schools. In fact, American infidelity goes back to the 1920s and 1930s, to situational ethics and notions of cultural relativity, along with a flirtation with communism at the highest levels of government. The point is not just that Americans have been bad and forfeited their entitlements. It is that unless they reform themselves in a hurry, something far worse may happen to them.[68]

Despite their deep mutual hatred for one another, many religious totalitarians end up supporting the same things. They all resent separation of church and state, despise secular culture, want to convert the entire world, hold on to Apocalyptic expectations, envision an afterlife in which their rivals will be tortured in hell, display an unusual passion for censorship, impose their moral ideals by law at any chance they get, support separate religious schools, reject evolution, and oppose uninhibited sexuality. In light of these common features, I fail to be excited by their supposed differences; they all seem like wannabe Talibans to me.

Let's Not Forget Fascists, Nazis, and Communists

Just to prove religious fanatics don't have a monopoly over totalitarianism, Fascists, Nazis, and Communists all stole a page from the playbook of repressive theologies to form their own secular exclusive claims to the truth. Even if we rule out the connections and occasional alliances between these movements and organized religion,[69] the similarities between them make it clear these movements are nothing but forms of political fundamentalism—different from religious fundamentalism in name only.

Thomas Paine was the first to notice the similarity between secular and religious fundamentalism. Commenting about the French Revolution, he wrote, "The intolerant spirit of church persecution had transferred itself into politics; the tribunals, stiled Revolutionary, supplied the place of an Inquisition; and the Guillotine, of the Stake."[70]

Similarly, Nazis, Fascists, and Communists never really challenged the premises of religious fundamentalism. They often resented it because they wanted to replace it as the dominant ideology, but they never really questioned its aims or its methods. Just like religious totalitarians, they had no problems forcing people to follow their dogmas. Whereas Christians, Muslims, and Jews attacked heretics, Communists would target any other leftist movements as well as people with alternative interpretations of Communism.

Despite their heated competition, both religious and secular totalitarians are after the same goal: they all want total control. They all want to reform society according to their priorities, they want everyone to submit to a single source of authority, and they are ready to trample freedom under their feet. In order to defend their ideals (take your pick on whether you prefer Biblical or Koranic concepts, or visions of a classless society or a pure race), violence is sanctified as a legitimate means.

The Totalitarian Attack on Freedom: From Censorship to the Inquisition

Censorship, squashing dissent, and limiting personal choices are at the essence of totalitarianism. Don't be fooled by the colors of their uniforms or by the different dogmas they spout: from Communist Red Guards to Christian fundamentalists, from Nazis to Islamic fanatics, members of the most extreme fringes of these movements are united in an effort to repress free thinking and eliminate different points of view. This is why they have all consigned thousands of texts to the flames.

This passion for book burning resurfaces anytime exclusive ideologies become more aggressive. In 390 CE, a Christian mob burned down the Library of Alexandria, where over 700,000 volumes had been carefully preserved. Little over a century later, the Byzantine Emperor Justinian the Great closed down the main schools of Greek philosophy. Non-Christian writings were banned throughout much of Europe, and many of them ended up permanently lost. When they conquered Mexico, Catholic Spaniards promptly set fire to

Aztec and Maya books, forever erasing a wealth of irreplaceable knowledge. Far from being the personal initiative of intolerant conquistadores, this was perfectly in line with the official policy of the Roman Catholic Church, as evidenced by their keeping a "List of Prohibited Books" to be eliminated (incidentally, the Church kept openly arguing for the utility of the list until the 1960s!). Even translating the Bible from Hebrew and Greek and making it available to the general population was enough of a crime in the 1500s that early translators, such as William Tyndale, paid for it with their lives. I could go on, but I think you get the gist.

C'mon, Bolelli, this stuff belongs to the past. No one burns books anymore, right? Yeah, just ask Chinese Communists. Better yet, go ask Salman Rushdie. Ever since 1989, Rushdie has had to live under police protection after Ruhollah Khomeini—that champion of Islamic fundamentalism and former religious leader of Iran—issued a death sentence against him, urging faithful Muslims to kill him on sight. His crime? Writing a book that offended the delicate sensibility of Islamic fundamentalists. In other words, Rushdie has been sentenced to death for nothing but expressing his opinions. Whereas Rushdie has been able to escape execution, several publishers and translators of his book have been assaulted and in some cases even killed. In a perfect gesture of solidarity among book burners, the Vatican as well as scores of Protestant and Jewish religious leaders reacted to this by criticizing Rushdie. In their eyes, he was guilty of provoking the violent reaction by fundamentalist Muslims.[71]

Even more recently, in 2005, when caricatures of Muhammad were published in a Danish newspaper, the fundamentalist Muslim world responded with its usual cool rationality and respect for freedom of expression. "Behead those who insult Islam," read the signs held by Muslim demonstrators throughout Europe. All together, the riots following the publication of the cartoons caused over 100 deaths. Just as with the Rushdie affair, the Vatican and other Christian religious authorities criticized the violence but criticized even more the blasphemy that triggered it.[72]

Blasphemy. . . it's hard to believe how many people have been murdered over such a bullshit concept. Someone says something about God or religion we find offensive, and we feel the need to burn them at the stake, disembowel them, or stone them to death. What kind of pathological insecurity makes totalitarians so ready to take offense, and unleash an orgy of blood? What makes them so delicate as to be unable to deal with freedom of speech? From Giordano Bruno to Jean-Francois de la Barre, plenty of people throughout history have been tortured and killed for the crime of expressing their opinion. In some countries (Pakistan, for example), blasphemy is still punishable with death or life in prison (Life in prison? Yeah, I know . . . these fundamentalists are getting soft.).

Blasphemy's evil twin, apostasy, has usually ignited the same kinds of reactions. In this case, nothing offensive is said at all. The believer in a certain faith simply decides to abandon it. That's it. Nothing else. According to the Hadith, a collection of traditional sayings attributed to Muhammad, this warrants the death penalty. Upholding this tradition, death is still the recommended punishment for apostasy in several Muslim countries, including the "Westernized" Saudi Arabia.

Accordingly, in 2006, when an Afghan man by the name of Abdul Rahman decided to convert to Christianity, he was charged with a capital offense. Shahnawaz Farooqui, a religious intellectual (I use the word "intellectual" very loosely here) perfectly explained the logic for the death penalty: "If somebody at one point affirms the truth and then rejects it or denies it, it would jeopardize the whole paradigm of truth. This is such a big offense that the penalty can only be death."[73] Jeopardizing the paradigm of truth?!? This is why fanatic followers of exclusive ideologies kill people?

But wait. Before you start thinking these are evil, blood-thirsty people, listen to the generous offer made to Rahman by the chief judge in this case: "The Prophet Muhammad has said several times that those who convert from Islam should be killed if they refuse to come back. Islam is a religion of peace, tolerance, kindness and integrity. That is why we have told him if he regrets what he did, then we will forgive him."[74] Understood? Since we belong to a religion of "peace, tolerance, kindness and integrity," we'll give him a chance to publicly squash his own opinions. But if he is stubborn, we'll kill him. Ah, yes, a heartwarming example of "peace, tolerance, kindness and integrity" at work.

Do Judeo-Christian scriptures prescribe the same brand of peace and tolerance? Judge for yourself. Here's what the Old Testament has to say, "Anyone who blasphemes the name of the Lord must be put to death. The entire assembly must stone him. Whether an alien or native-born, when he blasphemes the Name, he must be put to death."[75] Damn . . . even the Taliban can't top this.

In another passage, the Bible confirms the same idea:

> If your brother, the son of your father or of your mother, or your son or daughter, or the spouse whom you embrace, or your most intimate friend, tries to secretly seduce you, saying 'Let us go and serve other gods,' unknown to you or your ancestors before you, gods of the peoples surrounding you, whether near you or far away, anywhere throughout the world, you must not consent, you must not listen to him; you must show him no pity, you must not spare him or conceal his guilt. No, you must kill him, your hand must strike the first blow in

putting him to death and the hands of the rest of the people following. You must stone him to death, since he has tried to divert you from Yahweh your God.[76]

Anyone who doesn't display the necessary murderous enthusiasm for the executions of religious dissidents and refuses to participate in the proceedings must be put to death as well.[77] Also, just so you don't give in to some wimpy, soft-hearted reformations watering down the laws, Deuteronomy 4:2 warns us to never alter these divine instructions.

These clearly are the kinds of passages that tickle the souls of people like the grandma from hell. Since I don't want to bury you under too many quotes from scriptures, I'll spare you. But if you are into this sort of thing, check out the Bible for yourself: it's full of pleasantries like this.

Drawing inspirations from these Biblical ideals, the history of Christianity is littered with acts of violence and religious repression. Shortly after becoming the official religion of the Roman Empire, the very Christian Emperor Theodosius banned all other religions (and alternative versions of Christianity) on penalty of death.[78] Cultural diversity and religious liberty were clearly not high up on his agenda.

The more than 600-year history of the "Holy" Inquisition picked up where Theodosius left off. For centuries, throughout Christian Europe, anyone holding unconventional opinions could be brought to trial, tortured in a million of highly creative and horrifically painful ways, and burned at the stake. Protestants were as active as Catholics in this endeavor. In 1553, for example, the great Protestant reformer Calvin had the theologian Michael Servetus burned at the stake for denying the Trinity. During the witch-hunt, both Protestants and Catholics murdered thousands of suspected witches.

Whereas the highest estimate for this carnage lists over 9 million deaths, the lowest argue for "only" between 50,000 and 100,000. Even if we assume the lowest estimates to be correct, the body count still adds up to a minimum of seventeen 9/11s piled on top of each other. Bin Laden, clearly, is just an amateur.

The same story repeats itself in any country controlled by fundamentalist versions of Islam and Christianity. Save for short-lived exceptions, a worldwide repression of Judaism, Buddhism, Hinduism, and indigenous religions has been the norm. Even relatively recently, between the late 1800s and the mid-1900s, in the supposedly secular United States, the fundamentalist intolerance for different traditions manifested itself in the banning of many American Indian religious ceremonies. Yes, you read right, deep into the 1900s, in the United States people could go to jail for practicing the wrong religion.[79]

Holy War!

The same desire to protect the "paradigm of truth" that has spawned Inquisitions, witch-hunts, and other forms of repression has also been responsible for many religious wars. For millennia now, the earth has shaken under the feet of self-styled armies of God marching to war on a quest to conquer the world and submit it to their One True Faith. "God is with us" has been the battle cry before unleashing hell on the enemy. Nazi soldiers had this motto emblazoned on their belt buckles. Mohamed Atta probably thought something along those lines right before he crashed a jet into the World Trade Center. Christian crusaders slightly paraphrased it ("God wills it") as the slogan for their own murderous activities.

The amount of blood spilled by these people, and the countless others who believed they were doing God's will, can hardly be measured. Once you believe you have been entrusted by God with the task of destroying evil, killing people becomes much easier. Your enemies are not simply human beings in competition with you; they are the Devil's minions. Can't you hear God's voice commanding you to wipe them off the face of the earth? Hitler himself justified his Final Solution by saying, "I believe that I act today in unison with the Almighty Creator's intention: by fighting the Jews I do battle for the Lord."[80] For those seeing themselves as God's warriors, armed conflict is no longer a means to an end. It's a sacred enterprise. It's a Holy War.

Just writing these words strikes me as deeply disturbing. Two words that were never supposed to go together somehow found each other, with very regrettable consequences for humanity. How can war be holy?

Inclusive ideologies don't believe it can. Taoists, for example, value fighting skills for last resort self-defense, but they would much rather get the job done without having to go to battle. Throughout the Tao Te Ching, weapons and soldiers are referred to as "instruments of evil." "Even in victory," Lao Tzu writes, "there is no beauty, and who calls it beautiful is one who delights in slaughter . . . The slayings of multitudes should be mourned with sorrow. A victory should be celebrated with the Funeral Rite."[81] At best, war is sometimes a regrettable necessity, but it certainly is never holy. Since they follow a similar thought process, inclusive ideologies have a nearly spotless record when it comes to initiating religiously motivated wars.

Exclusive theologies, on the other hand, embrace the notion of a holy war as the logical outcome of the cosmic battle between the forces of good and evil. Judaism developed this theory with a passion but only very rarely had the power to carry it out. So it was up to the other two main Western religions to inherit the theology of a holy war along with the means to actually wage it.

According to exclusive theologies, war is a sacred duty, a wonderful occasion to extend the borders of God's kingdom on earth. This hyperaggressive belief has spurred them to expand by conquering the lands of unbelievers. Christianity and Islam are the two most widely practiced religions in the world today. They are also the two with the most blood on their hands. This is not a coincidence, for their popularity has been won at the tip of a sword. Holy wars and forced conversions have been their main proselytizing tools.

Something doesn't seem to add up. Wasn't Jesus the one who advised to love your enemies and turn the other cheek? Wasn't he the guy who, as he was being arrested, urged one of his followers to renounce violence and put away his sword, because "all who take the sword will perish by the sword"?[82] How can a religion inspired by such a man end up glorifying a perverted concept such as a holy war?

Unfortunately, besides including these very peaceful ideas, Judeo-Christian scriptures also contain extremely brutal celebrations of religious warfare. All Christian holy warriors need to do in order to justify themselves is forget the former and quote the latter. Some passages of the Bible, in fact, tell us that God himself sometimes enjoys a good act of genocide. Remember Phinehas, the guy who skewered a Jewish man and his wife with a single spear thrust while they were making love? Shortly after that episode, Moses put him in charge of an army marching against a rival pagan tribe, the Midianite, as God commanded. As it turns out, even Phinehas is too soft for the job, since he *only* kills all the adult males among the Midianites, but brings back as prisoners of war the women and children. This infuriates Moses who promptly Moses orders his army to "kill every male among the little ones, and kill every woman that has known a man by lying with him."[83] To add the icing on this genocidal cake, Moses also sanctions rape by ordering to "keep alive for yourself" the female virgins.[84]

God also orders the Jewish armies to carry out holy wars of extermination on a few other occasions as well. Here is some sweet advice straight from God: "you shall consume all the people which the Lord your God shall deliver to you: your eye shall have no pity upon them."[85] Or try this: "Now go and smite Amalek, and utterly destroy all that they have, and spare them not, but slay both man and woman, infant and suckling."[86] Hungry for more? OK. "You shall save nothing alive, but you shall utterly destroy them."[87]

Jesus' pacifist advice is easily lost in this orgy of bloodshed. Considering how many times God openly sanctions murdering even the infants among the enemies, we may understand why Christian holy warriors find plenty of inspiration in the Bible.[88] The war of extermination against the Cathars, the Crusades, and the religious conflicts between Catholics and Protestants that turned Europe into a bloodbath are but leaves in a forest of violence. Even the colonization of the Americas can be seen as an extension of this holy war mentality, since massacring Indians and stealing their land was typically justified as part of a religious duty to bring new territories under the control of God's religion.[89]

If genocide were an Olympic event, however, Islam would be giving Christianity a tough competition for the gold medal. After a long and successful career, Christian fundamentalists have now lost a step when it comes to killing thousands of people in acts of holy war. Muslim fundamentalists, on the other hand, show no signs of slowing down. Just in the last few years, their "Holy War World Tour" has passed through Russia, Spain, England, the United States,

Bali, China, and plenty of other countries. At every stop, scores of civilians have paid with their lives.

For some bizarre reason, many Western fans of multiculturalism plagued by a sense of guilt over their colonial past have tried to justify these acts of terrorism by writing them off as unfortunate reactions to the imperialistic policies of Americans and their allies. According to them, religion has nothing to do with it. And yet, as author Sam Harris has pointed out, the United States has caused much more suffering throughout Latin America than they ever did in Muslim countries, but you don't see Guatemalans bombing American civilians.

Religion has nothing to do with this, eh? Just ask Mohammed Bouyeri, the man who shot the Dutch filmmaker Theo Van Gogh and cut his throat for making a movie criticizing the treatment of women in Islam in 2004. "I did what I did purely out of my beliefs. If I ever get free, I would do it again," Bouyeri said. Addressing his victim's mother, he added, "I don't feel your pain. I don't have any sympathy for you. I can't feel for you because I think you're a non-believer."[90]

Clearly, not all Muslims are wannabe terrorists dreaming of wiping unbelievers off the face of the earth. If you look for them, you'll find in the Koran several passages counseling peace and tolerance.[91] But peace and tolerance are intermixed with advice such as, "When you meet the unbelievers, strike off their heads."[92] Far from being something to be regretted, righteous war is a duty, for in an echo of the biblical, "Cursed be he that does the work of the Lord deceitfully, and cursed be he that keeps back his sword from blood,"[93] the Koran admonishes the faithful: "If you do not fight, He will punish you severely, and put others in your place."[94] In the hands of Muslim fundamentalists, all the Koranic passages showing contempt for unbelievers, and praising martyrdom in the name of God, have provided the necessary rationale for Holy War to this day.

The One True Way and Victimless "Crimes"

In that beautiful hymn to freedom entitled "Burn One Down," Ben Harper sings,

> My choice is what I choose to do
> And if I'm causing no harm
> It shouldn't bother you
> Your choice is who you choose to be
> And if you're causin' no harm
> Then you're alright for me

This sounds to me like a perfect ethical law. You are free to do whatever you want as long as you don't infringe on somebody else's freedom. The government's role should be simply to protect common goods (i.e., the environment) and the rights of individual citizens. Nothing more and nothing less. For, as the Tao Te Ching warns, "The more prohibitions there are, the poorer the people become."[95]

This libertarian philosophy is much easier for those who live by inclusive worldviews to accept than it is for those who want everyone to obey the dictates of their One True Way. Yet another legacy of the exclusive mentality, in fact, can be seen in the existence of laws designed to enforce morality. I can't think of a better litmus test for one's commitment to freedom than support or opposition for laws legislating personal choices. It always cracks me up when the rhetoric of freedom comes from people who would like nothing better than to prohibit anything outside their accepted standards. "We love freedom!" they say. "But if you use it in ways we disapprove of, we'll send you straight to jail." Even though they like to pay lip service to liberty, the reality is they don't value freedom nearly as much as having their ideals imposed on everyone else.

The same impulse that pushes people to wage holy wars also makes them prone to pass laws upholding morality—that is, *their* morality. If God spells out moral standards for human beings to follow, then allowing people the freedom to make their own choices is a sin. As fundamentalist theologian R. J. Rushdoony wrote, "Freedom as an absolute is simply an assertion of man's 'right' to be his own god; this means a radical denial of God's law-order."[96] The idea that every aspect of life needs to be brought under God's control gives exclusive ideologies a good push toward totalitarianism.

This horrendous threat to freedom rests on the illusion that we know exactly which behaviors enjoy God's stamp of approval and which ones don't. The censor, as an agent of God, knows what's best, and limits choices in the public interest.

This conflict between moral crusaders and defenders of free choice is still raging today, but over the last few decades the moral crusaders have been losing ground. The Comstock laws targeting any printed discussion of sex, the Mann Act that allowed the prosecution of an unmarried couple crossing state lines together, and the prohibition on alcohol are long gone. The right to divorce and the right to use birth control are now no longer threatened. But the ghost of a state-enforced morality survives in the laws on euthanasia, prostitution, gambling, and drugs—just to name a few.

The War on Drugs, in particular, shines as a glowing example of the irrational determination to pursue a failed policy in the name of fighting against "sinful" behaviors. Despite a price tag of many billion dollars a year, the War on Drugs manages not to affect the supply of, or demand for, drugs. Some of its only tangible effects are the early releases of violent criminals from overcrowded jails to make room for nonviolent drug offenders, and a gift of sizeable profits to criminal organizations. But in an effort to hold the line against "sin," our government keeps flushing money down the toilet prolonging a suicidal policy.

If we are so determined to prohibit things that are bad for us, why don't we outlaw fast foods? Why don't we force people to eat broccoli and exercise three times a week under the watchful eye of a government employee? If nothing else, this would show consistency rather than a selective application of moral outrage.

Regardless of the specific examples, though, the desire to shove by law one's ideals down everyone's throats is a glaring indication of insecurity on the part of the moral crusaders. If they had any faith in the attractiveness of their message, in fact, they wouldn't need laws to force people to follow it. You believe your way is the best? Fine, but why not have the honor and the guts of trying to convince others by words only, and ultimately letting them choose for themselves?

Open-Minded, Yet Strong

Pluralism is the lifeblood of the modern world. The once heretical idea of allowing individuals a wide range of choices on how they want to live their lives is becoming more common. And yet, this is planting fear in the hearts of millions of people throughout the world. In their minds, pluralism opens the door to a loss of morality, and a descent into absolute relativism. With no dogma to guide them, they feel lost. This is the reason why, paradoxically, fundamentalism is growing at the same time as pluralism is expanding. One is a reaction to the other.

The irony is that the fundamentalist rhetoric of claiming unshakeable, absolute truths puts on an impressive show of confidence, but it has very limited success in producing positive, tangible results. Exclusive fundamentalism rarely produces a stronger moral order, but it regularly delivers wars, squashing of freedoms, and bloodshed. Fundamentalists are masters at projecting the illusion of solid morality. Too bad they are not as skilled at promoting the real thing. Both within the United States and throughout the world, the places where fundamentalism is strongest are also the places with the worst statistics of social dysfunctions (from abortion to sexually transmitted diseases, from murder to rape). In the United States, bulwarks of conservative religion like Kentucky and Arkansas have twice the divorce rate of liberal Massachusetts.[97]

Having said this, if someone can manage the difficult task of believing there's only one right way to follow but is at the same time willing to allow others full freedom of choice, I have nothing against them. Unlike the grandma from hell and the cannibal settlers of Jamestown, I respect everyone—regardless of their ideology—as long they behave decently toward me. I value actions over stated beliefs.

My problem is with the far too common cases in which exclusive claims to absolute truths give way to flirting with totalitarianism. Whether we are talking about Osama bin Laden or Stalin, Moses or Hitler, it makes little difference: anyone willing to impose their ideology by force is equally an enemy of freedom, and a danger to everyone else. Tolerating their repressive efforts is not a sign of open-mindedness, or enlightened multiculturalism. It's just stupid.

Tolerating those who want to ban tolerance is plain suicidal. Freedom doesn't extend to those who wish for nothing better than to restrict the freedom of others.

Much of the world is stuck in a sad dichotomy pitting tough, strong-willed fascists against sweet but feeble liberals. Too often, when people rid themselves of dogma, they turn weak and lose a sense of purpose. The challenge we face is to combine the ability to be open-minded with an iron will. Openness without strength is useless; strength without openness is oppression. The love for freedom needs to go hand in hand with strong values. The future of our world depends on developing religions able to bring these qualities together.

CHAPTER 6

ON A ROUND BALL FLOATING IN SPACE: THE RELATIONSHIP BETWEEN HUMANS, NATURE, AND THE UNIVERSE

Nature in World Religions (Part I): Anthropocentrism

A tiger knows how to do one thing very well: be a tiger. The same story goes for any other species on earth; their natural instincts guide their paths. Humans are unique in having a greater range of conscious choices regarding their relationship with nature. They can embrace it or reject it, preserve it, or dramatically alter it. No other living being is quite in the same position.

Most religious traditions have addressed the question, how should humans interact with nature? Even though the nuances in these answers are many, they can be broadly divided in two camps. On one side, we have those worldviews placing human beings on a pedestal, above all other forms of life, somewhat removed from nature (anthropocentrism). On the other side, we have those ideologies considering human beings a part of nature, just one interesting species among many.

Typically, anthropocentrism has been a staple in Western religions. The Judeo-Christian-Islamic tradition tells us that only human beings were created "in God's image." This clearly marks them as something other than animals. Moreover, only humans have an immortal soul, whereas plants and animals do not.

This hierarchical view is clearly expressed in both the Bible and the Koran. In the Koran, Sura 36:71 recites, "We have created for them [humans] the beasts of which they are masters. We have subjected these to them, that they may ride on some and eat the flesh of others; they drink their milk and put them to other uses."[98] Judeo-Christian scriptures echo this sentiment at the very beginning of Genesis. Here, we find divine instructions for Adam and Eve to "subdue" nature and "have dominion over the fish of the sea, and over the fowl of the air, and over every living thing that moveth upon the earth."[99]

Should we take these passages to mean that humanity is entitled to everything that exists? Do these verses give God's stamp of approval to a rape-and-pillage, exploitative approach to nature? Or do they mean that humans are being charged with an enlightened stewardship of the earth's resources? We'll return to this controversy later because it carries very important consequences. But for now let it suffice to say that the more exploitative interpretation won the popularity contest for much of history.

This view has pushed Western religions to embrace the most extreme forms of anthropocentrism. Think of the earth as a giant, divinely created mall, with plants, animals, and natural resources made exclusively for the use of humans. All other creatures are not living in the same way humans are. They have no consciousness and no special purpose other than being consumed by us. They are just commodities to be used, no different than the items lined along the supermarket shelves. As master of the earth, mankind can do as it pleases.

James G. Watt, a conservative Christian who served as US Secretary of the Interior for Ronald Reagan in the early 1980s, spells out this view with chilling clarity. In his writings, he made it clear his faith pushed him to see the earth as "merely a temporary way station on the road to eternal life . . . The earth was put here by the Lord for His people to subdue and to use for profitable purposes on their way to the hereafter."[100] Mmhmm. It makes me feel warm and fuzzy to know this man was placed in charge of managing national parks and public lands . . .

Exploiting the earth is a symptom of a general uneasiness about everything that's natural. The wilderness has been viewed by these guys as the playground for heathens, demons, and dangerous animals; and followers of "civilized" religions better stay clear of it. When they do venture out there, they should do so with an axe in order to make more land suitable for the dwellings of "God-fearing people." Cut down forests, set up farms, surround yourself with man-made stuff—and only then will you be safe.

But nature is not just a physical place out there. Its dangers also hide in our very bodies. Particularly in Christianity, the fear of nature is intimately tied to the war waged by good Christians against wild, uncontrolled instincts. In the same way we should be taming and "civilizing" the wilderness, we should also be taming and civilizing ourselves. For if our physical instincts are left unrepressed, they open the door to sin. The same mentality responsible for the largely negative image of nature itself is also pushing Western religions toward a very strict view of sex and the body. It's the same issue; only the examples change. This is a war between body and soul, nature and culture, earthly pleasures and an otherworldly afterlife.

However we define it, in fact, nature is seen as something to be improved upon and ultimately transcended. If we fail to act accordingly, we sink to the level of animals, whose instincts are unconstrained—a heinous crime in the eyes of an anthropocentric worldview. Repress natural instincts instead, and you rise above all other forms of life and become worthy of God's approval.

Part of the horror of seeing ourselves as animals goes back to the very human fear of death. As far as the eyes can see, everything that lives in a body is destined to die. The more one is tied to the physical world—as animals very obviously are—the more the inevitability of death becomes real. The idea that we are different from animals, driven as they are by their natural instincts, offers some hope to defeat death. If we are unlike any other creature, if we alone have a soul, if we are able to transcend nature and the physical world, then we'll be able to escape Death's fangs, for we'll go on living as disembodied spirits long after Death has devoured our bodies. Rising above what's physical and earthy, then, is the pathway to keep alive our hopes of outrunning death. God will take care of us because we are His favorite creatures, goes the cry. He won't let us die along with our bodies.

Unfortunately, the illusion of being disconnected from the natural world and immune to the laws governing other living creatures has gone to our heads. This belief has convinced us that we can manipulate natural forces to our liking without ever having to pay a price for it. At some point, much of humanity began to believe its own propaganda, and think that the effects of exploiting the planet will not reach beyond the safety of our homes. However, as the evidence of a polluted planet all around us indicates, this illusion—born out of a desire to escape death—can paradoxically end up causing our collective extinction.

This religious separation between the earthy, organic aspect of existence and the idea that humanity is destined for higher purposes has sometimes infected scientists as well. Influenced by this prejudice, some scientists have operated from the same assumption that human beings are somewhat unlike all other animals. Descartes, for example, justified vivisection on the grounds that animals—unlike humans—are incapable of feelings, and are insensible to pain. In his view, "animals were clocks . . . the cries they emitted when struck were only the noise of a little spring that had been touched, but . . . the whole body was without feeling."[101] Can you think of a better example of anthropocentrism at work?

Other times, however, scientific discoveries have seriously challenged the anthropocentrism found in Western religions. A classic anthropocentric idea once held that the earth is at the center of the universe and all other planets rotate around it. If human beings were indeed creation's crowning jewel, it only made sense that their planet would be located in the position of honor. The astronomical discoveries made by Copernicus and Galileo, however, knocked a big hole in this inflated sense of human self-importance.

Humanity's bruised ego had to undergo further downsizing at the hands of Darwin, who showed how humans are very much related to other animals. It's difficult to maintain too many illusions of being separate and different from animals when science demonstrates you share 98.5 percent of your DNA with chimps.

Nature in World Religions: Animism and Interconnectedness

Not all cultures, however, have embraced anthropocentric worldviews. Whereas some Western religions consider natural instincts something to tame or overcome, Taoism invites us to shed artificial behaviors and rediscover harmony with nature. Rather than "subduing the earth," Lao Tzu asks, "Does anyone want to take the world and do what he wants with it? I do not see how he can succeed. The world is a sacred vessel, which must not be tampered with or grabbed after. To tamper with it is to spoil it, and to grasp it is to lose it."[102]

Much like Taoism, Animistic religions emphasize a deep level of interconnectedness among all forms of life. Lakota Sioux ceremonies often end with the prayer *Mitakuye Oyasin,* which can be translated as "We are related to all things." In this view, plants and animals are not separate from human beings, but are their relatives. "Mitakuye Oyasin" is literally a prayer acknowledging kinship with everything that lives and breathes.

While the anthropocentric world is a lonely one, where only human beings are believed to have souls and everything else is just dead matter, the Animistic universe is filled with spirits. The very word "Animism" refers to the belief that animals, plants, rivers, mountains, and all other natural forces are spiritually alive no more and no less than human beings. Rather than promoting a hierarchical view of life that gives humanity the right to exert its dominance, Animistic ideas demand people to strike a balance with all other beings. If anthropocentrism sees life as a pyramid of power, Animistic religions see it as a circle of relationships, a complex web connecting different forms of life to each other.

This does not mean that Animists refrain from taking anything from nature. Everything that lives derives nourishment from something else; this is the cannibalistic truth of life. If we are to eat, it means someone else—animal or plant—has to be our lunch. But accepting this fact doesn't mean we should be callous about it. In theory—if not always in practice—a cultural ideal in many Animistic societies requires a good hunter to be respectful to the animals he is going after. He should pray to them, explaining his family's needs, and ask for permission to hunt. He should then do his best to avoid cruelty and not insult the animals by wasting any part of them.[103] At the end of a successful hunt, ceremonies are in order to give thanks to the spirit of the animal and to pray for its welfare in the afterlife.

Besides encouraging a respectful attitude toward the environment, these worldviews consider nature as something to be studied in order to learn the secrets of life. Whereas anthropocentric religions require us to tame nature, Taoism, along with many Animistic traditions, invites us to harmonize ourselves with nature.

In a classic example of anthropocentric thinking, Plato wrote that trees and open country have nothing to teach us.[104] In his mind, the only knowledge we can gain comes from other human beings. This is the exact opposite of what Lao Tzu, Heraclitus, Thomas Paine, and many other Animists feel. For example, Ikkyū, the most radical thinker in the history of Zen, wrote, "Every day, priests minutely examine the Dharma and endlessly chant profound sutras. Before this, though, they should first read the love letters sent by the wind and rain; the snow and moon."[105] Inspired by a flash of Zen that must have gotten lost in the English countryside, even a Western poet such as William Blake wrote of seeing "the world in a grain of sand" and "heaven in a wild flower."[106]

It's not that these guys believe in a Disney, tree-hugging version of nature, where furry animals of the forest are our best friends, and everything is benign. They are fully aware of how scary nature can be at times. In their view, nature is the foundation of everything that exists. Rather than drawing wisdom from man-made abstractions, they believe all the essential principles of life can be discovered by observing the natural world.

Similar sentiments are echoed among Zen Buddhists, American Indian tribes, Shinto priests, and Western Deists. Tribal elder Matthew King, for example, said, "He [the white man] has his Bible, but to us the hills and the sky and the water make our Bible. That is what the Creator told us, to watch the natural things; that is where we will learn how God wants us to live."[107] Along the same lines, Zen Buddhists declare, "The Universe itself is the scripture of Zen."[108] The point that all of them are trying to drive home is that in order to be attuned to life, a religion needs to be in tune with nature. And for those religions that believe in a creator God, there is no better place to learn about a creator than in creation itself.

Not surprisingly, the diametrically opposite attitudes existing between this worldview and anthropocentric religions are reflected in what they consider sacred places. In most Western religions sacred places are temples, churches, and synagogues. Apparently, the Western God doesn't like to get wet; for you won't find too many open-air places of worship. Nature is typically not deemed a suitable place to hang out with God—a fact that prompted Alan Watts to write, "I can feel like a Christian only when I am indoors. As soon as I get into the open air, I feel entirely out of relation with everything that goes on in a church—including both the worship and the theology."[109] In addition to worshipping in man-made buildings, Western religions also value places where events historically relevant to their beliefs have taken place (e.g., the site of Jesus' crucifixion, or the place where Muhammad received his first revelation). In either case, no place is sacred in and of itself.

The opposite is true in Animistic cultures. Tribal sacred places are usually part of the wilderness. They may come in the shape of rivers, springs, lakes, woods, and mountains. Roman writers, including Julius Caesar, were often puzzled by Celtic rituals, which always took place in the woods rather than in temples.[110] The sacredness of a place in Animistic eyes has nothing to do with human activity or historical events. It's inherent in the place itself. Some locations are simply charged with energy unlike anything you can find anywhere else. You won't find any sign hanging at the door telling you "You are entering sacred grounds" because (*a*) there is no door (since there is no building), and (*b*) if you need a sign to tell you, it's because you wouldn't recognize sacredness if it hit you on the head. It's something you feel in your guts, when you walk onto such a stretch of land. Sacred places induce a sense of reverence; these are places where you can almost smell an invisible power lurking in the air; places where the boundaries between different dimensions seem to be thinner. The first time I visited the Black Hills, for example, I felt as if I had stepped into the center of the world. The mountains were beautiful, sure, but they didn't look all that different from other beautiful mountains I had seen. And yet, they possessed a type of energy that was richer, deeper, and more powerful than anything I had ever known.

It's for the sake of tapping into this natural power that Animistic people gather at these locations to perform their ceremonies. The power to be found in groves of trees, rivers, and mountaintops is more raw and vibrant than what exists among tiles and bricks. Rather than keeping nature at bay, Animistic cultures include it as an integral part of their sacred life.

In the origin stories of anthropocentric and Animistic religions, the differences between them are clear. Western religions speak of nature as a very beautiful, benign place. . . for about five minutes. But everything changes once the first human couple is unceremoniously kicked out of the Garden of Eden for their transgressions. From then on, nature will no longer be their friend. Food will no longer come easily, but only through great labors. As God declares, "Cursed is the ground for thy sake . . . Thorns also and thistles shall it bring forth to thee."[111] The earth turns into a place of trial and suffering—a stepping-stone before making it to a better place in the afterlife. Plenty of Animistic origin stories, on the other hand, describe nature as a Garden of Eden, but don't feature any divinely sanctioned expulsion.

These opposite attitudes toward the earth have no single, simple explanation. Many factors are probably at play. One theory that's worth considering argues that the physical environment in which a religion originates may have a lot to do with its outlook on nature. The Judeo-Christian-Islamic tradition is born out of the desert. Whenever I read about the desert, it always sounds beautiful and poetic. But when I've spent time in it, any romantic image I had constructed in my mind quickly went down the drain. All I wanted was to crawl between two rocks praying that my brain wouldn't start oozing out of my ears. Despite not being usually too big on technology, it wasn't long before I had visions of flying refrigerators coming to the rescue. The intense heat, the lack of water, and the limited vegetation make it clear that, in a desert, nature is not your friend. If you go looking for water in the wrong direction, you're history. The competition for scarce resources among animals and humans tends to be fierce. If your religion is born in the midst of beautiful mountains, flowing streams, and abundant resources, on the other hand, it comes as little surprise that your view of nature may be more positive. There are of course exceptions to this theory. For example, some tribal people living in the desert hold nature in high regard. But it's still very possible that our environment may be giving us a push toward certain ideas.

The differences between anthropocentric and Animistic world-views have created never-ending arguments between starry-eyed fans of Animistic religions, who view tribal peoples as the perfect environmentalists, and critics who dismiss these ideas as overly romantic stereotypes. Both sides throw around conflicting historical evidence to support their claims. As fun as playing this game can be, we have much bigger problems at hand. Whether most tribal people were really able to achieve a perfect harmony with nature is not the point. The only thing that matters right here, right now, is whether *we* are able to do so. Regardless of which ideological framework we adopt, the end result should be a worldview guiding us to protect the planet we live on and find a balance with all living beings. We can debate theology from here to eternity, but the ongoing destruction of our global ecosystem is telling us something needs to change fast.

Energy Wars and Eco-suicide

One of the greatest wars of the century is one most people aren't even aware exists. This is a war that is being fought on a daily basis and in every continent. It causes countless casualties and threatens the survival of humanity and the entire planet. Incredible amounts of suffering and destruction are tied to the competitive quest to tap into sources of nonrenewable energy: oil, coal, electricity, uranium, and all the other substances forming the lifeblood on which industrial societies run. Both governments and multinational corporations go to battle to gain an advantage in this struggle because, as Henry Kissinger stated . . .

Sorry for the interruption, but after naming Henry Kissinger, I had to rush to wash my hands. OK, now that I'm done, I can finish the previous sentence . . . because as Henry Kissinger stated, "Control energy and you control the nations."[112]

Historically speaking, even slavery could be seen as an extension of these energy wars. In the past, the desire to exploit the energies of human muscles caused the devastation of a worldwide slave trade. Today, the legacy of the energy wars can be seen in the extinction of an increasing number of species, the clear-cutting of forests, the melting of the ice caps, horrendous air and water pollution, and global warming.

Religion is only part of the story behind this war. Even though embracing a theology that looks down on nature may reduce any inhibitions toward overexploiting the earth, practicing a more ecologically minded religion doesn't always translate into more enlightened behavior. For example, Shinto is one of the most environmentally friendly, pro-nature religions in the world. And yet it has not been able to prevent Japanese industries from causing many major environmental disasters.

Economic philosophies are also at play. Communist regimes have ruined many ecosystems just as effectively as the most rapaciously capitalist countries. Marxism advocates exploiting the earth no less than capitalism. The only difference rests on how these two philosophies plan on dividing the spoils of their pillage.

In this war, greed speaks louder than any ideology. But at the same time, we can't forget that few forces can move people and stimulate them into action as much as religion. So encouraging the development of an earth-friendly theology, creating a culture that rewards conservation over consumption, and making environmental protection a religious priority may help change the current tide.

On the surface, it seems puzzling that we even have to have this discussion. Regardless of race, class, gender, political preferences, or religious affiliation, it would seem logical to assume everyone would greatly value protecting the ecosystem we depend on for all our needs. It should be a no-brainer, and certainly not a political issue. Theoretically, environmentalism should be something everyone agrees on. After all, we depend on a delicate ecosystem for all our needs. Environmentalism is not exactly a radical idea. It is simply the notion that it is not wise to poison the water you drink and the air you breathe. Who could have a problem with that?

Unfortunately, we have created societies that run on very polluting and fast-disappearing nonrenewable energy sources. Like junkies who haven't found an alternative, we keep returning to these sources to get a fix, even though we know we are hurting ourselves in the process. And anywhere there are junkies, you are going to find pushers. There's plenty of money to be made in the business of destroying the earth. Since a sizable amount of cash increases your political weight, energy corporations are regularly able to buy the complicity of governments throughout the world.

The political ties between government and big business are a fairly straightforward affair: a politician uses his or her influence to help a company make money by weakening environmental laws. In exchange, the politician will get much-needed campaign contributions for the next election, and perhaps even a comfy job at the end of their political career.[113] This mafia-style alliance is not necessarily limited to the borders of one's country, either. The role played by the CIA in organizing coups in Guatemala, Chile, and Iran (just to name a few cases) for the sake of advancing the interests of private corporations offers a perfect example of this.

But even if we rule out conspiracies (and that's not always wise, since they are the daily bread of energy politics and environmental policies), many people honestly feel that protecting the earth is a luxury that is antithetical to a healthy economy. On the surface this may appear as a legitimate conflict, but it only demonstrates a deep ignorance of both ecological *and* economic principles. The reality is that in the long run not taking care of the environment messes up the economy far more than sound environmental policies. By clear-cutting a forest, for example, a logging company will make money today, and its employees will have a job for a few months. The Gross Domestic Product (GDP) will go up, but with no plants to hold the soil in place, soil erosion is inevitable. At the first rain, the destruction caused by mudslides will net economic damages exceeding the money made by logging in the first place. The cost of clean ups and healthcare bills to treat the diseases caused by pollution outweigh all the economic benefits created by polluting.[114]

Environmental protection laws were definitely not some soft, fuzzy idea born out of a romantic view of nature. It's what smart self-interest is all about. Good environmental policies benefit us, first and foremost. In 2003, the Pentagon—not exactly an organization of tree-huggers—released a report naming global warming the greatest threat to American national security—greater than terrorism and international drug trade combined. The Pentagon report stated that many natural resources are dwindling. The amounts of supplies available, from oil to clean water, are declining day by day. Given the basic imbalance between supply and demand, the Pentagon report outlines the likelihood of food shortages, epidemics, and wars in the near future for access to energy sources.[115]

Nature and Humanity Go to Marriage Counseling

After being on the brink of divorce for so long, humanity is going to have to find a way to rekindle its relationship with nature. Whether we like it or not, we need to live closer to the land than we have over the last few centuries. This is not moral advice or some "it would be good if . . ." type of statement. It's going to happen, one way or another. The current model is destined to collapse. An economic system based on the notion of limitless growth simply can't survive in a world where natural resources are finite. We already consume more than the earth produces, and the human population keeps growing. This can't go on forever.[116]

In recent years, more industries are seeing the writing on the wall and are responding to popular demand by taking a more eco-friendly approach to business. This new approach seeks to make money without sacrificing the earth and its people along the way. Maybe this change could usher in an age in which we figure out a way to combine the best insights of animistic cultures with technological innovations and modern comforts. If we are feeling very optimistic, we could even envision a future where a country's success is measured not only by its GDP, but also by the happiness of its people, its sustainability, and a higher quality of life. The level of sensibility for environmental issues has grown tremendously over the last couple of decades. Whether this signals a momentous shift in global awareness or it represents a case of too little, too late, remains to be seen.

Catastrophe-lovers predict a doom and gloom future. They say humanity has hopped on a train in collision course with disaster: a quick ride on the Apocalypse Express before going out with a bang. Maybe they are right, but maybe we are going to survive after all, albeit by dramatically scaling back our current levels of consumption. No one can know for sure how things are going to change. The only thing we know for certain is that things will change.

How do we go about developing new, cleaner, less destructive technologies to help humans and the world? How do we limit population growth without applying the Chinese "we'll bash you on the head if you have more than one child" model? How do we break the corporate hold on government, and encourage more enlightened long-term environmental policies? How do we begin to undo our addiction to overconsumption? Where do we find the money to pay for the enormous damage already caused? How do we convince more corporations to forgo the appeal of immediate profits earned through short-sighted actions in favor of greener, more eco-friendly models? All of these steps are needed. All are possible. None are easy.

The very real problems we are facing require specific, practical solutions. So it would be easy to assume only scientific discoveries, new technologies, or different approaches to business hold the keys to this story. And it would be equally easy to consider religions as having virtually no role in our quest to create a sustainable future. But a change in our collective mindset, in our way of perceiving our place in relation to everything else in the world, is just as essential a contribution—if not more so—than all the others. As American Indian author and theologian Vine Deloria Jr. writes,

> It is becoming increasingly apparent that we shall not have the benefits of this world for much longer. The imminent and expected destruction of the life cycle of world ecology can be prevented by a radical shift in outlook from our present naïve conception of this world as a testing ground of abstract morality to a more mature view of the universe as a comprehensive matrix of life forms. Making this shift in viewpoint is essentially religious, not economic or political.[117]

Our environmental crisis was not caused exclusively by religious ideologies, so we can't expect religious ideologies alone to solve it. But hardly any force possesses religion's unparalleled power to shape people's culture and values, and ultimately mobilize them into action. So, religions today are faced with a choice. They can either avoid the issue and miss an opportunity to play an important role in facing the greatest collective threat to our survival, or they can put helping human beings at this critical juncture at the top of their priority list. The battle is raging. Will religions get in the trenches or sit on the sidelines?

If religions decide to get down and dirty, they have many fields of battle where their participation is badly needed. The biblical injunction to "be fruitful, and multiply,"[118] for example, may have been necessary in a past when premature deaths threatened human survival. But when overpopulation is pushing us to the brink of a Malthusian nightmare made of more mouths to feed and fewer resources, this message is in dire need of revision. A new theology preaching birth control, a voluntary reduction in population, and an emphasis on quality over quantity when it comes to having kids is very much in order.

Even more important, religions need to teach what science is beginning to discover: that everything on earth is interconnected and interdependent. Any life-affirming religion wanting to play a meaningful role in our future needs to place a deep reverence for nature as one of its cornerstones. Celebrating nature is the place to start. Moving from reverence and celebration into action to protect the earth is the next step for a religious, environmental movement.

One of the defining characteristics of Buddhism, for example, is a commitment to show compassion to all people, and to all other living creatures as well. This determination to try to avoid causing pain to anybody and anything is simple and beautiful. It makes it harder to justify slaughtering people across the border to get to their resources. It makes it harder to destroy entire ecosystems in search of profit. And it makes it harder to throw a live lobster in a pot of boiling water for the sake of a juicier dinner. If more religions were to adopt this view, our relationship with the world may radically change.[119]

The very recent changes at play in Christianity also offer a ray of hope: eco-friendly Christians. The newborn environmental Christian movement points to several passages in scriptures that make environmental protection a religious duty. Revelation 11:18, for example, promises God's wrath against "those who destroy the earth."[120] If the earth is God's creation, in fact, hurting it by mismanaging its resources is nothing short of a sin against God.

On this issue, as usual, the Bible offers ammunition to both sides. I don't particularly care to debate theology; I'm interested in results. And the environmental consequences of the different interpretations of Christianity speak loud and clear. One side casts Christianity as one of the prime enemies of human survival on earth. The other side offers us a Christianity that can work as positive force in the fight against extinction. It doesn't take a genius to figure out which version we should support and encourage.

Whether people embrace Animistic ideas, an environmentally friendly Christianity, or any other religion makes no difference to me. As long as one's beliefs drive them to protect the only planet we have, they are fine with me.

We need new rituals to awaken us to the fact that we are not separate from the land, water, and sky. We need ceremonies putting us back in touch, and urging us to conserve the resources that give life to everything in existence. We need to once again think as part of something greater, to view reality from a place higher than the narrow confines of a shortsighted ego. Empathy toward other living things should be one of the very first lessons instilled by all religions.

Rather than encouraging a materialism built on overconsumption and accumulation, the religions of the future have the mission to entice us to follow a whole different type of materialism. It's the materialism that finds joy in the world of living matter, that looks at the material plane as a source of living beauty and inspiration. It reminds us that nature is essential medicine for the human psyche. Moved by a deep appreciation for the physical universe, it shakes us away from dangerous delusions, and brings us back home to live here and now, on this awe-inspiring round ball. If we want to have a future, we need to nourish this religious reverence reminding us of the ecstasy of what it means to be a human being, standing between earth and sky.

CHAPTER 7

BODY AND SENSES

There is more reason in your body than in your best wisdom.

—Friedrich Nietzsche, *Thus Spoke Zarathustra*

Run, Daniele, Run!

Once upon a time, writing this book had seemed like a good idea. After years of taking notes and tossing these ideas in my head, I couldn't wait for the moment when I would finally sit down to write. But that was about a thousand work hours ago. Now the only thing I feel is that I have been sitting at this damned computer for too long. My eyes are glazed, my back aches, and my muscle tone is packing its bags, ready to walk out on me. Out of the window, summer in Southern California is in full bloom, but I might as well be in the depths of winter in Alaska because the computer screen gets jealous anytime I look away. It screams, cries, and threatens divorce and is only placated when I promise that from now on it will have my undivided attention.

And so I am trapped in this room, surrounded by thoughts, words, and books—not enough fresh air coming through here. Too many hours of mental strain are aging me prematurely. I swear I can hear the sounds of the neurons in my overworked mind reaching a boiling point. The body, in the meantime, is left behind, forgotten, sinking in the chair, its desperate requests to go out, move, and play falling on deaf ears.

Every minute that goes by, my mood gets worse, and my energy goes stale. If a good preacher got a hold of me now, it wouldn't take much effort to convince me that I'm a worthless sinner in need of redemption. I'm just a few steps away from confessing my sins and asking for forgiveness. Hell, I feel so bad I have almost degenerated into a scholar, one of the gloomy ghosts haunting the halls of academia—their lives, and the lives of anyone coming in contact with them, ebbing away under the weight of too many theories and not enough action.

But then . . . as I await a coup de grace to free me from my misery, something inside reminds me I still have a spine. Not all hope is lost. My destiny is not to be bossed around by a psycho, domineering computer with control issues. If you have a problem with it, screw you, evil, glowing screen. I'm out of here. The computer goes hysterical, calls me names, and throws dishes in my direction, but I'm long gone.

For the next three hours, I lull my mind to sleep as I stretch, pump iron, run six miles, and sweat enough to cause a minor flood. Inside the temple that is the gym, I remember my barbaric nature. I remember I'm a healthy, adult mammal, with raw, powerful energies flowing through my veins. I am more than my brain. I'm tendons, muscles, and ligaments. I'm nerves, bones, and blood. I feel the joy of vitality at last returning.

By now, you may be wondering what's the point of all this. Why this overly dramatic tale of a sick, symbiotic relationship with a control-freak computer? Why the gross story of finding solace in sweating like a pig? Where am I going with this stuff?

It's about bringing the body to the forefront. Every philosophy and religion that ever existed has had to come to terms with the physical dimension of existence. Our bodies have been the object of scorn and disdain by some, and fascination and attraction by others. But in either case, our beliefs and attitudes about the body affect our lives profoundly.

If I was planning to keep my argument as a big mystery and reveal it only at the end of this chapter, I'm afraid the preceding paragraphs just blew it for me. Psychic powers are clearly not required to figure out what stance toward the body I'll be supporting. But despite the lack of a climactic, surprise ending, I hope the next pages can help clarify how different religious outlooks on the body lead to dramatically different consequences.

Religions' Attitudes Toward the Body

This is not the time and place to delve into an extensive overview of the ways in which the human body appears in the eyes of world religions. The topic is so rich and so vast that entire scholarly books can be written about it. Anyone seriously interested would do well to explore the already existing literature on this issue. Here, at the risk of being overly simplistic, we'll just skim the surface in order to focus on the results caused by certain beliefs.

As a good rule of thumb, typically the more emphasis a religion places on spending eternity as a disembodied soul in the afterlife, the less importance it will attribute to the body. In their view, the body is little more than clothing shed by the soul as it will move on to bigger and better things. This can be seen in many branches of Christianity, to a significant extent in Islam, some versions of Judaism, and at least a few schools of Buddhism and Hinduism. On the opposite side of the spectrum are the many Animistic cultures that focus primarily on life in this world.

In the West, Judaism and Islam praise the body and the physical nature of reality. This enlightened outlook, however, is often negated by innumerable, very restrictive rules regarding what we can and cannot do with our bodies.

Similarly, no single, clear-cut position on this issue characterizes all Asian religions. Depending on which variation of Taoism, Hinduism, or Buddhism you practice, you may find a very relaxed, life-affirming celebration of the body or a rigorously ascetic approach which views the body as a source of dangerous distraction that can keep the soul from reaching its transcendental goals. A strong dualism pitting the soul against the body is clearly alive and well in some of these traditions. But in Buddhism, Taoism, and Hinduism, for every push toward denying the senses and denigrating the body we also find other currents pulling in the opposite direction.

But no major religion has consistently expressed a harsher view toward the body than Christianity. Saint Paul spells this out very clearly. "While we are at home in the body, we are absent from the Lord," he wrote, quickly adding how preferable it was to "be away from the body and at home with the Lord."[121] Paul's condemnation of the physical aspects of reality ended up shaping the very character of Christianity through the ages.

So, what is that bugged Paul so much about the world of the senses? Well, he arrived to Christianity carrying heavy baggage inherited from certain currents of Greek philosophy. Even though, traditionally, Greek culture honored the ideal of physical and mental health, some philosophical schools—Orphism, for example—preached a stark dualism pitting body and soul as bitter enemies. According to Orphists, the human body is a prison for the soul. The physical is an obstacle to overcome in order to become truly spiritual. These thoughts were shared by only a minority of Greeks at the time, but they struck a chord in Paul. He introduced them into Christianity with momentous consequences, altering the future of this religion, and the history of the Western world. After appropriating these ideas for his new religion, Paul colored them with overtones of Christian theology. Body and soul in his view were competitors in a tug of war, with the soul yearning for heaven and the body trapping it on earth. But because the life of the body lasts only a few years whereas the soul is eternal, the soul will pull through and win the contest. If we accept this premise, it only makes sense to take the next step along with Paul, and consider the body as a hindrance standing in the way of dedicating our limited time and energies to spiritual pursuits.

This dualistic idea of competition between body and soul was heightened in Paul's mind by what he perceived to be the imminent end of the world. In several passages throughout the New Testament, Paul makes it clear that—like many early Christians—he expects the apocalypse to be knocking at the door any minute. This sense of urgency is what spurred Paul to take the mind-body opposition in more a more drastic direction. If at any moment the curtains may fall and the show can end, the logical consequence is to dedicate all of one's being to spirituality.

Let's give up the world of the flesh, preaches Paul, in order to commit ourselves 100 percent to the spirit. In the battle between good and evil that is at the theological roots of Christianity, the body and the world of the senses take attention away from the spiritual. With its dazzling show of colors, shapes, sounds, taste, and very intense physical drives, the world of the senses gets us lost in the sensual experience of life and induces us to chase what Paul considers temporary gratification at the expense of eternal salvation. Even pleasure, according to this line of thinking, can easily turn into a tool for the Devil to lead us away from a purer, more spiritual lifestyle. And so, propping up these ideas as articles of faith, Paul sets the stage for a negative view of the body to prevail throughout much of Christian history.

Following Paul's lead, many early Christians turned self-repression into a path toward sainthood. Extreme physical deprivation, and the occasional act of self-torture, often characterized the lives of Christian hermits who turned to the desert to escape the temptations of the flesh while they waited for Judgment Day to come. Perhaps in an effort to repel the Devil by grossing him out, early hermits ate the most foul substances, and competed with each other for who could do the weirdest, most disturbing things to their own bodies. For example, the Church Father Origen castrated himself; Ammonius burned his skin with red-hot irons for the sake of keeping sensual temptations at bay.[122] Approaching these holy men downwind was risky business even for demons, since stinking beyond belief and never bathing were regarded as badges of spiritual progress. Why? Because paying too much attention to the body was seen as immodest and downright sinful. Viewing cleanliness as the doorway to hell didn't exactly do wonders for hygienic conditions, and this attitude indirectly contributed to the spreading of diseases.

Thanks to Paul's influence, from its inception Christianity declared war on the human body and its instincts. The battle between the material and the spiritual raged on throughout the West even more viciously than it did among the body-hating, world-denying traditions of East Asia. But even though Christianity takes the gold medal in this contest, many are the religions that dismiss the concrete, physical, biological dimension of existence as a primitive condition that we need to transcend. In their eyes, our nature is something to be improved upon thanks to intellectual and/or spiritual detachment from the material world. The goal of these religions is to repress natural instincts in favor of what they consider civilized behavior. Ultimately, what they want is to domesticate human beings.

In case it's not clear, I am not a big fan of this way of thinking. By approaching the body with awkward discomfort, instilling shame about sexuality, promoting horror for everything that is natural, and rejecting the senses as distractions, these religions are against life. Condemnation and scorn for the flowering of physical energies are the symptoms of a mindset that sees life as a sin to be amended.

Their ideology is so odd, masochist, and counterintuitive as to make us wonder, why the hatred for nature? What's so bad about the human body? Why repress our instincts and distance ourselves from the physical world? There are several possible answers, but one stands out in my mind as the most likely candidate. The fear of the body comes from the refusal to recognize our animal nature. And the obsessive desire to view ourselves as something other than animals stems from the biggest fear of all: the fear of death. It is no mystery that any physical body that breathes and lives is destined to die and decompose. Clearly, the annihilation of our bodies—one of the defining characteristics making us who we are—doesn't sit well with most people. So, what to do . . .

Here we go: problem solved. As long as we believe that, unlike other animals, we are more than our bodies, then we can hold on to the notion that death will not be able to strike us down. It may dismantle our bodies, but it won't reach our essence because our disembodied souls will go on living. Diminishing the importance of the body and emphasizing the belief in a pure, immaterial spirit is a way to deny the power death has in our lives. As we are about to see, however, this choice of not enjoying fully the physical nature of our world comes with many very unpleasant side effects.

When the Body Goes Missing in Action Part I: From Descartes to Academic Learning

To be fair, religion is not the only pursuit that has promoted alienation from the body. Even though usually it casts the body in a less negative light, science has sometimes substituted the religious soul versus body dichotomy with its own mind versus body problem.

This contrast is no doubt a little less extreme than the religious one. While science does not identify the body as a source of sin and shame, the idea that we have a body but are not our body, remains. According to this view, our true self is our mind. As Descartes, one of the pillars of Western mechanist scientific thought, famously stated, "I think, therefore I am."[123] By identifying exclusively with his mental activities, Descartes makes the ultimate argument for the superiority of the mind over the body. In Descartes' view, thinking is a process that is completely detached from our somatic experience. True reality is not made of muscles and blood, but of thoughts and ideas existing separately from the physical world. With this statement, Descartes ties himself to a long tradition of thinkers, such as Plato, who place the ideal over the real, the abstract over the tangible.

This combination of religious and scientific prejudices has affected human life in hundreds of ways. Despite some tremendous advances made over the centuries, modern medicine only acknowledges to a very limited extent the interconnectedness of mind and body. In Western medicine, health and sickness are usually considered purely physical issues with no relation to our emotions, states of mind, and overall spiritual wellbeing. Healing is the result of fixing a series of mechanical systems. Doctors trained with this mindset are little more than mechanics who relate to the human body as if it were a car, or any other complex machine devoid of consciousness.

Walk into any classroom and you see the same logic being applied to education. Remember the pain and boredom of having to sit most of the day in little, uncomfortable chairs facing forward, listening to some teacher speak for hours on end? The body, forced into an unnatural immobility, is left to atrophy while the mind is engaged. Our physical energies beg us to get up, stretch, and move, but one of the primary requirements of classroom learning is to become skilled at repressing these impulses. The pedagogical message couldn't be clearer: the only thing worth educating is your mind. The body has nothing to do with your full development as a human being. It's little more than an accident of nature—irrelevant to who you truly are. The basic assumption underlying this approach to education is that the quality of our thoughts is independent of our physiological states.

I was never able to buy into this idea. As a student, anytime I looked into the eyes of the people who were supposed to "educate" me, I would feel like something had gone seriously wrong. So many of them looked like they had escaped from the set of a scholarly version of a zombie movie. They were already dead, but someone had forgotten to notify them. I could sense the staleness of the energy flowing through their veins. They moved like achy librarians who had lost the address to their bodies long ago. They smelled of old books and decaying flesh. Listening to their lifeless lectures, I couldn't help but think that their words were direct extensions of their bodies: dry and hunched over. These were the people I was supposed to learn from?!? They were the ones in charge of feeding my mind and expanding my being?

As I looked around for help, I realized some heretical thinkers throughout Western history must have felt exactly the way I did. Take Nietzsche, for example. He says:

> We do not belong to those who have ideas only among books. It is our habit to think outdoors—walking, leaping, climbing, dancing, preferably on lonely mountains or near the sea where even the trails become thoughtful. Our first questions about the value of a book, of a human being, or a musical composition are: Can they walk? Even more, can they dance? . . . Almost always the books of scholars are somehow oppressive, oppressed; the "specialist" emerges somewhere—his zeal, his seriousness, his fury, his overestimation of the nook in which he sits and spins, his hunched back; every specialist has his hunched back. Every scholarly book also mirrors a soul that has become crooked.[124]

Right on, Friedrich! Tell those gloomy freaks that nothing good will ever come from people who are more familiar with the dust of the library than with the light of the sun.

To clarify, let me say I don't believe you need the physique of a Greek deity to be a smart, loving, or otherwise pleasant person. Many individuals have molded wonderful personalities despite facing some very serious physical limitations. Stephen Hawking is a perfect example of what a brilliant mind and an undefeatable spirit can achieve even without the aid of a healthy body. But just because exceptional persons can reach high on mind and spirit alone doesn't mean their lives couldn't be easier, or better, if they could also rely on a vibrant physical energy.

What I am advocating here is not some anti-intellectual glorification of athleticism and popular wisdom against the elitist "high" culture of academia. Few things are as pathetic as those who consider reading books a waste of time and wear their lack of refinement as a badge of pride. My issues with much of the world of academia derive from the opposite. It is precisely because I do value intellectual pursuits and view them as essential that I am disturbed by traditional academic learning treating the body as something superfluous. It is hard to develop a healthy mind without also developing a healthy relationship with one's body, and with the physical world in general. As Thoreau put it, "A man thinks as well through his legs and arms as his brain. . . . Indeed, the mind never makes a great and successful effort without a corresponding energy of the body."[125] In my own experience, I have noticed that any time I feel physically at the peak of my health and strength, my mind works better. When my body is tired and weakened, the mind doesn't flow as well.

This is why I firmly believe that personality is influenced by the body—possibly even more than by our thoughts and values. Nietzsche again says it best when he writes, "give no credence to any thought that was not born outdoors while one moved about freely—in which the muscles are not celebrating a feast, too."[126]

By overlooking the body, we are doing more than just damaging the body; we are also limiting our intellectual potential. The alchemy of body and mind working together transforms knowledge into wisdom. Not only does it change the quality of our thoughts, but it changes also the way we walk, talk, and act. Knowledge ceases being a heavy load of notions we carry in our heads, and turns into a practical source of empowerment to help us lead better lives. Reason and instincts complement each other. The union of muscles, intellect, and spirit makes us more complete human beings than if we were to develop only one of these areas at the expense of the others. Combine athletic talent with great intelligence, and the odds are you'll have greater depth than anyone who is only familiar with half of the experience.

When the Body Goes Missing in Action Part II: The Supersizing of Humanity

The effects of the lack of connection between mind, body, and spirit in our culture are not limited to the confines of medicine or academia. The material conditions of postindustrial society have radically changed our relationship with our own bodies. In the not so distant past, the vast majority of human beings had to rely on physical labor to make a living. Today, for the first time in history, this is no longer the case.

In many ways, this is a wonderful transformation that spares us sometimes insanely harsh and exhausting working conditions. We are now free to do something more than be beasts of burden; we have extra energy now to pursue leisure, a fairly new concept. At the same time, though, this evolution has furthered the divide between mind and body. It is not at all uncommon for people to hardly ever move their bodies. No longer being forced to engage in physical labor, many people only remember they have a body when it's time to feed it. Many citizens in industrialized nations drive from home to work, sit at a desk somewhere all day, then get back into the car and drive home. There, physical inactivity continues as people unwind from a long day at the office. They melt into their couches and watch TV, surf the Internet, and stuff their faces with food. The walk from the couch to the fridge is the longest many people take on any given day.

No longer having to chase one's meal through the forest, or dig it out of the earth, comes at a heavy price. The combination of lack of movement with easy access to enormous amounts of food is paradoxically turning into a liability. Too much comfort can be as bad as too little. Today, people in industrialized nations are getting fatter by the minute. Far from being purely a problem of appearance and resulting emotional pain, the supersizing of the human population has triggered one of the biggest health crises today. Thousands of people die every year as a direct result of being morbidly overweight. Obesity is also more likely to be a contributing factor in deaths from heart disease, certain types of cancer, diabetes, and high blood pressure. The annual health care costs of tending to this epidemic are in the tens of *billions* of dollars.

As horrifying as they are, these statistics are the logical consequence of a change in material conditions (less physical work and more easily available food) combined with the negative view of the body promoted by many of our religions and philosophies. Laws curbing the abilities of certain industries to profit by peddling junk food, and campaigns designed to encourage people to adopt healthier lifestyles (a.k.a. the "move your ass for a change and quit eating so damn much" campaign) are positive steps, but they are not enough. They target the consequences of the problem, but not the root cause: the lack of a mind-body-spirit connection. This is a philosophical problem that begins in the heart, mind, and muscles, and then it manifests in bad habits and poor choices. We can diet from here to eternity, but little is going to change until we alter our whole attitude toward our bodies.

The Marriage of Body and Soul

Energy is eternal delight.

—William Blake

I can only have so much in common with people who have never been in touch with their bodies. Some of them may be very pleasant, smart, and sweet individuals. Maybe we share similar tastes and opinions, but our connection can only go so deep, since we relate to life in radically different ways. To them, the body is little more than an afterthought. For me, it is a primary source of insight: an essential part of who I am.

But to make things more complicated, I also don't necessarily have much in common with people who dedicate plenty of time and attention to their bodies. If my psychic powers are up to speed, I believe the questions you are looking for right now are: why do you have to be such a pain in the ass? What's wrong with those who worship the body as much as you do?

Plenty of people obsess about their bodies, and obviously consider them crucial to their self-esteem. The billions of dollars spent annually in fake boobs, botox injections, liposuctions, steroids, diet programs, and a whole array of other products and medical procedures attest to that. But this has nothing to do with the relationship with the body I am advocating. All these artificial efforts to enhance one's physical appearance indicate a relationship with the body that is no different from the relationship one has with one's clothes, or with a car: nothing but another product to take care of for the sake of attracting attention and showing off.

Even those who don't turn to plastic surgery and other shortcuts, but mold their bodies through old-fashioned sweat share the same mentality. Most people who work out do so for one of two reasons:

either to improve their looks or their health. I can fully appreciate that being healthy and attractive is preferable to being ugly and sick. These are very legitimate goals, and I find nothing wrong with them. But then again, this reminds me of how people treat their cars. They change the oil regularly and perform all the needed maintenance to ensure the car's "health," and paint it, wash it, and wax it to make it look its best.

Well-being and beauty are great, but why stop there? The body is much more than health and looks. It's not a product. It's an experience offering a pathway to expand our perceptions and forge our character. We can turn the body into a way to shape our very essence. Working out becomes a way to transform our whole being. Forget drugs. The body is the ultimate psychedelic agent. Through the body, we can dramatically change our state of consciousness.

Have you ever had one of those nasty, painful days when it feels like the weight of the world is on your shoulders, and sadness, anger, and frustration are pinning you to the floor? More likely than not, working out is the last thing on your mind. All you want to do is disappear into the couch and dive into a pint of the most fattening ice cream on earth. But if through some titanic effort of the will you manage to walk away from your den of misery and head to a gym, interesting things may start happening.

For the next hour or two, the flow of your thoughts slows down while all your muscles are awakened by the intensity of the training. At this point all the negative emotions begin to fade away; as your breathing changes, tension is literally sweated out of your body, and the endorphins come out to play. Once you are done, your problems are waiting for you, still as big and scary as when you left them. But in the meantime your attitude has changed. Instead of feeling overpowered, you are ready to stare them down, and tackle them with renewed energy. If you have had this experience, you know exactly what I mean when I say body and mind are interconnected. And if you haven't, this may be a good time to put down the book and head for the gym. I'll be waiting for you when you get back.

If you are really morally opposed to sweating and working out, you can try a different experiment. Next time you are depressed and bummed out, pay close attention to your posture and your breathing. Open up your chest rather than caving it in, and substitute shallow breaths with deep ones. Sit straight rather than slouching. The odds are you'll realize that being depressed is hard work, for it requires adopting very specific physical postures. Without them, it will be hard to remain depressed for too long.

After we understand that the body can affect our thoughts and emotions as much as thoughts and emotions can affect the body, we can learn to use physical exercise as a religious ceremony for mind and soul. Martial arts, lifting weights, and running are some of my rituals of choice. For a little while, they free me from any excess of thoughts and mental heaviness. They allow me to fully embrace my animal nature. These are not simply ways to work out. Through them, I celebrate the pure, unrestrained joy of the muscles tensing as they put on the line the last ounce of energy they have. What we are worshipping here is raw energy, vitality, and the primitive powers of which life is made.

Seen in this light, weights stop being just something you lift to build muscle; they turn into tools for meditation. The same goes for running or martial arts. I find it much easier to center myself when my body is fully engaged. I love to sweat in the heated competition of combat sports, when everything but you and your opponent disappears from your consciousness. I crave intense activities challenging every last fiber in my body.

Maybe it's because I'm a barbarian, but I have a hard time meditating by sitting down in complete stillness. Despite my rough, uncivilized tendencies, however, even I can appreciate that there are more delicate ways to relate to the body. Yoga and Tai Chi are beautiful forms of mediation in motion. Something as simple as starting the day with a brief yoga routine such as a Salute to the Sun is a surefire way to wake up balanced and energized. Receiving a treatment by a first-rate osteopath also rates as one of the most spiritual experiences I have had. One moment I'm lying on a table awaiting treatment, and just minutes later, I pass out completely. By the time I wake up, I feel reborn, centered, happy, in love with life. By working on the subtle energies in my body, she helped me reach a state of consciousness that is very difficult for me to achieve on my own.

But let's not get too attached to specific examples. There are hundreds of ways of working through the body. It's up to you to figure out which ones work best for you. The point remains the same: using the body to reawaken the senses and expand your awareness. Once your senses are brought back from the lethargy most people let them slip into, everyday events become more intense. The ordinary suddenly appears extraordinary as color, shape, texture, taste, sounds, and scents come to life. Those who pay little attention to the five senses have no idea how damn amazing the world can be.

When speaking of physical energies changing our perceptions and shaking us to the core, we cannot forget about what is possibly the most powerful of them all: sex. I can almost hear the horndogs among you suddenly waking up, and deciding that this chapter may be worth your attention after all. Sorry to disappoint you, but we are not going there. Don't despair though. This is too juicy a topic to dismiss in a few lines, so hang on: a whole chapter dedicated to it is coming up.

In an effort to prevent you from abandoning me before the end because you are too busy flipping to the sex chapter, I'll cut this short. Just hang with me for a few more lines.

All these examples point to the same conclusion: the notion that the body is the enemy of the soul is a silly superstition we need to finally shake off our collective consciousness. The idea that the mind is superior to, and works independently of, the body is an equally dangerous pitfall we need to avoid. Too much is at stake here. This is no secondary issue. It's at the core of the way we perceive the world and relate to it. Listening to the voice of muscles and tendons is an art that needs to be taught in school. Let's be suspicious of any religion that doesn't encourage us to sweat.

CHAPTER 8

SEX, SEX, AND MORE SEX

From an author's perspective, writing about sex is risky, because if you write well enough, evocatively enough, vividly enough, you make the reader want to put the book aside and go get laid.

—Tom Robbins, *Wild Ducks Flying Backwards*

I don't want to live in a society where I get stoned for committing adultery. I want to live in a society where I get stoned. And then commit adultery.

—Ibn Warraq

Let's Get It On

Let's lower the lights, break out the wine, and play some music—maybe Marvin Gaye's "Sexual Healing," or, better yet, Ben Harper's version of that song. Candles, perhaps? A log in the fireplace? Whatever helps you get in the mood, I'm game. The time has come for us to switch gears, bid goodnight to laughter and pleasant conversation, and open the door to something more primal, raw, visceral— something that unleashes our natural instincts, drives sweaty bodies on a collision course with each other, hardens the nipples, and simultaneously sends a tingling to your groin and to your soul. Entirely beyond logic and sober rationality, it speaks a language made of juices, tongues, muscles, and skin. As Marvin Gaye, the bard of lust himself, would say, it's time to get it on.

I interrupt this introduction to let you know that my computer just ate a piece of buffalo jerky. It fell on the keyboard in the gaps of the buttons, and, before I could retrieve it, the computer promptly swallowed it up and burped satisfied. I hope it gives this machine the energy to carry on, since the topic of this chapter will require its best efforts. What we are playing with here, in fact, is sex.

I can almost hear the neurons in the heads of my readers who were about to doze off suddenly jumping up, fully awake and ready to give me their undivided attention. If it is true that religion ranks in the top five in the hit parade of humanity's interests, sex is certainly there to keep it company. Time, place, and cultural context matter little: in all times, all places, and all cultures, sex has the power to captivate minds and make heads turn. People can deny it or embrace it, but at the end of the day sex is hardwired in their very DNA.

Perhaps out of jealousy and fear of a tough competitor, religions have often done their best to bring sexuality under their control. Sometimes, they have openly waged war against it. Sometimes, they have tried to domesticate its power through a million rules. But hardly ever have religions been in a position where they could afford ignoring it. If you ignore sex, after all, what's left? So, before we get to the juicier parts of this chapter, let's warm up by taking a quick look at what world religions have had to say about sex.

Sex in World Religions

Go back to the dawn of civilization, and you'll find Mesopotamian temples set on fire by steamy sex rituals. Despite the limited evidence we have, ceremonial sex celebrating fertility, and symbolically uniting earth and sky for the welfare of all that live, was a staple throughout much of the ancient Middle East. Still millennia later, before the monotheistic version of Judaism eventually stamped them out through a bloody civil war, Jews practiced similar rituals as part of the cult of the goddess Asherah.[127] But this promising intersection of sex and religion has largely been forgotten, buried under centuries of theology going in the opposite direction. So, let's keep our story simple and to the point. What do modern mainstream world religions have to say about sex?

Asian religions don't seem overly concerned with pushing a single official view of sex. When it comes to sex, they tend to engage in the curious habit of arguing one thing and its very opposite at the same time. If we wanted crystal clear coherence (damn, do I like alliterations or what?), we'd be better off looking elsewhere. Taoism is a perfect example. The philosophical roots of Taoism seem to almost require a very sex-positive attitude. For example, take the Yin-Yang symbol. It may not be graphically sexual, but what it lacks in explicitness it more than makes up for in other ways. After all, the Yin-Yang is about a celebration of opposite energies playing with each other. Rather than being separated by a puritanical straight line chaperoning the meeting between the feminine essence (Yin) and the masculine (Yang), and telling them to keep their hands to themselves, the symbol of Taoism follows a curve allowing the two essences to joyfully merge into each other.

In case you are not into symbols, Taoism spells out its worldview even more clearly by inviting us to follow our natural instincts. So it would seem quite counterintuitive for Taoists to want to stifle sexuality, which is one of the most powerful natural instincts within our bodies. But among the Taoists, we find ultra-puritanical sects advocating celibacy and detachment from the senses as a path to enlightenment as well as those who approach sex with enthusiastic indulgence. The former may seem at odds with the foundations of Taoist philosophy, and may be influenced by neo-Confucianism and Buddhism more than by the Tao Te Ching; and yet they are nonetheless among the existing variations of Taoism. But even if we discount them as aberrations and only look at those who reject celibacy, the picture would still be murky. Currents of Taoism viewing sex as a beautiful part of life to be enjoyed live side by side with others teaching a cold-hearted form of sexual vampirism aimed at absorbing the energy of one's sexual partners in order to increase one's own vitality and longevity.[128] And to add yet more confusion, some sects devise super-complicated techniques to have sex without ejaculation because they consider any loss of semen as extremely dangerous, while others view this as an unnatural obsession. (Incidentally, this same bizarre, mostly medically unsound concept also exists among Hindus, Buddhists, and followers of other religions as well.)

The story doesn't get any clearer if we switch to Hinduism. The many traditions that make up Hinduism can't agree about sex any more than they can agree about anything else. Hinduism has produced elaborate sex manuals like the Kama Sutra, created temples covered in erotic sculptures, like the Khajuraho Group of Monuments and the Konark Sun Temple, and given birth to torrid mythological tales about the sexual escapades of gods and goddesses.[129] At the same time, some branches of Hinduism exalt celibacy and extreme self-denial as essential spiritual practices, believing that the world of the senses is an illusion keeping us from enlightenment. The more puritan, orthodox forms exist side by side with schools of Tantrism that consider physical pleasure as a stepping-stone toward enlightenment.

In more recent times, partially due to the influence of Muslim and Christian invaders, and partially because of changes internal to Hinduism itself, many modern Indians seem to be more comfortable with Victorian standards of morality than with the pages of the Kama Sutra.[130] And most forms of Hinduism have always endorsed the most classic sexual double standard: female sexuality is severely repressed, while men are considerably freer to do as they please (as long they don't set their sights on women who "belong" to other men).

Despite being born in opposition to orthodox forms of Hinduism, Buddhism follows the same confusing script in regards to sex. What Buddha actually thought on the topic is largely a matter of speculation. One of the few points everyone more or less agrees on, however, is that growing up as the son of a king, Buddha spent his youth having an inordinate amount of sex with hundreds of beautiful concubines. After well over a decade of this, being a bit extreme and unable to find lasting fulfillment, Buddha made a 180-degree turn by taking up the most severe forms of self-mortification. Enlightenment, however, continued to elude him until he adopted a middle path between indulgence and self-denial.

Here is where the story gets complicated. Some Buddhists believe that sexual energy inevitably creates attachment and distracts us from the spiritual path. In their view, avoiding extreme passions and whatever ties us to this world is essential, so they argue that sex and enlightenment are incompatible. True Buddhists—according to them—are to be celibate, for only in this way will they develop the energy and focus to work for the benefit of all living beings.[131] This antisex take on Buddhism seems to have become more extreme over time.[132]

In direct conflict are Buddhists who believe that the essence of Buddhism is manifested through insight and compassion, and that these qualities can be developed without having to sacrifice one's sex life.[133] Enlightenment is not some mystical, remote dimension, but something to be discovered and embodied in the midst of the passions of ordinary life. Much like in the case of Hinduism, Buddhism also includes in its ranks some versions of Tantrism that believe sexual energy can open the doors to enlightenment.

The golden rule bringing peace among these competing interpretations of Buddhism is found in the principle of non-injury: as long as a certain action does not hurt any other living being, it doesn't need to be censored, and it is a matter of individual preference. This is why Buddhism usually allows a high degree of free choice in regards to sex. Even when it endorses seemingly strict rules, it tends to leave plenty of room for exceptions.

The opposite is true for Confucianism. Despite the fact that Confucius said next to nothing about sex, later forms of Confucianism elaborated a strict code of conduct looking down not only on sex, but also on any type of public displays of affection. The rules changed once you were in your own home, though. Confucianism never condemned sex per se—at least for men. The familiar patriarchal formula endorsed by Confucius' fans allows men the freedom to have sex with their wives as well as concubines and prostitutes. Women, on the other hand, have to follow an entirely different set of rules, since they are required to be 100 percent faithful to their husbands, and otherwise forget about sex.

Moving from East Asia to the domains of Western religions doesn't change these double standards one bit. Scriptures don't even bother raising an eyebrow when they tell us the patriarchs of Judaism had sex with multiple wives, slaves, and prostitutes, while also regularly threatening any woman who is as free with her sexuality with death. Adultery is grounds for capital punishment.[134] But for a woman, adultery means having sex with anyone other than her husband; for a man, it means having sex with any woman who is the "property" of some other male—which leaves one's own slaves and prostitutes as fair game.

Besides prohibiting adultery, Jewish scriptures also apply their enthusiasm for the death penalty to homosexuality.[135] This differs from the position taken by most world religions only by degrees, since the majority of them disapprove of homosexuality more or less strongly. In addition to this, Jewish scriptures include laws against having sex during a woman's period, as well as many other possible sexual infractions, which is a little odd when you consider that all these strict rules and moralizing come from the same scriptures that allow the rape of war captives.[136] This particularly distasteful passage is not an isolated incident either, for the Old Testament is full of very unpleasant sex tales. Among the stories that will probably be skipped in Sunday school we have episodes of incest,[137] gang rape,[138] incest and rape simultaneously,[139] public rape on the rooftops of Jerusalem,[140] and quite a few other disturbing anecdotes.

These ugly and violent images of sex show up in yet another way. Over and over again, the prophets compare Jews who didn't share their enthusiasm for monotheism to women deserving horrific punishments for adultery. Jerusalem itself is often metaphorically portrayed as a whore who betrays her legitimate husband (God) by having sex with everyone (worshipping other Gods). In his role as a rejected lover, God himself rails against those unfaithful to him by promising that their fate will be like that of two promiscuous sisters that he eventually caused to be raped, mutilated, and stoned to death for their sexual affairs with foreigners.[141] Mmmm . . . nice, just the kind of speech to inspire love for such a God.

Despite all of this, Judaism does not characterize heterosexual sex as sinful or bad in and of itself. Sexual pleasure is highly regulated (particularly for women), and infractions are punished unmercifully, but as long as it stays within the prescribed laws it is approved by Judaism.

A very similar attitude is also found in Islam. Much like in Judaism, sex during a woman's period is taboo. Much like in Judaism, homosexuality is outlawed. Much like in Judaism, fornication results in harsh physical punishment: but whereas the Old Testament prescribed death by stoning, the Koran sentences the guilty individuals to "only" 100 lashes.[142]

And again, much like in Judaism, Islam also endorses the familiar double standards in the accepted sexual behaviors of men and women. Muslim men can marry non-Muslim women, but Muslim women can only marry Muslim men. Additionally, in some parts of the Muslim world, an obsession with severely controlling female sexuality continues to result in practices not found in the Koran, such as clitoridectomies and honor killings, as well as those sanctioned by the Koran, such as wife-beating.[143] Male sexuality, by contrast, doesn't evoke the same level of violence and anxiety.

If you can get past all these obstacles, you may be able to get a glimpse of Islam's sensual side that has not been covered under the burqa and veils. The Koran, for example, provides a much more vivid description of heaven than any of the other monotheistic religions. Plenty of physical delights await good Muslim men in the afterlife. In a passage that makes it clear even God is a boobs man, we are told, "But for the God-fearing is a blissful abode, enclosed gardens and vineyards; and damsels with swelling breasts for companions; and a full cup."[144] This same theme of Muslim males being able to enjoy eternity in the company of very hot, very available women is repeated multiple times throughout the Koran.[145] Even in this life, Muslim men are given the green light to enjoy sexual pleasure as long they do so without breaking the rules.

Moving away from the pattern of Western religions, Christianity adopted a whole different type of sexual theology. Throughout much of its history, in fact, Christianity has been the only one among Western religions to declare open war against sexual pleasure in all of its forms. Whether Jesus would have approved of this or not is anybody's guess, since the New Testament tells us next to nothing about his view of sex. The writers of the Gospels don't even tell us whether or not Jesus was married. It would have been highly unusual for a Jewish man at that time *not* to be married, but this clearly is not enough evidence to conclude that he was. Knowing that a good mystery always attracts attention, the Gospels chose to remain silent (to the benefit of Dan Brown, who ended up making millions imagining what might have been in *The DaVinci Code*).

What the Gospels *do* tell us, however, is that Jesus' mom managed the considerably tricky business of getting pregnant without having sex. Did I say that the Gospels report this? Well, that's partially correct. The Gospels of Matthew and Luke include the wild story of the virgin birth, but Mark and John, the authors of the other two Gospels, must have slept in the day that this tale was being told, for they forget to mention it. Despite being missing in action from half of the Gospels, and being related in very different ways in the other half, the virgin birth is an article of faith for most variations of Christianity. This is particularly important because—united with the belief that Jesus never married, and presumably never had sex—this idea of immaculate conception seems to cast a negative light on sex in general. As many Christian groups have later elaborated, the fact that Jesus was not born in the old-fashioned sperm-meets-egg way implies, at least indirectly, that sexual passion is inherently sinful.[146]

Adding fuel to this fire is a quote attributed by the Gospels to Jesus:

> You have heard that it was said, "Do not commit adultery."
> But I tell you that anyone who looks at a woman lustfully has
> already committed adultery with her in his heart. If your right
> eye causes you to sin, gouge it out and throw it away. It is better
> for you to lose one part of your body than for your whole body
> to be thrown into hell. And if your right hand causes you to
> sin, cut it off and throw it away. It is better for you to lose one
> part of your body than for your whole body to go into hell.[147]

Some Christians interpret this quote to mean that sexual thoughts are as sinful as actions, and that Jesus makes the already super-strict sexual mores of Judaism even stricter. Others believe Jesus is teaching a master course in *reductio ad absurdum*—taking an argument to its extreme consequences in order to discount the argument. In other words, the former, literal interpretation presents Jesus as being ultra-conservative about sex. The latter, more metaphorical interpretation suggests he is having a good laugh at those among his audience who swear blind obedience to the laws rather than focusing on love and compassion. According to this view, Jesus is challenging the Pharisees and other devotees of strict legalism to take their views to the next level. Why stop at stoning people to death for adultery? Aren't words and thoughts as bad as actions? Why not go after those as well? Given the impossibility of what Jesus suggests, the message of his speech would seem to be to lighten up—which is the exact opposite of what many Christians interpret it to mean. Unfortunately, the Gospel writers fail to tell us whether Jesus was smiling or foaming at the mouth while speaking those words, so we are left wondering whether this passage is an example of great humor or exhibit A in a theology of self-repression.[148]

Given Jesus' relative silence about sex, then, how did Christianity come up with its ideas on sexual morality? The early Christian community was divided about this issue, just as it was about nearly everything else. At one extreme were those who viewed any type of physical pleasure as a trap set by the Devil; at the other people like the followers of the Christian teacher Carpocrates engaged in wild sex orgies in order to free the soul.[149]

In the midst of these very different standards, one man was more influential than any other in turning his own ideas about sex into official Christian doctrines. The man who hijacked Christianity . . . ehm, I meant to say, the man who *affected* Christianity so strongly was a former persecutor of Christians who became known as Saint Paul.

Paul's worldview was shaped by Judaism and certain branches of Greek philosophy such as Orphism and Neo-Platonism that taught a rigid dualism between body and soul. This approach viewed the human body as nothing but a prison, and physical pleasures were considered dangerous distractions clouding both mind and soul. So, the logical consequence was adopting a strict ascetic lifestyle that shunned worldly joys. In the Greco-Roman world, however, these ideas didn't go very far and were mostly restricted to a tiny minority of obscure philosophers until Saint Paul injected them into his very successful brand of Christianity.

In 1 Corinthians 7, Paul breaks down his theology of sex: abstinence from all sex is the best option; if you are too weak to pull off celibacy, then you are allowed to have sex within marriage in order to avoid the more deadly sin of sex outside of marriage.

In addition to the gloomy branches of Greek philosophy mentioned earlier, Paul's extreme take on sex was influenced by something most Christians expected to happen any day: Jesus would return and the world as people knew it would come to an end. As Paul writes, "What I mean, brothers, is that time has become limited, and from now on, those who have spouses should live as though they had none . . . because this world as we know it is passing away."[150] If physical pleasures are a distraction, reasoned Paul, and we are running out of time for the end of the world is about to knock on the door, then it only makes sense to reject sex and anything else tying us to earth in favor of dedicating ourselves 100 percent to prayer and spirituality. Celibacy, therefore, should be the one and only ideal Christian behavior. In light of this, it's hardly surprising to notice that sexual love is never mentioned in positive terms throughout the entire New Testament.

But Paul and his fans didn't stop there. They turned sex into a crucial topic in Christian theology. Throughout the Greco-Roman world, 99 percent of the population considered celibacy unnatural and downright impossible to achieve, since the sex drive was just too powerful to resist. Taking this as a challenge, Paul's supporters argued that celibacy was indeed impossible *unless* one received God's grace—the only force capable of freeing humans from being slaves to their natural instincts. Being able to resist sexual urges was seen as proof of divine help. Sex was thus transformed by Paul and his followers into a battlefield between the forces of good and evil, a true test to see if believers could reject the pleasures of this world for God. Incidentally, this is why celibacy has become a requirement for priests in the Catholic Church down to this day—something that allowed vast amounts of wealth to flow into the Church's coffers, since priests couldn't have legitimate heirs. Those of you who enjoy a good conspiracy theory can take this and run with it.

Paul's argument is what pushed many early Christians to flee to the desert and become hermits. But things didn't necessarily become simpler there. Tormented by visions of everything they were trying to avoid (everything from naked women to great-tasting food,) some turned to creative forms of self-torture such as burning themselves with fire every time sexual desire stirred in their bodies.[151] Oddly enough, the sexual morality of cave-dwelling, apocalypse-fearing hermits from a tiny Jewish sect eventually ended up spreading all over the world. Aah . . . the last 2,000 years could have been quite a bit more fun had most Christians taken their cues from Carpocrates rather than from Paul.

The kick in the groin that is Paul's view of sex was later reinforced by another giant of early Christian theology: Saint Augustine. Celibacy, Augustine confirmed, is the best possible behavior. Sex within marriage for the purpose of procreation is a regrettable necessity—but you better not enjoy it, for that would be a sin. Knowing full well that the majority of his listeners would fall short of his commands, Augustine added that they should feel very bad about themselves for falling prey to lust, and that this proved they were sinners at heart and in need of redemption, but if they groveled enough they could be forgiven. Those, however, who had any kind of sex outside of marriage were guilty of a deadly sin. Sexual pleasure, in his view, was a disease to be avoided at all costs.[152]

This negative obsession with sex left an indelible mark on Christian history, causing deep psychological wounds in millions of people around the world. Any time they thought about sex, Church authorities told them, they were in danger of buying a one-way ticket to hell.[153] The heaviest forms of self-repression and shame about natural instincts were thus ingrained in the hearts of countless men and women. But the machine of oppression targeted women much more than men. Like in all patriarchal societies, exceptions to these super-stringent rules could be made for men, but the same courtesy was not applied to women. For many centuries, following the advice of some theologians, public opinion considered ". . . any woman who did not blush at the very thought of sex . . . a whore."[154]

In addition to breaking the Catholic monopoly over Jesus' message in the West, Martin Luther gave Protestantism a radically different set of sexual ethics. Luther argued that celibacy is unhealthy and will most likely drive you insane. In his view, the clergy should not be required to abstain from sex, and sexual pleasure within marriage was not sinful. Any kind of sex outside of marriage, however, was still met with the most severe punishments in this world and the next. What Luther did was bring back the Protestant variations of Christianity within the framework of the sexual theology espoused in the West by Judaism and Islam. Unlike Catholicism, in fact, Protestantism, Judaism, and Islam rejected celibacy, approved of sex as part of marriage, and harshly condemned it in all its other forms. Even though this is clearly a step ahead compared to the rabid sexophobic views cherished by Saint Paul and Saint Augustine, the improvement is only relative. Much of the uneasiness and shame about sex created over the centuries remained unaltered. And by promising hell to anyone enjoying sex out of marriage, Protestantism kept alive a culture of fear surrounding sexual exploration.

The Harvest of Repression

I have a quiz for you. Check out the following quote and tell me who is speaking.

> Humanity today is living in a large brothel! One has only to glance at its press, films, fashion shows, beauty contests, ballrooms, wine bars, and broadcasting stations! Or observe its mad lust for naked flesh, provocative postures, and sick, suggestive statements in literature, the arts and the mass media![155]

Too hard? I'll make it easier. You don't need to tell me the name of the speaker, just which religion he belongs to.

OK, I admit it; I am a tricky bastard and my question is a trap. The description of modern society that emerges from the previous quote, in fact, could come from the lips of any religious fundamentalist, since ultraconservative members of most religions seem to be reading from the same script. In case you are wondering, the words above were penned in the mid-1900s by Sayyid Qutb, one of the father figures of modern Islamic fundamentalism. But they could just as easily have been spoken by a biblical prophet 3,000 years ago, or by Pat Robertson yesterday. Enraged by the individual rights offered by many modern societies, religious fundamentalists from different traditions are all particularly offended by the greater degree of sexual freedom enjoyed today by millions of people around the world.

I don't think it is a coincidence that the most vocal, hostile opponents to a more open sexuality are also fond of the most aggressive, dogmatic, intolerant, holy war—waging interpretations of certain religions. After all, if you are busy getting laid and having joyful orgasms, you are less likely to be so damn angry all the time. Sexual repression and fundamentalism are made for each other.

The fundamentalists' fear of sex is a running theme in their war waged against modernity. The fields of battle in this conflict are many. The availability of birth control is a prime example. For the Catholic Church in particular, birth control is deeply troublesome since embracing sexual pleasure and separating it from the possibility of having kids flies in the face of their dogma that sex is condoned only for the sake of having children. Perhaps even more troublesome, it enables human beings to take charge of their reproductive destiny rather than leaving it "in the hands of God." This is precisely why the Catholic Church still officially outlaws birth control to this day, despite the fact that an overwhelming majority of Catholics conveniently ignore this prohibition. Not to be outdone, some Orthodox Jews and Muslim fundamentalists are just as opposed to birth control. And it was only a few decades ago that many Protestants supported laws imposing jail time on those teaching the public about birth control.

Sex education is still viewed by most religious conservatives as the gateway to perversion and immorality. The idea that unmarried teenagers may learn how to enjoy sex while avoiding unintended pregnancies and sexually transmitted diseases is enough to make them recoil in horror. "Just say no to sex" is the beginning and end of their version of sex education.

Good old-fashioned censorship is yet another approach favored by religious conservatives in their losing battle against "unregulated" sex. If we were to pick one man to carry the banner for sex censorship, the prize would go to Anthony Comstock. After coming across some pornographic pictures as a young man in the mid-1800s, Comstock was forever haunted. "Like a cancer," Comstock wrote, "it fastens itself upon the imagination, defiling the mind, corrupting the thoughts, leading to secret practices of most foul and revolting character, until the victim tires of life, and existence is scarcely endurable."[156]

Wait . . . all of this because he saw images of naked men and women having sex? Damn . . . Sayyid Qutb would be proud.

Tormented with guilt by his fascination for porn, Comstock dedicated his life to fighting it. He successfully lobbied Congress to pass censorship laws, became a postal inspector who opened other people's mail looking for "sinful" material, destroyed tons of books, was responsible for over 4,000 arrests, and drove over a dozen people to suicide as a result of his persecution. Comstock's censorship efforts included everything from medical anatomy textbooks to the works of writers like George Bernard Shaw and Walt Whitman.[157]

In the United States, it wasn't until the 1960s that Comstock's spiritual heirs saw the tide turning and their repressive policies being overturned.[158] But Comstock still has plenty of soul mates throughout the world: from Muslim advocates for the strictest interpretations of Islamic law to Chinese politicians influenced by a deadly combination of a Confucian historical heritage with a Communist present, many are those whose hearts flutter at the thought of burning books and squashing anything having to do with sex.[159]

Oddly enough, even in the United States, the same conservative Christians who normally adore free-market capitalism clamor for government intervention imposing more restrictions when the law of supply and demand responds to the public thirst for sex. In one of the most bizarre examples of skewed priorities, many religiously strict parents voice little objection if their kids play video games where you have to mow down your opponents with machine guns, or chop their heads off with samurai swords: boys will be boys—they believe—and a little blood and gore won't do them too much harm. But their relative tolerance for extreme violence doesn't extend to sexual themes. Whereas ultraviolent video games are usually considered appropriate for teens, any type of nudity, even within otherwise mellow, nonviolent games, have parents jumping up and down screaming for the strongest possible restrictions against this blatant attempt at corrupting the minds of their kids. I don't know if it's just me, but this seems more than a little counterintuitive. After all, which would you rather see coming at you in a dark alley—an AK-47–wielding ninja assassin or boobs?

While you visualize yourself in the proverbial dark alley and ponder your options, you may also want to consider the enthusiasm with which certain religions have endorsed "vice laws." In the city where I am writing at this moment (Long Beach, California, once home to the indigenous Tongva people and now home to great Thai food, a sizable gay community, and Snoop Doggy Dogg), less than a hundred years ago it was illegal to kiss or even hug someone in public. Six months in jail and heavy fines were used to discourage such "sins."[160]

Around the same time, Congress passed the Mann Act. Originally intended to target men taking women across state lines to sell them into forcible prostitution, its purpose was expanded by the Supreme Court under pressure from various churches. Under the new guidelines, it became illegal for an unmarried couple to cross state lines together. This meant that, basically, any man bringing his girlfriend across state lines was guilty of a federal felony. The way the good people from the churches viewed it, forcible prostitution and consensual sex out of marriage were morally equivalent, since any kind of unmarried sex violated their idea of morality.[161] For that matter it was only very recently that laws against "unnatural" sexual acts, such as oral sex, were abolished in the United States.

This same desire to impose one's sexual ethics on everyone else is what led to worldwide stringent laws against prostitution, despite the fact that wherever it is legal and regulated prostitution results in fewer abuse cases and fewer incidents of sexually transmitted diseases than where it is illegal and unregulated. But this matters little to moral crusaders as long they get to force the rest of society to follow their standards. Consider that a few decades ago Christian fundamentalists opposed research to find a cure for venereal diseases such as syphilis. Even today some maintain the same attitude about HIV, since they consider STDs divine curses sent to punish sinners and bring humanity back to the "right" path.[162]

It is perhaps sobering to notice that most of the examples of repressive theology at work come from the modern West, which is usually condemned for its excessive sexual permissiveness by most of the Muslim and Hindu world, as well as by those countries were Confucianism runs rampant. The relatively more open attitude found in the West doesn't exist because Western religions take a more relaxed and positive view of sex, but rather *in spite of* the sexual ethics of Western religions.

Sex, Sake, and Zen:
The Philosophy of Ikkyū Sojun

Since our little journey through the sexual morals of world religions may have bummed you out by now, I'm here to come to the rescue and offer you some water in the midst of the desert. Just when you start thinking that all religions have been shaped by sexophobic freaks, I'll give you three examples to show you otherwise. The one and only Tom Robbins introduced me to the first.

The hero of our story is a Japanese monk from the fifteenth century—hardly a promising start if you're looking for sexual redemption, but don't despair. Appearances in this case are very deceiving. The life of Ikkyū Sojun was wild from the beginning. Born in 1394 as the illegitimate son of the Emperor of Japan and a lady of the court, Ikkyū barely survived a political conspiracy aimed at wiping out possible heirs to the throne. After being banished from the court, his mother placed him in the care of a Zen temple when he was only five years old—a desperate move made in an effort to save his life. Despite being considered a genius by his peers, Ikkyū seriously flirted with suicide on a couple of occasions. But in a way his early existential troubles made him much stronger, since he would eventually become renowned for his ability to find joy in the midst of the most desperate circumstances.[163]

Ikkyū's sharp intellect and intuitive grasp of Buddhism made him a likely candidate to climb the religious hierarchy within Zen temples, but Ikkyū instead chose to raise his middle finger toward the religious establishment of the day and create his own path. In an act of rare defiance, he burned the certificate of enlightenment (think of it as the Buddhist equivalent of a spiritual PhD) given to him by his teacher—a daring gesture since the certificate was a requirement for the higher offices in temples. *Certificate of enlight-*

enment? Has spirituality turned into some bureaucratic perversion? Screw this, I don't want any part of it, thought Ikkyū.

Then Ikkyū found yet another way to burn his bridges with the religious orthodoxy. Despite his earlier iconoclastic behavior, he was named abbot of a temple. He disappeared a little over a week later. When the other monks went looking for him, they only found a poem he left behind which said if anyone wanted to see him, they could find him at the sake shops or the local brothels!

It wasn't that Ikkyū was giving up on Zen in favor of a life of drunken parties and hookers (though sex and sake-drinking were among his favorite activities). Rather, choosing the life of a vagabond teacher wandering the countryside was for him an extension of his Zen insight. It's precisely because he loved what Zen could be that he couldn't settle for what Zen in the temples had become. Given a choice between the power politics, corruption, hypocrisy, and blind devotion to empty formalisms that characterized many Zen communities and the freedom to actually live and embody Zen in the midst of a world rich with passion and contradictions, Ikkyū didn't hesitate. Earning his nickname "Crazy Cloud," Ikkyū chose freedom. This total freedom made him shunned by most monks, and at times it could be dangerous and lonely, but that didn't bother him. Monks and other religious officials annoyed him anyway. In their hands, Zen had stopped being a living experience and had turned into a ritualistic dogma. Hookers were much more fun to hang around—more down to earth, more genuine, more real. As he wrote,

> The sound of priests piously intoning sutras . . .
> How their empty words grate on my ears!
> Lost in elegant dalliance
> And love-talk, we . . . scoff at grim ascetics.

With a young beauty, sporting away in deep love play;
We sit in the pavilion, a pleasure girl and this Zen monk.
I am enraptured by hugs and kisses,
And certainly do not feel as if I am burning in hell!
Stilted koans and strained answers are all you have.
Forever pandering to officials and rich patrons.
Good friends of the Dharma, so proud,
But a brothel girl in gold brocade has you beat by a mile."[164]

The blood pressure of Ikkyū's Zen comrades must have gone through the roof. Most Zen texts hardly ever mentioned sex, and when they did, it was always with stern, puritanical words of warning. Ikkyū dismissed the strict mainstream Zen view of sex as a superstition created by unstable minds afraid of truly being alive. Taking pleasure in the body to him was a natural, healthy antidote to the mental neurosis afflicting most "spiritual" people. As he wrote, "The autumn breeze of a single night of love is better than a hundred thousand years of sterile sitting meditation."[165] And in another passage that can't be accused of ambiguity, he states, "Don't hesitate: get laid—that's wisdom. Sitting around chanting sutras: that's crap."[166] Now, these are words to live by. Take that, sexophobic freaks!

One of the things that bugged Ikkyū the most was the artificial distinction between what's sacred and what's profane, separating spiritual virtues from raw, earthy living. Contrary to the conventional Buddhist wisdom of the times, Ikkyū felt passion and enlightenment went hand in hand, for enlightenment was nothing other than daily life experienced in all of its intensity, with full awareness. By awakening us to the here and now through intense pleasure, sex could be considered no less than the holiest of rituals, and an orgasm could be as powerful and deep as the most solitary mystical vision.

For a devotee of joy-no-matter-what such as Ikkyū, they were one and the same.

The puritan souls in the Zen community were horrified, but many other people from all walks of life, fascinated by his disarming honesty and zest for life, naturally found themselves gravitating toward Ikkyū. Eventually, a wide circle of artists, poets, actors, and musicians formed around him. And so, between sweaty sessions of mind-altering sex and epic sake-drinking bouts, Ikkyū managed to find the time to shape the cultural history of Japan by influencing the tea ceremony, theater, calligraphy, poetry, and painting. In Ikkyū's own words, all of this was accomplished while ". . . tasting life and enjoying sex to the fullest."[167]

Bible Porn

Our second example comes from . . . the Old Testament!

You can stop rubbing your eyes now. You have read right. The same Jewish scriptures that contain all the moralizing precepts discussed earlier are also home to one of the most unashamed celebrations of sex ever found in religious literature.

When I first ran into this composition, I was floored. I was eighteen years old, and I'm not sure what had gotten into me, but I had decided I would read the entire Bible cover to cover. I wanted to find out for myself what the whole big deal was about, so I was determined to read every passage in every chapter, even those parts that would go on page after page listing genealogies of unpronounceable names.

After several eight-hour days of reading non-stop, I began to think that maybe I had bitten off more than I could chew. My stamina was running out. If I read about one more story of God demanding bloody punishment against the unbelievers, I was going to lose it. But just when my determination seemed to have reached its limits, I stumbled onto the Song of Songs. When I was done, I read it again. And again. I kept trying to figure out just how this could have possibly made its way into the middle of the Bible. My theory was that one of the original scribes who wrote down scriptures one night got mighty drunk, and mistakenly swapped whatever religious book he was supposed to copy for something out of his personal stash of literary porn.

OK, maybe it wasn't the best theory ever, but none of the other theories made much sense either. Here was a book completely unlike anything else in Jewish Scriptures: The Song of Songs was a series of very explicit love poems, the majority of which were written from a woman's perspective. This represents possibly the only time in scriptures where, in defiance to patriarchy, a female voice takes center stage. This is exciting on its own, but it gets even better. The lovers who are the main characters of the Song couldn't care less for God, rituals, priests, or the law since they don't bother mentioning them much. The identity of this couple is a mystery: it's not even clear if they are the same man and woman throughout all of the sections. At times, it sounds like they are a bride and groom at a wedding party, perhaps even King Solomon and one of his queens, but in other moments they are a couple of shepherds. And in some parts they are clearly not married.

What is unmistakable, however, is their enthusiasm for sex. Not sex for procreation, mind you. But the sex that drives a man and a woman insane for each other—completely swept away by overwhelming passion. Unlike Adam and Eve, the Song's couple is not at all ashamed by their nudity. Quite the opposite. Line after line, they celebrate each other's beauty in verses that seem to caress every part of the lovers' bodies. From feet to thighs, from eyes to breasts, there's hardly an inch of their bodies where their gaze doesn't stop. Their desire-filled descriptions enlist all of the five senses to fully embrace the very physical dimension of love.

"Those who restrain Desire do so because theirs is weak enough to be restrained," wrote William Blake.[168] Had he spoken to the lovers of the Song, Blake would have wasted his breath, for their desire knows no bounds. In order to fulfill it, they are willing to challenge the control of their families and of the authorities. The woman of the story runs through the streets of Jerusalem at night looking for her lover, with little care for the night watchmen chasing her. Even more radically, she is unafraid to defy her brothers' attempts at controlling her sexuality. As she sings, "My mother's sons were angry with me; They made me keeper of the vineyards; but my own vineyard I have not kept."[169] And later she adds, "But my own vineyard is mine to give."[170] (Hint: it's not a literal vineyard she is talking about!) Absent from the words of this most assertive woman is any sense of guilt, shame, or sin. She is going to make love with whomever she wants, and she is not about to let family duties, gods, laws, or men stand between her and her lover.

Embarrassed by the obvious physical lust that literally drips from the pages of the Song of Songs, both Jewish and Christian theologians have performed the most complicated mental contortions in order to justify its place in scriptures. All this talk of body parts and sexual metaphors should not be taken too literally, they say. Those passages are really just images expressing the loving union between Israel and God (in the Jewish version), or between Jesus and the Church (in the Christian version), or, as some suggest, between the soul and God (in both the Christian and Jewish variations).

Talk about earning your black belt in the art of bullshitting. Consider this: "My beloved put in his hand by the hole of the door, and my insides were moved for him. I rose up to open to my beloved, and my hands dropped with myrrh and my fingers with sweet smelling myrrh, upon the handles of the lock."[171] Or this, "A bundle of myrrh is my beloved to me; he shall lie all night between my breasts."[172] Or this, "Your breasts are perfect; they are twin deer feeding among the lilies."[173] Or this, "In his shade I took great delight and sat down, and his fruit was sweet to my taste."[174]

The union of the soul and God? Really?

Great sex doesn't need any justifications, nor does it need to stand as the metaphor for anything besides what it is. It's great sex. Why complicate something so beautiful?

Where Gods and Goddesses Go Have an Orgy

The same desire to make apologies for an example of burning sexuality within their tradition is also found in Hinduism. This time sculptures, not words, have embarrassed prudish theologians—hundreds of sculptures decorating the walls of some temples at Khajuraho and Konark. Just like in the Song of Songs, what we have here is an extremely graphic representation of sexual love—even more graphic perhaps than in the Song of Songs, since the sculpted stone leaves nothing to the imagination. Dozens and dozens of very well-shaped male and female figures have chosen the walls of the temples as the site for a full-on orgy, enacting just about every possible variation on heterosexual love, from acrobatic positions to multiple partners.

Troubled by the super-explicit enjoyment of sex for sex's sake, several people have rushed to argue that the sculptures are not of gods and goddesses getting it on, but rather, they represent human activities. Others have added that these statues are a warning to leave sexual thoughts outside the temples. Ha! If this were true, it would be one of the worst strategies in recorded history, for everyone would hang out by the external walls and not in the temple itself. Plus, the sculptors obviously had a little too much fun with their subjects for us to think they were just trying to admonish us against sexual pleasure.

No, the sculptures at Khajuraho and Konark are not there to preach and lecture us (it's kind of hard to lecture while you are naked and are pleasuring three partners at the same time . . .) What they do is remind us that, much like the deepest spiritual experiences, sex can open the doors to pure bliss. They tell us that lovemaking is the key to making rigid, separate egos melt into a place of relaxation, happiness, and unity with the energy of the universe. Ikkyū and the mysterious author of the Song of Songs would have understood this.

Sexual Healing

For far too long, many religions have weighed us down with all their hang-ups. Thousands of years of whispering in our ears that there is something wrong with delighting in sex have planted a deep neurosis into our psyche. This relentless negative feedback has taught us to be ashamed of our sexual desires, ashamed of any spark of passion, and even ashamed of our very own naked bodies. Once internalized, this message creates a schizophrenic conflict between our instincts and our religious beliefs, and ultimately leads us to declare war against ourselves. "What we want to do" and "what we think we should do" fight each other in a never-ending battle within our consciousness. What could and should be a beautiful experience is ruined, for it becomes difficult to have a great orgasm with so much guilt hanging in the air.

This is the inevitable result of listening for too long to religions seeking to put a leash and muzzle on our sexual nature. Many of them will tell you that by keeping sex within the confines of marriage, they are preserving it for its proper context and thereby honoring it. They'll add that they consider the body as a holy temple. But these are just empty words. What does it mean for these religions to hold the body as "sacred"? We should remember only after we are married that we are sexual beings. Until then, don't touch, don't look, don't feel: these are the proper ways to honor the body—indeed a very strange logic that equates alienation and repression with holiness.

Nietzsche writes, "Every kind of contempt for sex . . . is the crime *par excellence* against life—is the real sin against the holy spirit of life."[175] When you take into account the amount of suffering and dysfunction caused over the centuries by sexophobic doctrines, it's hard not to agree with Nietzsche in seeing this as a horrendous crime against humanity.

Perhaps the people responsible for this were/are just scared by the powerful emotions that sex can ignite. Or maybe—if you are in the mood for a good conspiracy theory—something darker is at play here. Many religions, after all, owe their popularity to offering a cure to various human problems, and playing doctor to different sorts of spiritual diseases. If people are healthy and happy, they are not going to line up at their door looking to buy their prepackaged salvation. But if you can convince them that they are sick and in need of redemption, you can ensure a wide supply of customers. Good sex is a threat to this because it builds self-confidence, injects you with self-esteem, and ultimately empowers you—the perfect antidote to people and institutions seeking control by making you doubt yourself. But if these same people and institutions can manipulate you into feeling bad about something as personal and inescapable as your sex drive, then the trap is set. They don't even need to recruit you, for you'll be begging to be taken in and saved. Once you become convinced that you are a sinner and need a cure, you'll be seeking them out.

Like all good conspiracy theories, this one is fun to entertain, but it doesn't explain everything. Reducing many religions' restrictive attitudes about sex to a cynical ploy to control people is much too simplistic. But the fact remains that good sex and increased self-esteem go hand in hand, and imposing severe limits on healthy sexuality is a guaranteed way to disempower people. So, whether this is done cynically or in a completely innocent manner, the end result is the same.

Worse yet, the more you repress natural instincts, the more they will emerge as perversions. The damage done by puritan ideologies is made evident by the long string of scandals involving those who preach for the harshest limitations to be imposed on sex. Not only are they often unable to live up to their own rhetoric, but when they fail, they go to the other extreme. Consider, for example, Ted Haggard, once president of the super-powerful National Association of Evangelicals (which represents over 45,000 churches). Very conservative guy that he is, Haggard regularly condemned any type of sex outside of marriage, but he ended up having to resign after tales began circulating of his crystal methamphetamine-laden meetings with gay hookers. Crystal meth with gay hookers?!? Wouldn't it have been easier to just be a little more relaxed about healthy ways to experiment with sex? Or consider the horrendous record of countless Catholic priests officially preaching against masturbation and the "sins" of consensual sex outside of marriage, but at the same time raping young kids. There's no escaping it: too much self-repression breeds perversion.

So, one of the very first steps to build a healthy religion is to do away with all the negative superstitions surrounding sex. Abstinence doesn't make one holy—just miserable, angry, and well on the way to insanity. All the emphasis placed on virginity all but ensures that most people's first times will be awful: too much pressure creates self-consciousness, and self-consciousness just kills the moment by making you too tense. And why should marriage be the one and only context in which sex is allowed? As long as everyone involved is adult and willing, why so many rules?

One of the things that bugs me the most about many otherwise very nice spiritually inclined individuals is their very annoying habit of coming up with complicated rationalizations to somehow justify their sexuality. When I hear them speaking of sex as a "loving spiritual connection," it makes me want to throw up. It's not that I'm a complete barbarian who doesn't see their point, but too often they seem to be trying too hard to find some respectable excuse for raw passion. It's almost as if sex needs to be domesticated before it can be considered acceptable.

Now, I am the first to be turned off by a vulgar, gross attitude, for that's just the flip side of puritan repression, and it ultimately spoils good sex. But at the same time, sex doesn't always have to be about a spiritual connection, or an expression of the deepest love. As long as it feels good for those involved, and they walk away happy, sex can be great in and of itself. Nourishing love and emotional connections through sex is obviously wonderful, but insisting that this is the only legitimate use for sexual pleasure may just betray some hidden sense of shame about openly enjoying the honest, sweaty, lustful side of life.

Good sex is the greatest antidepressant ever invented. It clears the mind, relaxes the body, and makes us more open to the beauty of it all. By removing stress and tension, it brings us to a happier place where being in love with life is easy. This is why laughter erupts spontaneously after an orgasm. And this is why the healthy thing to do is lift the heaviness under which religions have buried sex. What we need is more joy and celebration, not rigid rules and self-repression.

CHAPTER 9

KILLING PATRIARCHY AND REWRITING GENDER ROLES

The Embarrassing Uncle in the House of Theology

A very unpleasant visitor showed up to play with us tonight. With its usual arrogant, bossy manners, it demanded a starring role in this chapter, and threatened not to leave my book alone until it got its share of the spotlight. Our most annoying guest is not the type we can convince that it's time to go home by yawning and claiming we have to wake up early tomorrow. And certainly, we will not be able to gently but firmly usher it to the door, either. Quite a number of people have already been trying to do that for a few millennia without any luck. And so here we are, tackling one of the forces that has done the most to squash dreams, deny what should be basic, inalienable rights, and enslave the bodies and souls of half of the human population.

The name of the beast is patriarchy—a dark, ever-present demon whose shadow never left the stage of history. Male domination and female submission are the ideological cornerstones on which it built its home in the consciousness of millions of people throughout the world. In modern times, most religions pretend to be barely acquainted with it. Gone are the days when they could openly support it without repercussions. Now, their former ally has turned into a public relations nightmare—better deny any familiarity with it, or what will the neighbors think? Patriarchy has turned into the embarrassing uncle in the house of theology, the proverbial skeleton in the closet of faith. But no matter how loudly they deny knowing it, the fact remains that patriarchy has been aided and abetted in its criminal activities by nearly all world religions.

To be perfectly honest, we should introduce a disclaimer: none of the modern world religions is responsible for creating patriarchy. Adam and Eve or Pandora's box are the mythological great-grand-kids of patriarchy—certainly not its creators. Patriarchy was alive and well long before Christianity, Islam, Judaism, Confucianism, Buddhism, Hinduism, and their colleagues ever showed up on the scene. But most, if not all, ended up giving patriarchy their blessing and support.

Before we turn to the obscene marriage between patriarchy and religion, let's figure out how the beast ever came into being. The first shocking thing about patriarchy is how widespread it is. Put your finger anywhere on the map, and the odds are that you'll see a place where patriarchy has set up shop. Across time and space, anywhere one gender has had preferential access to power, it has always turned out to be men having more power than women. No matter how hard you look, you'd search in vain for a female-dominated society. What you'll find instead are either egalitarian societies where men and women have equal rights, or male-dominated societies where an exceptional woman could attain status and power *despite* her gender. The tales of the Amazons make for a great myth, but they don't find a home in historical reality. And the same can be said about the utopia of nature-loving, nonviolent, goddess-worshipping societies from a very distant past, when sexism and hierarchy didn't exist. According to this story, these societies lived in peace and love for centuries before being wiped out by hyper-aggressive, nomadic warriors who introduced the exclusive worship of male gods.[176] Even though it is true that goddesses played a key role in the religious life of plenty of people around the globe, the existence of powerful goddesses often didn't translate into peaceful or women-friendly societies. Just because a female deity existed didn't mean the people couldn't be chauvinist toward the actual flesh-and-blood women living among them.[177] The reason why many badly like to believe otherwise is clear: the ideal of peaceful, women-honoring, goddess-worshipping societies offers a great counter-myth to the oppressing patriarchy peddled by most religions. If it happened in the past, then it could be done again in the future.

Unfortunately, history tells us that it probably didn't happen in the past. But there's no reason we can't take the best aspects of this myth and create something beautiful here and now. In any case, this detour through Amazons and goddesses still has not answered our question: where does patriarchy come from? As much as I resent biological explanations of human behavior, if something shows up all over the world regardless of cultural context, I am afraid biology has something to do with it. Our most distant ancestors were clearly influenced by biology when they decided to divide labor along gender lines assigning men the task to hunt and women to gather. Why? Because women can breastfeed and men can't. It's as simple as that. Babies, therefore, could afford to have their father be gone on long hunting expeditions, since they didn't have to be glued to their nipples night and day, while mothers had to remain in constant contact with their infants in order to feed them. And this precluded hunting, since a baby could not be safely taken on a long trip to stick a spear through the ribs of a pissed-off mammoth. It made sense, then, for women to focus on a safer, less travel-intensive activity like the gathering of plants, and for men to hunt.

And because men gained great familiarity with weapons through hunting, they would be the best candidates to specialize in fighting against rival tribes. The fact that they naturally had greater muscle mass than women was an added bonus.

Despite all of this, the majority of hunting and gathering societies remained egalitarian: women among them were as respected and powerful as men. But the fact that mastery over weapons and violence had become a male monopoly meant that any time a society moved away from egalitarianism, men would have the upper hand. Patriarchy, in this sense, is the almost inevitable consequence of this. When only one gender possesses the skills and the tools to crack open the heads of anyone they disagree with, you can bet that they are not going to be the ones being disempowered. Violence speaks louder than words. So, it's no surprise that societies around the world are either egalitarian or dominated by men. At the end of the day, men have always had the means to impose their will by force; women have not.

The Love Affair Between Religion and Patriarchy

The previous lines may have tricked us into thinking that religions play little or no role in this debate. But just because no specific tradition has laid the egg that spawned patriarchy does not mean that religions don't have plenty to say about the roles of men and women.

And unfortunately, the harsh reality is that patriarchy has been a running thread throughout the history of world religions.

Since we have to start from somewhere, we might as well take on the big boys right away. Let's begin by hunting down patriarchy where it hid within the Judeo-Christian tradition. If it is not overly traditional for you, we'll start at the beginning. And by beginning, I mean it quite literally—as in the creation of humankind according to Judeo-Christian scriptures. With its usual clarity, the Bible gives two different accounts of creation. In Genesis 1:27, God creates the first man and the first woman at the same time. But in Genesis 2:7, *one page later,* the biblical narrative starts over again, telling us that God creates the first man only—Adam. The first woman enters the picture later, once God realizes that poor, lonely Adam needs a "helper," and that none of "the beasts of the fields and the birds of the air" are qualified for that job. This is no joke. In Genesis 1:27 it seems like women were part of the original divine plan, on equal footing with men. But in this second account of creation (told in Genesis 2:18–23), Eve is an afterthought, fashioned out of Adam's spare rib just to ease his loneliness. Had Adam been into animals, women would not exist.

If this is bad, don't worry. Things in Genesis are only going to get worse for women. Eve has barely been created when she promptly disobeys God's order not to eat a certain forbidden fruit, and manages to convince Adam to go along with her. Our Judeo-Christian God responds by having a fit, yelling: "I will greatly increase your pains in childbearing; with pain you will give birth to children. Your desire will be for your husband, and he will rule over you."[178] The very first thing that Eve does brings about the fall of humanity and their expulsion from the Garden of Eden.

This is Patriarchy 101, right there. Not only are Eve and all women after her sentenced to a painful childbirth, but also men ". . . will rule over you." In the Judeo-Christian tradition, then, women's subordination to men is not simply a cultural choice or a sociological accident, but a divinely ordained part of God's plan. According to this tale, rejecting patriarchy means preventing God's sentence from being carried out. This is what prompts the author of Ecclesiasticus to add a cherry to the cake of misogyny by writing, "Woman is the origin of sin, and it is through her that we all die."[179] This is also what inspires Martin Luther's conclusion in regards to proper gender roles:

> The rule remains with the husband and the wife is compelled
> to obey it by God's command. He rules the home and the state,
> wages war, defends his possessions, tills the soil, builds, plants,
> etc. The woman, on the other hand, is like a nail driven into
> the wall. She sits at home . . . The wife should stay at home
> and look after the affairs of the household as one who has been
> deprived of the ability of administering those affairs which are
> outside . . . In this way Eve is punished.[180]

We could go home at this point, and close the book on the Judeo-Christian tradition, because after such an emphatic endorsement of patriarchy in the very first few pages of scriptures, what more evidence do we need? But since I'm in the mood for overkill, bear with me and let's look further.

Throughout the pages of the Old Testament, we run into few women worthy of note, and most of them are mentioned for their evil qualities. In particular, the recurring theme of foreign, polytheistic women leading good, monotheistic Jewish men astray is a recurring theme that keeps resurfacing in the Hebrew scriptures. Much venom is directed at them, page after page.[181]

But even Jewish, monotheistic women don't fare much better. In the text of the Ten Commandments, for example, God orders men not to covet their neighbors' homes, wives, slaves, animals ". . . or anything else that belongs to your neighbor."[182] According to the Ten Commandments, then, women are to be considered the property of men much like cattle or real estate—a fact that is also underscored by the charming story of God causing King David's concubines to be raped in public. What was their crime? Absolutely nothing. They are simply pawns used by God to punish David for *his* crimes. Rape, in fact, was not seen as a violation of the woman, but of a man's property. The final, lovely touch to this edifying tale is that David will later punish these women for being raped.[183]

Besides what we find in the Ten Commandments, several other biblical regulations help clarify what God thinks of women. For example, we read that after giving birth to a boy, a woman is considered "unclean" for seven days and requires going through thirty-three days of purification. But if she gives birth to a girl, she is unclean for fourteen days, and needs to be purified for sixty-six days.[184] Apparently, in the eyes of God, girls are twice as dirty and polluting as boys.

Deuteronomy 22 offers us another pearl of chauvinism. Here, God instructs his people on what to do if a newlywed wife is accused by her husband of not being a virgin: she better produce some evidence (e.g., bloody sheets) that she was indeed a virgin, or ". . . she shall be brought to the door of her father's house and there the men of her town shall stone her to death. She has done a disgraceful thing in Israel by being promiscuous while still in her father's house. You must purge the evil from among you."[185] Curiously, God does not seem to be equally worried about male virginity, since no equivalent rule exists for men.

OK, so it's safe to say that the Old Testament is not the most female-empowering book ever written. But surely things get better once we move to the New Testament, no? The quick answer is: no. Try this example from 1 Timothy 2:11–15:

> Let the woman learn in silence with all subjection. But I suffer not a woman to teach, nor to usurp authority over the man, but to be in silence. For Adam was first formed, then Eve. And Adam was not deceived, but the woman being deceived was in the transgression. Notwithstanding she shall be saved in child-bearing.

Many, many other passages in the New Testament echo this one,[186] but I realize that if I continue at this rate quoting all the hyper-patriarchal passages in Judeo-Christian Scriptures, I will end up causing the end of life on earth for we would have to cut every tree left on the planet to produce enough paper to contain them all. (I admit I may have a mild taste for hyperbole, but you get my point.) So, in an effort to avoid killing you and the rhythm of this chapter under a mountain of quotes, I invite those among you who have a perverse desire to read more of the same to refer to the notes at the end of the chapter. There, I'll serve you a few more plates of New Testament patriarchy. And, truth be told, the quotes above don't tell the whole story. Shortly after Jesus' death, the early Christian community was divided on just about everything. Jesus, in fact, had not spelled out his thoughts on gender roles as well as many other contentious topics, so different factions bickered about what exactly Jesus would have wanted them to do and believe. Quite a few Christian groups were convinced that Jesus' worldview included the equality of women and men. Women, after all, had stood by his side when all his wimpy male disciples had deserted him. Women had gone to his sepulcher when the men were too busy drowning in fear and desperation. Over and over again, Jesus had reversed traditional expectations regarding social hierarchy, so it wasn't such a stretch to imagine him swimming against the current when it came to gender roles.

But there were just as many Christian groups who still held on to some ultrapatriarchal views. This male-dominated version of Christianity found its paladin in Saint Paul. Influenced by a very misogynist current of Greek philosophy and raised with the usual dose of Jewish patriarchal prejudice, Paul thundered against those factions who allowed women to take positions of leadership. Women equal to men? Women as leaders??? Not on my watch—thought Paul, who campaigned tirelessly against these wild notions. When the dust settled Paul's brand of chauvinist Christianity came out on top and proved more popular. Whether this truly reflected Jesus' vision or it shamelessly hijacked it is anybody's guess, but from then on the mainstream branches of Christianity spent the next couple of millennia walking hand in hand with patriarchy.

This deep disdain for women shows up in the pillars of all denominations of Christian theology: we go from Protestant reformer Martin Luther ("Girls begin to talk and stand of their feet sooner than boys because weeds always grow up faster than good crops")[187] to Catholic Saint Thomas Aquinas ("A woman is inferior in her essential biological and psychological nature. She is weaker physically, lacking in moral self-control and inferior in reasoning power")[188] to one of the early Church Fathers, Saint Jerome, ("Woman is the gate of the devil, the path of wickedness, the sting of the serpent, in a word a perilous object")[189] to his saintly colleague Augustine ("What is the difference whether it is in a wife or a mother, it is still Eve the temptress that we must beware of in any woman").[190] Misogyny drips from the pages of more Christian texts than I have room to name here.[191]

In the eyes of most Christian theology, a refusal of patriarchy was an insult to God's plan for humanity. It was the first woman's stupidity, after all, that had opened the door to the Devil. Feminine nature was seen as childlike, immature, weak, less able to reason, and more susceptible to sin, so it was necessary for women to be under male authority in order to prevent evil from spreading. Good women were those who readily submitted to their fathers and husbands. And what about the ones who didn't? Well, it may be time to go look for our whips. . . . Those who insisted on asserting their independence were guilty of sinning against God and nature.

Faithfully following in the footsteps of its elder siblings, Islam, the youngest child in the family of Western religions, adopted a similar stance on gender roles. Even in the present day, chilling stories about the status of women regularly emerge out of the Muslim world: from the countless women every year who have their throat cut by family members during "honor" killings to the courts of Saudi Arabia that, out of deep concern for Islamic morality, sentence a rape victim to six months in jail and 200 lashes because, when she was attacked, she was in a car with a non-relative male. (This is a heinous crime under the Saudi version of sharia law.[192])

Apologists for Islam tell us that these are aberrations, and Muhammad single-handedly improved the status of women in Arabic society. In part, this may be true. Muhammad outlawed female infanticide and gave women the rights to inheritance and divorce, the ability to independently own property, write a will, and several other freedoms women would not be able to enjoy until centuries later in parts of Christian Europe. In light of these reforms, apologists insist that the true message of Islam was positive for women but was later distorted by people wanting to reverse many of these gains.[193]

While it is true that the Koran doesn't advocate practices such as veiling and female circumcision, it would take a black belt in self-delusion to believe that it champions the rights of women. Isn't the Koran the same book that gives males twice the inheritance of females,[194] argues that men are superior to women,[195] suggests that two female witnesses are equal to one male witness,[196] compares women to "weak men" and "children,"[197] prescribes house arrest until death for "lewd women,"[198] and suggests that the wives of sinful husbands should go to hell with them regardless of their own personal conduct?[199] Oh, and I almost forgot the best part. Isn't the Koran also the book that offers precious advice regarding when it's appropriate for a good husband to beat his wife, if she dares rebel against his authority?[200] I rest my case.

It would be nice to believe that virulent misogyny is a disease confined to Western faiths. It would be nice to believe that religions born in other parts of the world are unaffected by this plague. But it's simply not true. Being born female in a country where Confucianism runs rampant, for example, would hardly be an improvement. Confucius, in fact, places the relationship between husband and wife on the same plane as the one that exists between ruler and subject. Followers of Confucianism built a social order where female submission to fathers, husbands, and adult sons is the norm, it is considered a waste to educate little girls since their only functions are to make babies and clean the house, and divorce or even the right to remarry for widows are simply not options.[201]

Confucius' fans, sadly, are not the only gender fascists in Asia. The fact that many goddesses are worshipped as part of the Hindu pantheon, for example, has not prevented several forms of traditional Hinduism from arguing that women are unable to achieve enlightenment. The best they can hope for is to accumulate good karma and be reborn as men. Heretical schools of Tantrism have offered Indian women asylum from a patriarchal social order, but these are but an oasis in the desert of Hindu history.

Buddhism offers a more promising start. Buddha went against the conventional wisdom of his times by arguing that women could become enlightened, but the familiar specter of misogyny soon reared its ugly head and made its presence known throughout much of Buddhist literature.[202] Nuns ended up being subordinates of monks. Celibate monks, in particular, would often blame women for their own inability to come to terms with their sexual feelings. And so many Buddhists began repeating the old refrain that being born female was the result of poor karma.

Other Buddhists countered this view by arguing that insight and compassion can be developed by men and women alike, and that both genders are equally capable of embodying the essence of Buddhism.[203]

The answer to which side is truly faithful to Buddha's message is the same thunderous "who knows?" we have already heard in regards to Jesus' thoughts on gender. The evidence is so ambiguous that one can make them say whatever they want.[204] What can't be doubted, however, is that historically speaking Buddhism has been at minimum guilty of tacit complicity with patriarchy.

In theory, Taoism has all the cards to be the shining exception in this story. After all, it is the one religion that emphasizes the importance of subtle, feminine Yin energies over the obvious, masculine Yang. Its philosophy is built around female images and metaphors. Its mythology is populated by rain goddesses who frolic amidst clouds and mountain peaks. And yet, the Chinese version of patriarchy managed to partially derail Taoism to the point that Taoist sects range from the very women-friendly to the "if-there-were-a-gold-medal-in-chauvinism-we-would-give-Confucianism-a-run-for-its-money" type.

Stockholm Syndrome

Anyone who was at least semi-conscious over the last few pages should have gotten by now that limiting women's choices is a very popular sport among the world's religions. But let's add some spice to our story. A particularly bizarre element in this equation is the extremely high number of women who have enthusiastically embraced even the most patriarchal religions. What are we to make of people volunteering to become accomplices in their own oppression? Are we witnessing a mass case of Stockholm syndrome?

The answers to this complex situation are many. But in my mind, one is racing ahead of the others. The vast majority of human beings don't like to question what they are taught. It takes too much work, too much courage, too much self-esteem to reject what is accepted by all around you. Equal parts of fear and laziness usually convince most of humanity to just play by the rules handed to them. So what's a poor little girl to do if, from the second she is born, she is told she is weak, vulnerable, and in need of male authority? No, actually, it's not even that easy—what if she is told from the second she is born that *God*, in His divine wisdom, has ordered her to follow male authority? Day after day, year after year, she is told that disobeying her father, husband, and (male) religious leaders is an affront to God. How likely is she then to challenge not only the rules of society, but God's will itself? The world is not exactly full of people with enough toughness and willpower to take on both men and gods. The results, then, are quite predictable.

The classic carrot and the stick approach used to train donkeys is at work here. If a woman learns to accept the role given to her by a patriarchal society, and reinforced by a patriarchal religion, she will receive the carrot of an identity as a respected mother and housewife, with all the protection, economic support, and divine approval that goes with it. She will be able to find a more or less comfortable niche for herself *despite* her being a woman. But if she doesn't accept this house-slave mentality, and decides to speak out against patriarchy, the stick is ready to put her back in her place.

So, it's hardly surprising that many women may have complained about the most flagrant abuses of patriarchy without ever questioning its foundation. What's surprising, instead, is the number of women who have decided to fight tooth and nail despite the very high price to pay for this choice.

Change: Patriarchy Heading for Retirement?

After holding the title of undefeated heavyweight champion in gender ideology for a few millennia, patriarchy, finally, seems to be with its back on the ropes. Despite taking a long time dying, the once all-powerful patriarchy is now hobbling along—still alive and dangerous, but wounded and weakened. Over the last 300 years or so, ideas that were always loved by a minority of people have become

mainstream: equal rights for all human beings, democracy, the sanctity of individual freedoms . . . wild notions that for so long were
but dreams you could only whisper about in secret have now broken
out of jail and found a home in the hearts and minds of millions of
men and women. With inexorable determination, they have hunted
down tyranny, authoritarian ideologies, and all those forces limiting
human freedom. Patriarchy's cousins, classism and racism, have had
to mount a steady retreat. They can certainly still bite, but they no
longer thrive the way they used to in a world that's becoming allergic
to flagrant injustices.

Much like its philosophical friends, patriarchy has seen its kingdom collapse. For all of its faults, modernity has brought to vast
numbers of women greater economic opportunities allowing them
to break the chain of dependency on men. It has brought them the
technology to choose whether to get pregnant or not. And it has
brought them the freedom to reject patriarchy.

Discussing how and why this change took place would take us
on a wild ride along the Mother of All Tangents. For the sake of staying on course, we will not go there. But we should at least mention
that religions have certainly not spearheaded this change. Rather,
most religious authorities joined patriarchy on the barricades trying to keep the barbarians out and, like all true opportunists, only
switched sides when they realized that the alliance with patriarchy
was a lost cause.[205] Wherever religion and politics were driven apart,
individual rights flourished. And still today, individual freedoms are
at their weakest wherever religion and politics go hand in hand.

As women have gained more freedoms, however, an increasing
number of religious figures have decided to adjust their theology
to a more balanced view of gender.[206] And most religions include
branches that are very vocal about women-friendly interpretations

of their own traditions. Oddly enough, this sometimes includes even women who are ultraconservative in every other way but make an exception for this one issue.[207]

But not everyone is ready to abandon the sinking ship. Patriarchy is still going unapologetically strong within much of the Muslim world and also finds a safe haven among many denominations of most other religions.[208] Try, for example, evangelical leader Pat Robertson, who still today writes that feminists encourage women "to leave their husbands, kill their children, practice witchcraft, destroy capitalism, and become lesbians."[209] And not to be outdone, the equally balanced and sober Jerry Falwell accused feminists of angering God, and thereby helping to bring about the 9/11 attacks.[210]

Without patriarchy to lean on, many men feel lost in a modern world made of more fluid gender roles and complex identities. Finding their macho role as providers and undisputed leaders of the family being taken away from them, they push back against this wave of change in the only way they know how: by longing for a return to the past, with patriarchy and its fixed gender roles still in place.

If feeling deprived of their very identity as men were not bad enough, add to their troubles the emasculating characteristics that always lurked in the background of their religions of choice. The male followers of quite a few religious traditions had to struggle with a theology that required them to pray on their knees, confess their weaknesses, surrender control, ask for help, and encouraged them to adopt "womanly" values such as forgiveness, mercy, tenderness, and a love relationship with a male deity. These issues were always a bit disturbing, but since women's rights have been gaining ground, and many males can no longer console themselves with the pacifier of a powerful macho identity, this uneasy sense of insecurity has become unbearable. Mad about being perceived as wimps, many men have been trying extra hard to inject virility in their theology by pushing their women back in the kitchen, cracking down on homosexuality, and threatening bloody violence against the unbelievers.

Heart and Balls[211]

If nothing else, this desperate attempt to keep patriarchy alive has sometimes gained in complexity and subtlety. Now that in much of the world it is no longer cool to openly advocate female inferiority, it has become fashionable in some religious circles to argue that women and men have separate areas of influence. This is the same old men-as-leaders, women-as-housewives model, but it is presented in a more acceptable light by removing the obvious hierarchy that used to go with it. Rather than speaking of male superiority over women, the new line is to emphasize both male and female contributions as equally valuable. What remains, however, is the idea that gender roles are biologically (and divinely) determined, and neither society nor individual inclinations should alter them.[212] Regardless of individual temper, talent, or character, all women are supposed to be emotional, sensitive, and nurturing, with an innate predisposition to taking on a full-time job as mothers; meanwhile all men are supposed to be strong, rational, assertive, and made to command. Individuality plays next to no role in God's master plan for each gender.

Now, obviously men and women *are* biologically different, but eliminating individuality from the picture, and reducing everything to some kind of biological determinism is pure fascism. This modern apology for patriarchy sounds very much like the "separate but equal" doctrine once embraced by the Supreme Court, and history tells us how well that worked . . .

I am not trying to deny biological reality. The problem is when gender roles force individuals to conform to a fixed model created by exaggerating these natural differences. Little girls are taught to be delicate, graceful, and pretty, while little boys are taught to wrestle, play in the mud, and act tough. Any boy or girl who doesn't fit the mold becomes an object of ridicule: a sorry example of gender confusion that will be unmercifully teased to death until he or she falls back in line. In this way, boys are taught to squash their more sensitive side, and instead develop exclusively toughness, aggression, willpower, and other "manly" virtues, and girls are taught to repress these qualities in favor of nurturing "feminine" qualities. This is how individuality is sacrificed on the altar of gender ideology. This is how society makes nature's formula much more extreme, and ends up shaping very one-dimensional types of human beings.

Many religions are built on a dualistic mentality that divides up existence in opposite, mutually exclusive categories: spiritual or physical, earthly or heavenly, civilized or wild, good or evil, logical or mystical. This harsh dualism is applied to everything, so it is hardly surprising to find it applied to gender roles as well. Rather than allowing for the possibility of so-called masculine and feminine qualities to complement each other, most religions have built an insurmountable wall between the two, and force them to live in a state of apartheid.

This rigid gender ideology is obviously bad for women since traditionally they've gotten stuck with the less glamorous and more dependent role, but is also bad for men, since they are trained to suffocate their feelings in the name of upholding a meathead, macho image. By following traditional gender roles, men may have more authority, but they also end up being a fraction of the complete human beings that they could be: tough and powerful, but insensitive and emotionally crippled.

Refusing to turn into the stereotypes of what men and women are supposed to be seems like the logical next step, but even this may not be the solution. Don't worry, I haven't suddenly changed my mind, and I'm not messing with your head for the fun of it. It's simply that the solution to our riddle cannot come from simply rejecting the traditional formula. Much of the modern world has been trying to move away from these stereotypes, and yet the results have not been ideal. In losing their macho posturing, many men may have become more pleasant and less abusive, but also whiny and weak. It's as if getting rid of chauvinism came at the price of losing their balls. It's as if they only knew how to be strong while they donned the armor of patriarchy, but when they took the healthy step of stripping it away, they found themselves lost and without an identity. It's as if the emergence of independent women were enough to throw male identity into an existential crisis.

What I am suggesting to counter this is not to turn back the clock and invite patriarchy to return. A strength built on putting other people down is no strength at all. What traditional male roles used to offer was the parody of strength—just a bossy, tyrannical façade that has nothing to do with real power. The new "separate but equal" recipe cooked by the fans of a neo-patriarchy is as pathetic today as it ever was. The solution we are looking for is not in rejecting feminine and masculine stereotypical qualities. It's about developing those qualities *and more*. It's about taking the best from each and combining them.

Once, a woman who happened to be a master in a particularly brutal form of martial arts told me she believed fighting helped her to be more feminine.[213] Needless to say, I was intrigued. How exactly does training to drive your knee into people's heads make a woman more feminine? I wondered. Many women, she said, are afraid to let their guards down and trust people, so it is harder for them to embody stereotypically feminine qualities such as being loving, warm, and affectionate. By becoming a good fighter, though, one can shed fear, which in turn frees you to be more relaxed and open to sharing your feelings despite the possibility that you may get hurt. Developing so-called masculine qualities such as toughness and a warrior's attitude, she concluded, can paradoxically end up enhancing a woman's femininity.

This marriage of seemingly contradictory characteristics is what can rescue us from an abusive patriarchy as well as the general weakness of modern gender roles. I found the same message on the skin of a woman I love very much: tattooed there, a tiger jumps out of a heart. The message couldn't be clearer: strength with no heart is mean-spirited and predatory, but a heart with no strength lacks the raw energy to burn with intensity. Only when the two go together do we have a real individual. What we need are toughness *and* tenderness, bravery *and* sensitivity, willpower *and* kindness—for these are not masculine or feminine qualities. They are human qualities. And all men and women who wish to be anything more than a living stereotype need to develop all of them.

To make up for their unforgivable historical support for patriarchy, modern religions can begin to teach people that abandoning stereotypical roles is not a loss, but a chance to be creating something better and more complete: individual mixes of "masculine" and "feminine" virtues that are much richer and more rewarding than traditional identities.

CHAPTER 10

INCREDIBLY SHRINKING CAMELS AND ZEN MOONS: WEALTH IN THE EYES OF WORLD RELIGIONS

Oh Lord, won't you buy me a Mercedes Benz.

—Janis Joplin

God and Gold

Nothing in the world can excite the minds of men quite like the two *G*'s—God and Gold. (The third *G* that boys dream about—Girls—ranks much higher than either of those on my personal priority list, but it has nothing to do with the subject of this chapter, so I'll try to keep my hormones in check and not get sidetracked.) If it is certainly true that religion is one of the most powerful forces driving our collective psyche, cold, hard cash is not far behind. God and gold are the objects of worship most revered by humanity. Countless people obsess about them, want them, crave them, and center their lives around them. For them, we fight, cry, and struggle. In the hope that they'll grant us their favors, we sacrifice on their altars unspeakable amounts of time and energy.

In the minds of some people, it may appear strange to discuss economic issues within the context of religion. But the relationship between religion and wealth is a complicated but meaningful one. Sometimes, they are bitter enemies competing for the hearts of human beings. Other times, they shamelessly flirt with each other. Religion would seem irrelevant if it were silent about such a key human concern; likewise, the quest for wealth is very much affected by religious attitudes.

The nitty-gritty reality of survival forces everyone to make choices about wealth. How much is enough for us to be happy? What do we want it for? What are we willing or unwilling to sacrifice for it? How much of our time will we devote to chasing it? The answers to these questions influence most other aspects of our lives, since any discussion of wealth is intertwined with the choice of what we'll do for a living. And inevitably, what you end up doing seven, eight, or nine hours a day will affect the person you become. Whether we like it or not, our job becomes one of our priorities. So it's naïve to expect religions to have nothing to say about such an important topic. Speaking of purely "spiritual" values without ever addressing economic issues means relegating spirituality to a corner, removed from day-to-day events. This is why most religions throughout history have expressed very strong opinions about money and wealth.

Incredibly Shrinking Camels and Zen Moons: Wealth in the Eyes of World Religions

Despite their enduring rivalry, when it comes to their attitudes about wealth, Judaism and Islam can lay down swords, Uzis, and atomic weapons, and find something they can all agree on. Both religions, in fact, advocate similar positions. Both stress the importance of

charity. In Leviticus and Deuteronomy we find passages commanding Jewish people to give away as a religious obligation a percentage
of their wealth to the poor.[214] Along the same lines, Islam elevates
charity as one of the Five Pillars of Islam. To varying degrees, they
both frown on charging high interest rates for loans, and they make
clear that the pursuit of wealth is subordinate to religious duties.
Other than that, they see nothing wrong with wealth in and of itself.

On the other hand, Christianity—the middle child in the
Middle Eastern monotheistic family—forcefully establishes its own
identity by adopting a very different stance from its siblings. Over
and over, the New Testament attacks the desire for wealth as fundamentally incompatible with Christianity. Jesus himself clearly forces
his followers to choose between God and wealth. "No one can serve
two masters," Jesus tells us unambiguously, "for either he will hate
the one, and love the other; or else he will hold to the one, and despise the other. Ye can't serve God and Mammon."[215] Reinforcing
the same concept, Matthew 6:19–21 reads:

> Lay not up for yourselves treasures upon earth, where moth
> and rust doth corrupt, and where thieves break through and
> steal: But lay up for yourselves treasures in heaven, where
> neither moth nor rust doth corrupt, and where thieves do not
> break through nor steal: For where your treasure is, there will
> your heart be also.[216]

Still not convinced? Try this then: "Woe to you that are rich! For
ye have received your consolation."[217] And just to make sure there
are no misunderstandings, other parts of the New Testament spell it
out for us:

> For we brought nothing into this world, and it is certain we
> can carry nothing out. And having food and clothing, with

these we shall be content. But those who desire to be rich fall into temptation and a snare, and into many foolish and harmful lusts which drown men in destruction and perdition. For the love of money is a root of all kinds of evil, for which some have strayed from the faith in their greediness, and pierced themselves through with many sorrows.[218]

Nowhere, however, does Jesus get any more radical about wealth than in Matthew 19:23–24. Communists are wimps compared to Jesus, who takes his attack against the love of money to new heights: "And again I say unto you, it is easier for a camel to go through the eye of a needle, than for a rich man to enter into the kingdom of God."[219]

One thing is for sure; good old Jesus could deliver a flowery speech. Easier for a camel to go through the eye of a needle than for a rich man to get into heaven? Wow. No one can accuse him of lacking imagination. But besides being funny, his metaphor is unequivocal in its meaning. Jesus' statement would make even Karl Marx blush. Read the last quote again and then consider how readily most Christians chase wealth. Tell me you see no contradictions. In regards to wealth, the majority of Christianity today seems to have conveniently edited Jesus' words out of their theology.

Baloo, the bear from *The Jungle Book*, embodies Jesus' spirit much better than popes or preachers. Baloo happily sings his anti-capitalist tune, inviting us to work less, not worry about the future, and enjoy the bare necessities of life that will fall in our laps when we stop struggling so much. This is the Sermon on the Mount sung by a furry animal coming to you courtesy of Disney. In one part of his most famous speech, in fact, Jesus preaches the exact same concept. Look at the birds of the air, and the lilies of the field, he says. They make no plans for the future. They don't stress about food and clothing, and yet they have more than they need. Learn from them and quit worrying.[220] Can you think of anything more contrary to the spirit of capitalism than this?

Jesus is in good company though. Besides Baloo, he can also find a kindred spirit in Lao Tzu, the mythological author of the Tao Te Ching. Much like Jesus, Lao Tzu had no inclination to mince his words. He writes, "There is no greater curse than the lack of contentment. No greater sin than the desire for possession."[221] "To be proud with wealth and honor," we find in another passage, "is to sow the seeds of one's own downfall."[222] Statements like these pop up all over the Tao Te Ching. Neither Jesus nor Lao Tzu are interested in winning a popularity contest, and that's why they say exactly what's on their minds without concern of pleasing the powers that be. Most rulers, according to Lao Tzu, being the greedy bastards that they are, overtax their people and let them starve in an effort to accumulate more wealth than they know what to do with.[223] This is what pushes Lao Tzu, long before Robin Hood, to argue, "It is the Way of Heaven to take away from those that have too much and give to those that have not enough."[224]

Similarly, the pursuit of wealth is also no friend of Buddha, who gave up his position as heir to the throne and kissed goodbye to a life of luxury in order to become a wondering monk. The otherwise easygoing Buddha condemned any job profiting from suffering— selling weapons, slavery, butchering animals, selling poisons and intoxicants—as being unequivocally contrary to a Buddhist path. But even more radically—just like Jesus and Lao Tzu—Buddha viewed attachment to wealth as fundamentally misguided. His problem was not with wealth itself, but with the attachment and the never-ending desires that usually accompany it. If one could enjoy wealth while remaining completely unattached to it, then wealth is no obstacle.

But according to Buddha, most people are incapable of this; they become dependent on wealth as the source of their happiness, and this attachment is the root of much misery.

It's this basic realization that pushed Zen monk Ryōkan to exclaim "Alone with one robe, one bowl—the life of a Zen monk is truly the most free!"[225] In another occasion, being the funny guy that he was, Ryōkan offered his clothes to a thief who had come to rob him but found nothing valuable to steal. After the thief left, Ryōkan sat naked, staring at the full moon. Feeling sorry for the thief, trapped as he was to live and die for material gain, Ryōkan commented, "Poor fellow. I wish I could give him this beautiful moon."[226]

This same theme echoes across time and space, among religious figures as much as philosophers. We find it in Diogenes ("To own nothing is the beginning of happiness"[227]), Heraclitus ("May you have plenty of wealth, you men of Ephesus, in order that you may be punished for your evil ways"[228]), Thoreau ("the laboring man . . . has no time to be anything but a machine. . . . Most of the luxuries, and many of the so-called comforts of life, are not only not indispensable, but positive hindrances to the elevation of mankind."[229]), and plenty others.

Why are all these guys so vehemently opposed to seeking wealth? What's wrong with good old-fashioned cash? Jesus, Buddha, and Thoreau all considered attachment to material goods as the doorway to self-inflicted pain. According to them, the thirst for wealth is never fulfilled. It breeds dissatisfaction. The more you earn, the more you want. In true addict fashion, you constantly crave more and can never have enough to be able to relax and enjoy life. Once hooked on this drug, people become the slaves of their possessions and get trapped in a struggle that will never end.

This is why Jesus, Buddha, and many other famous figures in the history of religions embraced voluntary poverty: none of them wanted to trade the time and energy needed to make money. Quite ironic, considering that many of their followers despair of never finding happiness unless they achieve a certain level of material wealth.

In Gold We Trust: The Invention of a Capitalist Christianity

The profit-seeking, money-dreaming capitalist in you needs not to worry, though. Despite religion's nearly unanimous opposition to striving after wealth, some religions have reinvented themselves to justify it—and in some cases even glorify it.

Christianity offers the most dramatic example of this. In a perfect case of hypocrisy, the hierarchy of the Catholic Church officially condemned greed for centuries while amassing huge fortunes at the same time. But as sociologist Max Weber famously pointed out, it was only with the development of certain branches of Protestantism that vast numbers of Christians found a way to openly justify having both God and gold.

According to Protestants, a virtuous existence in no way guarantees an admission ticket to heaven. Their gloomy outlook on life held that human beings are horrible sinners undeserving of salvation, and only through faith and divine grace can anyone get their unworthy ass into Paradise. This means that no one could ever be sure of being saved. Since self-esteem boosting seminars were not available back then, early Protestants found relief from their anxieties in the idea that success in the world was a sign of divine favor.[230] God intervenes in human affairs, they reasoned, so achieving success means being the recipient of God's blessing. Private property, as Martin Luther pointed out, is what separates humans from beasts, so the more of it you have, the more advanced you are.[231] If you are poor, on the other hand, it's because you are barely better than animals, and God probably hates your guts. The pursuit of wealth, then, became valuable not for its own sake but in order to prove one's standing in God's eyes. The door for the accumulation of wealth without any sense of guilt was finally open.

This marriage between Christianity and capitalism continues to be celebrated today by countless preachers arguing that God wants good Christians to be rich and successful. Fundamentalist leader Rod Parsley, for example, regularly condemns laws limiting unchecked capitalism, and famously stated, "one of the first reasons for poverty is a lack of knowledge of God and His Word."[232] Others, such as Reverend Robert Schuller, are even more blunt: "You have a God-ordained right to be wealthy. You're a steward of the goods, the golds, the gifts that God has allowed to come into your hands. Having riches is no sin, wealth is no crime. Christ did not praise poverty. The profit motive is not necessarily unchristian."[233] Needless to say, this message has been enthusiastically received.

As these examples demonstrate, it turns out that if you push hard enough, the camel can go through the eye of the needle after all. If you ever wanted proof that most people make up their own religions as they go, the Christian contortionists bending the Bible to say what they want it to say offer it to you on a golden plate. I can think of good arguments to defend both the accumulation of wealth as well as Jesus' radical critique of it. I have no problem with people choosing to be Christian *or* capitalists; but embracing both at the same time while claiming to follow the Bible literally is only possible if you shamelessly edit scriptures to justify your own self-interest.

My Take Part I: Windigo

Armed with some very strong opinions that exist out there about wealth, it's now my turn to tackle this issue. The message broadcasted by Lao Tzu, Buddha, and Jesus certainly resonates with me. The line between moneymaking as a priority and greed is sometimes a very fine one. My own experience tells me this. Every time I have focused my attention on the dollar sign, I have felt this insatiable hunger growing in me. It's not that I think there is anything morally wrong with wanting a more comfortable living, but I just don't like this feeling of longing. I don't think it's a coincidence that I tend to be more interested in money anytime my self-esteem is on a leave of absence. It's as if I'm trying to make myself feel better by looking at how much I've made: pride in oneself based on a number in my bank account. In the far more numerous occasions when I'm in a good mood, money is no more than a passing thought.

When European explorers first made contact with the Ojibwa tribe, they were often warned against the Windigo, a human turned demon who stalked the woods and fed on human blood. The Windigo's passion for cannibalism, however, wasn't the worst part of it. What could be worse than a flesh-eating demon? Every time the Windigo ate someone, it would grow in size so that it could never get full. Its appetite only increased by eating. For this reason, Windigos would never rest. Always hungry, always on the prowl, they were constantly looking for new victims to consume in a cycle without end.

Not finding any evidence for the existence of the Windigo, Europeans laughed it off as some savage superstition. Big mistake. They were the ones who were blind to reality. Windigos are all around—they were just too blind to see it. A Windigo is anyone who gives in to that urge to consume in order to fill a void that can never be filled: compulsive consumption without enjoyment. That Windigo drive is what today is pushing us to devour the very planet we live on. It pushes us to devour animals, trees, the earth, resources, communities, other people, and, in an act of self-cannibalism, our own time and energy. But all of this is to no avail because, in classic Windigo fashion, the hunger is never satisfied. Give us more money, more wealth, bigger houses, bigger cars; just give us more food to feed the beast.

The consequences of letting this hungry monster run loose are for everyone to see. Centuries of chasing profits have poisoned the very system we depend on for living. In an effort to convert everything into a marketable resource, we have gone after the environment with a giant fork and knife, overconsuming air, water, and the very earth we stand on.

Despite all the lip service we pay to them, community, friendship, family, and social life are usually sacrificed next to feed the monster. There are only twenty-four hours in a day, so inevitably the more time you dedicate to work and money, the less time you have for community and friendship.

Nowhere is this contrast of values clearer than in an obscure piece of legislation passed by the US government in 1887 in an attempt to "civilize" American Indian peoples. The Dawes Act basically required native tribes to divide up reservation land into parcels of private property instead of owning it communally. Senator Henry Dawes delivered the rationale for this:

> The head chief told us that there was not a family in that whole nation [Cherokee] that had not a home of its own. There was not a pauper in that nation, and the nation did not owe a dollar. . . . Yet the defect of the system was apparent. They have

got as far as they can go, because they own their land in common. . . . There is no enterprise to make your home any better than that of your neighbor's. There is no selfishness, which is at the bottom of civilization.[234]

I must have missed an important day in school as a kid, because I was taught that selfishness is not a very good thing. When did being selfish suddenly turn into a foundational point of civilization? What the hell was Dawes talking about?

His ideas actually flowed directly from the theories of Adam Smith, one of the godfathers of capitalism. Smith argued that it is human nature to accumulate wealth, so any culture that does not make the accumulation of wealth a top priority is uncivilized, and not fully human.[235] The time you spend with family and friends is time taken away from the business of making money. So forget about those fuzzy things, and focus instead on working hard to have a bigger house than your neighbor. This, according to Smith, Dawes, and their disciples, is what life is all about.

Faithfully following in their footsteps, plenty of people today dedicate only slivers of time to cultivating friendships, since they are too busy offering the bulk of their energies to the altar of work. Many pop out babies just out of habit, for the sake of patting themselves on the back for having passed their genes to the next generation, but they'll spend very little time building a relationship with their children. Let school, babysitters, and TV raise them. Work, after all, comes first.

But the environment and our social lives are not the only victims in our quest for money. We usually are our own first casualty. I'm always reminded of this when I think of a conversation I had when I was a student at UCLA. Had I been honest with myself, I would have had to admit that the woman I was chatting with gave me a really bad vibe. Something about her didn't feel right. But she was ridiculously hot, so being honest with myself didn't seem that important at the moment. I tried really hard to silence the annoying little voice warning me of the very nasty energy surrounding this woman. Being physiologically incapable of small talk, I asked her pointed, personal questions to cut the bullshit and get a sense of who she was. At some point in the conversation, she said "I don't have time to figure out what makes me happy. I just want to make money."

Damn. I don't care how hot you are, no one looks good enough for me to put up with this. A twenty-something woman finishing college tells me she has no time to figure out what makes her happy. When does she think she'll ever have the time? When she starts working forty, fifty, or sixty hours a week, for fifty weeks every year, over the next four decades? Before she knows it, years will fly by, and she'll never find out what she likes, or how to make herself happy. She'll live someone else's life, and then she'll be food for the worms.

I have nothing against money. If you, dear reader, feel like buying twenty million copies of this book, I won't protest—I promise. I have no moral objection to buying stuff. What disturbs me is the very dangerous trade required in order to make money. The price tag is our time and energy, and there's only so much of those I want to dedicate to chasing wealth.

The trap the hot-but-annoying woman was bound to fall into is the most typical of vicious circles. You are not happy and don't know how to find happiness, so you work like a dog in hopes that the newly found wealth will allow you to afford whatever fun thing you want to do or own. But the problem is that soon enough you'll work so much you won't have the time or energy to find out what makes you happy. So what to do at this point? Just go out and buy yourself something pretty to give you temporary comfort, and bring a little color to your otherwise miserable life. And this is where your problem becomes even bigger, because spending a bundle of cash means you now have to head back to work in order to make more money to continue the cycle of consumption. Material goods become a painkiller to dull the edges, a consolation prize in place of a real, fulfilling life. Why do so many people willingly jump headfirst into this trap? Because running after short-term gain is much easier than creating something beautiful with your life. It doesn't require any talent, and, like any good drug, it dazes you enough to make existence bearable.

When I look around me, I see overconsumption as a way of life. Spending, spending, and spending some more is the name of the game.[236] Money junkies are everywhere I turn. Despite their anti-drug rhetoric, most of humanity is divided into pushers and addicts, so I remind myself daily to do my best not to join their ranks. My approach to life tells me that any work that doesn't bring joy is self-imposed slavery. It may be very well-paid slavery; it may be the kind of slavery that makes you famous and admired by other slaves; but it is slavery nonetheless. When you do something you like, making money is a by-product. If I can't make a living doing what I love, and necessity dictates I absolutely have to do slave labor, I'll try to get away with doing as little of that as I possibly can. I'll trade just enough time and energy to provide for basic needs—but not an ounce more.

My Take Part II: Screw Poverty

As much as I agree with Jesus and Buddha that wealth is one of the most dangerous drugs in the world, I am not one to glorify poverty, and I don't find anything particularly spiritual in it. Quite a few people who share my views regarding work and consumption come to the conclusion that poor people are somewhat nobler than the rich because they are uncorrupted by an obsession with wealth. If there were a prize for taking a good premise and turning it to crap, this idea would be a promising contender.

Yes, vast numbers of rich people are addicts who can't kick the money habit because they have too much to lose. It's also true that poor people by definition don't have much to lose. But this doesn't mean in any way that they are necessarily less addicted to wealth than the rich. Obsession is in the mind, not in one's bank account. Being rich or poor is really not the issue. Being obsessed is, and obsession is available to everyone equally. Money is not good or bad. It's just a tool: everything depends on how it's used.

Learning how to approach money without falling into the trap of indulgent addiction or cheap self-denial is a balancing act. Tilt too much to one side and you lose all perspective. I got an early start in the game as a kid, courtesy of my parents. Despite being very young and not exactly swimming in gold, they would always let me make my own decisions as soon as I was old enough to understand the implications of my choices. They made it clear that as long as they had the bare minimum necessary to pay for food, rent, and the like, they would let me have the final word on whether I wanted to buy myself toys or not. Would this particular toy make me happier? Would I still be playing with it long after the initial rush was over, or would it only be fun for a moment? The choice was mine. And so here I was, at five or six years old, feeling very honored by the responsibility I was given and thinking hard about whether a toy was worth my parents' money or not. Early on, I learned not to deny myself what I truly craved while at the same time not to waste money on nonessential stuff. And it turned out that, after thinking about it long enough, not too many material things were essential to my happiness.

In my way of thinking, there are two ways to be rich. One is to be rich. The other is to be perfectly happy with few material possessions. The end goal, after all, is to be happy. If you don't need much to get there, great. If you need a lot, but you get there anyway without trading all your time and energy in the process, that's great too. I have nothing against indulging oneself. But I want to be equally comfortable playing with expensive toys if they are easily available, and not thinking about it twice if they are not. Basically, I strive to make sure my state of mind is not determined by my bank account. If wealth comes in my direction, my life will certainly be a little easier, but if it doesn't, I don't want to stress over it.

As it is hopefully clear by now, the reason why I emphasize frugality so much is not because I find something inherently sinful in wealth; it's because if you have few needs, it's much easier to fulfill them. If your needs are many and expensive, they can be easily fulfilled only if you win the lottery, marry rich, or are lucky enough to be paid lots of cash to do something you love. Otherwise, they'll turn into a prison forcing you to give away a big portion of your life in order to afford them. Learning how to be content with less, then, can be one of the most liberating things one can do.

It was after listening to a lecture by John Li Schroeder, a professor in Asian philosophies at Santa Monica College, that I decided my time was simply too valuable to waste it becoming the errand boy to a million different needs. From then on, I wouldn't be after wealth for wealth's sake. I would be after living comfortably *and* having plenty of time to do what I want.

After I made that choice, life got much easier. Now, I work thirty-two weeks a year doing something I like. And since this is still too much effort, during those thirty-two weeks, I work only four days a week, for perhaps no more than twenty-five hours a week. This is enough to provide for all my needs. The rest of the time, I'll work if I feel like it, playing with things I love to do—such as writing this book.

On plenty of occasions, when I've shared my priorities with someone, I get responses along the lines of "You are so lucky to be able to live like that," or "I wish I could do the same." At first, I feel bad for these people, but after I ask them a few questions, they almost invariably end up pissing me off. They usually make much more money than I do, and they don't have any major obligation forcing them to work so intensely. There is no village whose survival depends on the money they make, no sick relative who needs a million dollar operation. Here are people who live in bigger homes, drive fancier cars, and indulge in many more luxuries, and yet they comment on how lucky I am??? Luck has nothing to do with my lifestyle, or theirs. It's a choice.

Although I understand the importance of warning people against greed-addiction, I don't fully agree with the hardcore condemnation of wealth expressed by many religious people throughout history. Even deeper, however, is my disagreement with those religious views praising moneymaking as a moral virtue. The religion I want to live by has one goal and one goal only: helping me lead the best possible life I can live. Being rich is no obstacle to this goal, but neither is it required for it. . . .

OK, I was just saying this stuff to sound cool. I need a mansion by the beach, damn it! Please send your contributions to the "Feed Bolelli" campaign. God will love you for it.

CHAPTER 11

TOWARD A GLOBAL IDENTITY

Nationalism is an infantile disease. It is the measles of mankind.

—Albert Einstein

Outcast (Literally . . .)

The whole country is standing still, holding its collective breath. From the balcony of my house the view is surreal: the normally noisy, insanely busy streets of the city are deserted and eerily silent. It looks like one of those post-atomic movies where only the buildings remain, but every trace of life has been wiped out.

Inside my house it's a whole different story. About thirty of my father's friends are piled up on top of each other in the tiny living room, their eyes all glued to the TV screen. It's one of the decisive games of the World Cup, and the Italian national soccer team is fighting a head-to-head battle with Brazil.

What am I doing out on the balcony at a time when everyone in the country is watching the game? I am a soccer refugee, a World Cup pariah, quite literally cast out of the house. A quick poll among those present resulted in my banishment. I am eight years old and only my age spares me harsher sanctions. My crime is clear and unforgivable. I brought it on myself. I could have kept my mouth shut, but I'm too stubborn for that. So when invited to join the pro-Italy chants, I repeatedly voiced that I was rooting for Brazil.

You are rooting for whom?!? Throughout the World Cup, some games I have rooted for Italy, and some games I've rooted for their opponents. Today, I'm for the opponents. Before a game, I look at who the players are, and, depending on how much or how little I like them, I pick which team to root for. I choose my allegiance based on the individuals, not on what passport they carry.

My sophisticated argument goes nowhere. In the entire country, there are probably no more than three other boys my age who don't root for Italy—strange freaks who will no doubt be dropped by their own families into the sea with a stone tied to their necks. I'm the lucky one. Normally, my father's friends like me a lot, and maybe that's why they don't murder me outright. But my offense this time is too heinous to go unpunished. It's red card time for me. And so here I am—in exile on my own balcony.

In case you are wondering, I swear there is a point to the story of my World Cup exile, and yes, it will eventually connect with religion, but not yet. Please indulge me just a bit longer.

I was recently reminded of this episode when a Colombian friend who spent too many hours watching the History Channel asked me if the achievements of people such as Leonardo da Vinci, Galileo Galilei, Ludovico Ariosto, Giacomo Puccini, Julius Caesar, Giuseppe Garibaldi, Caravaggio, Marco Polo, and a million others made me proud of my Italian heritage. I must admit that when foreign women project their Italian stallion romance-novel stereotypes on me, suddenly being Italian seems like a good deal. When they look at me with dreamy eyes and comment how much they like my accent, I gladly bask in the benefits of coming from an Italian heritage. But as much as I love being at the center of a woman's attention, the very idea of national pride strikes me as too stupid for me to embrace. And so this is exactly what I told to my surprised Colombian friend (by the way, Axel, pick up the damn phone once in a while, you bastard . . .).

If I am to be proud of my heritage because I was born in the same nation as all the amazing individuals he mentioned, what should I feel about being born in the same nation as a fascist dictator like Benito Mussolini, a serial killer like Il Mostro di Firenze, and countless mafia bosses? Aren't they also part of "Italian heritage"? And just so we don't get too stuck on Italy, isn't it true that pretty much any other nation in the world has produced some wonderful individuals and some very evil ones, along with plenty of mediocre people?

As my World Cup experience proves, I guess I was weird from the start. But I still fail to see any appeal in concepts like patriotism, nationalism, or ethnic pride. They seem to me different names for the same disease: prepackaged identities that divide human beings along racial or national lines.

The Connection Between Religions and Ethnic/National Identities

Tribal Gods

There is a strong connection between religion and patriotism, nationalism, and ethnic pride. If we reach into the past far enough, we find ourselves in an age when religion and ethnicity were inseparable. Everything revolved around our tribe, our people, our god(s). What better way to nourish ethnic pride than the idea that our god(s) is/are better, more powerful, stronger, and wiser than our neighbors'? About three millennia ago, tribes in the Middle East were the chess pieces in a competitive game among the local deities. Each tribe had its own set of gods and would proclaim their superiority over the gods of their rivals. The point wasn't to convert foreigners—though occasionally that did happen. The point was to reinforce one's sense of identity by claiming to be the favorite tribe of the best gods in the neighborhood.

Ancient Jewish tribes took this game to a whole new level, and much of the Old Testament is a chronicle of the squabbles between these competing factions. The most monotheistic among the Jews—which, incidentally, were not always the majority, since polytheism thrived among them for a very long time—argued that their tribal God was not just the best among many, but the *only* true God. The gods of other tribes were either illusions or demons. As a corollary to this radical thought, the architects of this religious revolution married monotheism to a virulent ethnic pride. "We are God's chosen people," screamed Moses' boys, "and as such we are entitled to a promised land reserved for us by the one and only legitimate deity." The fact that the promised land was occupied by other tribes didn't make it any less promised. It only meant that God thought chasing them out would be good exercise for His chosen people.

The idea of a chosen people and a promised land is a strong example of the union between religion and ethnic identity. It is not a coincidence that these terms appear in the Old Testament along with other pearls of ethnocentrism, such as prohibitions against intermarriage with foreigners and religious sanctioning for genocidal "holy" wars of conquests against rival tribes. They are the bedrock of a supernationalistic theology.

Once claiming divine approval for racial superiority fell out of fashion, many Jewish and Christian people had to eventually rework the words of the Old Testament to alter some of its obviously racist meanings. In its original context, the idea of a chosen people was tied to claiming title to the land of neighboring nations and enforcing racial purity by law—things that the modern world doesn't look kindly upon. Even though there is an occasional nutcase around who will still defend the original interpretation, most modern apologists of monotheism have dramatically altered the meaning of "chosen people" from racial entitlement to an emphasis on sacrifice, responsibility, and service to God.

Others have opted to not try to salvage what they considered a broken concept and have decided to abandon it altogether. The great Jewish scientist Albert Einstein, for example, wrote:

> For me the Jewish religion like all others is an incarnation of the most childish superstitions. And the Jewish people to whom I gladly belong . . . have no different quality for me than all other people. As far as my experience goes, they are no better than other human groups, although they are protected from the worst cancers by a lack of power.[237]

Transition

Springing straight out of the heritage of Judaism, Christianity had to grapple with this problem from the beginning. With their usual clarity, the Gospels offer room for very different interpretations about the "chosen people" issue. Matthew 10:5–6 quotes Jesus telling the Apostles, "Go not into the way of the Gentiles, and into any city of the Samaritans enter ye not. But go rather to the lost sheep of the house of Israel."[238]

Further strengthening the idea of Jesus as a prophet strictly for Jewish people, Matthew 15:22–28 reports a fairly disturbing dialogue between Jesus and a non-Jewish woman. Having heard of Jesus' abilities as a healer, a woman asks Jesus to help her daughter. Jesus refuses, saying, "I am not sent but unto the lost sheep of the house of Israel." When the woman insists, Jesus again refuses, adding a delicate touch of comparing of foreigners to dogs: "It is not meet to take the children's bread and cast it to dogs." In this passage, he basically tells the woman that his skills are reserved for the Jewish people ("children" of God) and not foreigners ("dogs"). After the woman suggests that sometimes dogs get to eat the crumbs that fall off the table, Jesus gives in to her quick wit and persistence and agrees to heal her daughter.[239]

Other passages, instead, tell a different story. Mark 16:15, for example, quotes Jesus urging his disciples to go preach to all nations around the world. Luke 10:30–37 contains one of the most radical of Jesus' parables, the story of the Good Samaritan. Here Jesus suggests that a Samaritan—a member of a neighboring nation that was often in conflict with Jews—can be capable of kinder behavior than the highest authorities of Jewish society.

These conflicting ideas fueled the fire of an enduring argument among early Christians on whether Jesus' mission was for the entire world or only Jewish people. After a few years of debates, the faction emphasizing the global scope of Jesus' message came out on top and forever marked the nature of Christianity from then on.

State Religion

This choice proved to be the key to the popularity of Christianity. As relatively ethnically homogenous tribal societies gave way to multi-ethnic nation states, the idea of a chosen people based on membership in a specific ethnic group turned out to be less and less useful. By moving away from it, Christianity took the first step toward becoming the official religion of the Roman Empire.

In the early 300s, Emperor Constantine found time in his busy schedule (murdering scores of political opponents and having his wife boiled alive and his own son executed is hard work . . .) to transform Christianity from a persecuted sect into the main religion of the Empire. It's not that Constantine had suddenly turned soft and fuzzy. His motives had preciously little to do with spirituality, and everything to do with his desire to find a religion that would create greater unity across the Empire. What he was ultimately after was greater control over its people. Ethnically, culturally, politically, and religiously, the Roman Empire was very much divided. Throughout it, plenty of languages were spoken, and plenty of gods worshipped. These divisions created problems for any ruler since the population didn't see many reasons to be attached to a central government. The only thing that connected these people together was the power of Rome's armies.

Being the smart politician that he was, Constantine decided something had to be done in order to create more unity among the citizens by the illusion—if not the reality—of shared values. Religion could provide this badly needed bond. Being a citizen would be more than an accident of fate; it would also indicate membership in a common religion. To serve Constantine's goal of mixing state and religion, monotheism seemed much more attractive than polytheism because it demanded strict obedience to a single source of authority—a prospect that had Constantine salivating.

When it came to picking which form of monotheism to sponsor, the choice was obvious. Whereas Judaism had too many ties to one specific ethnic group to work well among an ethnically mixed entity like the Roman Empire, the more inclusive Christianity could serve as the perfect candidate. Making it painfully clear that religious piety was not his primary concern, Constantine promptly moved to squash any alternate interpretations of Christianity other than the one he endorsed. The rubber-stamped version of Christianity was to be used as a tool to tighten his grip on the reins of power.[240]

The sense of common identity created by the "chosen people" idea had worked great for a large tribal society. A Christian identity tied to Roman citizenship could serve a similar function on the much larger scale—the Roman Empire. Rather than one religion for a single ethnic group, there would be a single religion for all people under the same state.

Even though ethnic pride is, by definition, tied to a specific ethnicity, whereas nationalism and patriotism are not, they all build a group identity that goes beyond the individual or the family level, but yet is not inclusive of all humanity. This pride in an identity built along ethnic or national boundaries is why I address here ethnic pride, patriotism, and nationalism together as different heads of the same monster.

For God and Country, and Other Totalitarian Perversions

Borrowing a page from Constantine's playbook, in collusion with church authorities, most rulers throughout much of Western history promoted the idea that political power derives its legitimacy from God. The writings of Saint Paul provided the necessary ammunition for this totalitarian nightmare since, as Paul wrote,

> Every person must submit to the authorities in power, for all authority comes from God, and the existing authorities are instituted by him. It follows that anyone who rebels against authority is resisting a divine institution, and those who resist have themselves to thank for the punishment they will receive . . . You wish to have no fear of the authorities? Then continue to do right and you will have their approval, for they are God's agents working for your good. But if you are doing wrong, then you will have cause to fear them; it is not for nothing that they hold the power of the sword, for they are God's agents of punishment bringing retribution on the offender.[241]

This perfect declaration of religious fascism is what allowed Constantine to consider himself "the vice-regent of God."[242] It also laid the groundwork for the long-lived symbiotic relationship between government and church.

History records several cases of extremely religious people who considered patriotism a form of idolatry since, in their minds, the ultimate loyalty should be reserved only for God. But this is far from typical. Within Christian countries, religion and patriotism have mostly gone hand in hand, resulting in plenty of "God Bless America"–type statements. The declaration by French patriot Joan of Arc, "He who makes war on the holy kingdom of France makes war on King Jesus,"[243] stands as the kind of sentiment fostered by the marriage of ultra-nationalism and religion throughout the history of Christianity. Similarly, Muhammad served as a prophet *and* ruler of the early Muslim community, setting the blueprint for the union of religion and politics within the history of Islam.

Eventually, in one of the great moments of human history, the Enlightenment finalized the divorce of church and state throughout Europe. This hasn't happened quite as decisively in the Muslim world. While in many countries this split is radical and real, in others separation of church and state doesn't run too deep, and religious nationalism still runs strong.

Whether the union of politics and religion is a cynical, Machiavellian strategy to gain more control over credulous peoples, or whether political figures really saw (and continue to see) themselves as God's agents is immaterial. The end result is the same. Once church and state are united, disobeying the government equals disobeying God. And when it's God Himself who is waving your national flag, it becomes much harder not to march along. Fascist movements are regularly born on the pillars of church and patriotism.

Creating a collective mythology with shared rituals and values is a great shortcut to totalitarianism. Hitler understood it well, and that's why he reworked the "chosen people" concept into his ideology on the superiority of the "Aryan race"—a bitter irony considering his venomous hatred for Jews. The Japanese government did a similar thing by temporarily twisting Shintoism into a nationalistic religion promoting the divine origin of the Japanese people and their equally "divine" destiny to rule over Asia. Both Communism and Nazism attacked traditional forms of religion because they sought to replace them as "secular religions." The Nazi slogan "One people, one nation, one leader" is a direct echo of Louis XIV's Christian motto "One king, one law, one faith."[244]

The Desire to Belong

If you are wondering what horrendous sin you committed to deserve having landed back in history class, I apologize for the previous several pages and will have pity on you. I was not trying to torture you with history just for the fun of it—I swear. This long-winded historical background was important to explain how even religions that are not tied to a specific ethnic identity often end up supporting scary forms of nationalism. If I haven't put you to sleep by now, hopefully you are beginning to see why patriotism and/or nationalism and/or ethnic pride make me cringe.

Anytime I run into masses of people gathered around a flag—any flag—invoking divine blessings for their country, I feel like I have been transported into one of those body-snatchers sci-fi movies where the aliens start screeching, hissing, and pointing fingers as soon as they discover that a non-alien is among them. Patriotism and religious fervor can be scary on their own, but when united together they kick wide open the door to self-righteous fanaticism. This combination is like steroids for mob mentality, since it's easy to find a justification for any action as long as it's done in the name of serving God and country. From the Rape of Nanking to the Thirty Years' War, from the conquest of the Americas to the Holocaust, much horrendous violence against civilians has been committed by a bad mix of nationalism and religion.

We don't need any strange conspiracy theory to explain why masses of people regularly jump on the bandwagon of religious patriotism. People are not brainwashed into giving their power away to political and religious authorities. They are happy to do it. At the root of it all is the very human desire to belong. Who doesn't want to be part of something greater than themselves? Most human beings crave the safety and sense of security that come from being part of a powerful group. Rather than having to solve life's problems on their own, people in need of guidance can find readymade beliefs, codes of behaviors, symbols, and creeds provided by the group. The price to pay is your individuality with its quirks and idiosyncrasies. A group, in fact, usually has limited tolerance for anyone departing from its core beliefs. Too much questioning is considered an act of betrayal.

As the fashion industry knows well, there is power in labels. Put a designer label on some clothes, and millions of people will pay insane prices for them. It's all in the name. Group identities are no different. Embracing them makes you feel special—something that people who are not special badly want. And out of all the possible forms of group identity, none are as strong as religion and nationalism. This is why they have attracted scores of human beings throughout history. They give you a sense of identity simply for being born in a certain country or into a certain culture and claiming to adhere to certain beliefs. But no matter how different they claim to be from each other, all these identities are nothing but masks we can wear to avoid having to find out who *we* are. Nations at war despise each other's flags but all agree on the importance of patriotism. They differ on which side they label good or bad, but they play the same exact game. For my part, I find them all equally pathetic.

Ethnic Pride, Nationalism, and Patriotism: The Fancy Clothes in the Wardrobe of Racism

Clearly not all forms of ethnic pride or nationalism or patriotism lead to violent fanaticism. I find nothing wrong with having a soft spot for the land where you grew up, and the places of your childhood. There's something natural and legitimate about feeling this type of emotional attachment. But as Lewis Mumford notes,

> The simple love of country and home and soil, a love that needs neither reasons nor justifications, is turned by the official apologists of the state into the demented cult of "patriotism": coercive group unanimity: blind support of the rulers of the state: maudlin national egoism: an imbecile willingness to commit collective atrocities for the sake of "national glory."[245]

Even if we dismiss the most dramatic excesses as aberrations, ethnic pride, nationalism, and patriotism still bug me to the core. Plenty of people are so pathologically attached to them that I'm sure my words will strike them as threatening and offensive. This is not my intention, but the topic is too important not to address it just for fear of hurting somebody's feelings. Every time I walk into the campus cafeteria at one of the colleges where I teach, and I see people of the same color self-segregating to different tables, I'm reminded that, far from being some abstract, academic debate, this issue very much affects us in our day-to-day lives. After all, these categories often determine whom we are willing to date, be friends with, and go to war against. Since so much is at stake, let's dig deeper to see what all the fuss is about.

After enjoying many centuries of popularity, today, in many places around the world, public displays of racism are no longer looked upon kindly. Why is racism bad? Because it assumes that all members of a certain ethnic group or nation share certain cultural characteristics, and these characteristics are bad or inferior, and for this reason we should hate these people. This is clearly a mean-spirited indulgence in the worst kind of stereotype.

Ethnic pride and patriotism, on the other hand, are usually touted as noble values. Religions gladly give their blessings to these forces with various "God Bless . . . [fill in the blank with whichever nation you want]" or "one Nation under God"–type statements. And how do ethnic pride and patriotism work? They assume that all members of a certain ethnic group or nation share certain cultural characteristics, that these characteristics are good or superior, and for this reason we should be proud to belong to this group.

Is it just me, or does this sound a lot like the flip side of racism? Both racism and patriotism share the idea that people belonging to the same nation, or having the same skin color, share a common culture. The only difference is that racists look out at another group and view their values negatively, whereas patriots look at their own group and are proud. The assumption of shared values remains the same in both cases. The reason why one is frowned upon while the other is exalted escapes me.

Canadians Love Tyranny

Are racists and patriots right? Are values really shared by the majority of people within any one group? In the United States, we are told that freedom is the essential American value. That's what this country is supposed to be all about. But the notion of tying to a single flag a value that is highly desirable to most human beings strikes me as weird. If freedom is the monopoly of the United States, does that mean Canadians cherish tyranny and oppression? Last time I checked, many democratic governments throughout the world supported the ideal of freedom. Many people under repressive governments love freedom as well. Freedom is one of those worldwide human values that is beneficial to life across the globe. A single nation, like a single ethnic group, is too small to appropriate something so universal.

And at the same time, just as they are too small to address human needs as a whole, nations and ethnic groups are also too big to embody the intimacy of those values shared by small communities. Nations and ethnic groups, in fact, are by definition not a family, a gathering of a few friends, or a tribe. Most certainly, they are not face-to-face communities. They are far too large for everyone to sit around the fire to discuss ideas. Whereas members of a small community spend their lives together, most people within nations and ethnic groups will never meet each other. And yet, they are all supposed to share the same cultural values. But what values do we share with a serial rapist who happens to carry our same passport or have our same skin color that we can't share with a foreigner? Do nations and ethnic groups really stand for something? Maybe it's just me, but any entity that is too narrow to embrace all of humanity and too broad to form a working community seems useless and hollow.[246]

The best proof of the futility of these categories is that our identification with them constantly changes depending on the context. Even in a small country like Italy, the notion of "Italian pride" is only useful when facing off against foreigners. But if no foreigners are in sight, the idea that we all stand for the same principles falls to pieces. People from a northern city like Milan will look down at southerners, and vice versa. "Sicilians are not real Italians," they will think. "Only the north embodies the true spirit of Italy." But visit Bergamo just a few miles away, and the north won't look so appealing. Suddenly, they'll remember how those guys eat funny foods, speak in a weird accent, and are simply not enough "like us." So it's time to switch gears: "It's our city, Milan, that we are proud of," they will say. "We are the best of what Italian identity is all about. Except for the outskirts of town . . . but those guys are white trash, so they don't count. The real city is the center of town. Please don't include my neighbors, though. Those assholes always play loud music late at night. I hate those bastards. So I guess the real source of identity and pride is my family . . . but not my siblings, ungrateful selfish pricks that they are." This is how a supposedly meaningful national identity can shrink back down to the individual level. When examined in this light, any illusion of shared values among the entire nation (but not among all peoples in the world) can't survive the filters of family, neighborhood, city, and region.

Despite my deep distaste for patriotism, occasionally even I am susceptible to its appeal. Being a foreigner on the West Coast of the United States, I get oddly sentimental sometimes when I run into the rare Italian. My first reaction is to open up to them and treat them as friends. Why? They are Italians—just like me. When I stop to think about it, though, disturbing questions come to mind. What exactly is the deep bond that connects us, and that's supposed to turn us into instant friends? The fact that we both like pasta? What else do we share? We grew up speaking the same language. We may have read the same comic books as kids. We probably have a few cultural habits in common. But this is pretty much as far as it goes. What we share by virtue of being Italian doesn't exactly go very deep, and it certainly isn't enough to turn a stranger into an immediate friend.

Patriotism and ethnic pride, on the other hand, take the few cultural characteristics that are usually shared throughout a population and overemphasize them to the point of building a whole mystique about them. This is the recipe for creating stereotypes. Only when we give up our individuality in an effort to mold ourselves to a fixed cultural image can those cultural ideals bear more than a very superficial resemblance to reality. But doing our best to fit stereotypes doesn't seem like a great plan. The individuals I am interested in tend to be much more complex than what the average member of a certain nation or ethnic group is supposed to be like.

Exceptions (Well . . . Almost)

To be fair, if you have suffered occasions when someone treated you horribly because of your skin color or nationality, it is understandable to react by developing an attachment to that identity. Perhaps you were trying to move beyond race and nationality, but someone pigeonholed you. Even if you didn't have much in common with others from the same nation or with the same skin color to begin with, now you *do* have in common the very real experience of discrimination. And nothing creates quick bonds like having a common enemy.

Under these circumstances it is normal and logical to want to band together for protection, for safety, for finding the company of people who understand what you are going through. A certain level of patriotism and ethnic pride may be psychologically important if you are the target of an attack, or if generations of your ancestors have internalized a sense of shame about their people. Yet, it's very easy for this to turn into a trap. Nothing is sadder than seeing those who have been oppressed turn around and dish out the same type of oppression against others the moment they have the power to do so. They opposed racism and stereotypes because they didn't like being their victims, but have no problem being the perpetrators.

Even when things are not so drastic, and we don't shapeshift overnight into virulent racists, overemphasizing pride in one's culture can be a problem. After all, we still fall prey to the same assumption of shared cultural values across all members of a group, which is at the roots of racism. Rather than allowing ourselves the freedom to mix whatever values bring us happiness, we feel bound by duty to conform to the expectations of a particular culture. We may even be embarrassed when we escape stereotypes and embrace our individuality because it could be perceived as betraying our roots, losing our identity, or becoming like "them."

No matter how good the justification, I still see all the identities that divide human beings along racial or national lines as prisons. I'm not about to give artificial categories and man-made borders the right to limit my ties with other human beings and dictate what values I should or should not embrace.

Global Religions Creating Global Identities in a Global World (Did I Use the Word "Global" Enough Times?)

Many religions have been promoting a collective, global, human identity for hundreds of years, so I'm not preaching anything new here. At the same time, other religions have been fighting tooth and nail to keep the very unholy alliance of religion and nationalism/patriotism/ethnic pride alive in the modern world. These guys are scared now. Their sacred cows were safe as long as humanity was stuck in a slow-moving universe, in which little was known about people in the next valley, and goods and ideas traveled painfully slow. But the game has changed, and we now find ourselves in a world of fast connections, unlikely cultural exchanges, and greater knowledge about other lifestyles than ever before. In an increasingly interconnected world, borders are falling as we speak. Traditional forms of identity, built as they are on separation, stand in the path of modernity.

The twentieth century took giant steps toward shrinking the power of racism. Let's not stop here. In a global world, the idea of loyalty to a single nation, or a single ethnic group, is anachronistic and useless; it's an obstacle that slows us down, an archaic heritage steeped in a fear of diversity. The time has come for a more open, more courageous way of facing the world.

A weak type of multiculturalism and the resulting spineless relativism are not what I am talking about here. We need to create new cultures, not simply mix old ones. Freed from our old, tired identities and a restricted sense of belonging, we can tune our antennas to a more global form of consciousness. The problems humanity faces don't respect borders: desperate environmental conditions, increased demand for declining forms of energy, overpopulation, international corporate pillaging, and the terrorist threat of religious fascists are not the issues of any one nation. They are human issues. The task of a healthy religion is to give us the courage to shed our old nationalistic skins and help us simply be human. If it weren't for the annoying fact that I would probably end up stoned to death, I would love to celebrate a ritual in which we burn the flags of every country in the world—none excluded. Genki Sudo, my favorite mixed martial artist, displayed a similar distaste for nationalism, expressed in a less pyromaniac and offensive manner. After his fights, he would parade around the ring waving a flag with a picture of the earth taken from space: one planet—no divisions. I cannot think of a better symbol for the religion we need today.

We have only one earth, and so far our narrow-minded "let's exploit resources before the people across the border get to them" mentality has done a royal job of screwing it up. Developing a global consciousness is the first step in taking care of the only planet gracious enough to allow us to play, sleep, and feed on it; it is the only planet we know of capable of giving us life.

About 2,400 years ago, Diogenes the Cynic, the wildest man in Greece,[247] and one of the most overlooked philosophers in Western history, coined the word "cosmopolitan." In the face of the Athenians' pride in their own city, he proclaimed, "I am a citizen of the world." More than two millennia later, it's time for religions to be more forceful in stirring humanity in this direction.

CHAPTER 12

I COULD ONLY BELIEVE IN A GOD WHO CAN LAUGH: WHY RELIGION NEEDS TO BE FUN

My faith is whatever makes me feel good about being alive. If your religion doesn't make you feel good to be alive, what the hell is the point of it?
—Tom Robbins, *Fierce Invalids Home from Hot Climates*

The gods too love a joke.

—Plato

Those who understand jokes are many; those who understand true laughter are few.

—Hakuin

When it comes to having a good time, churches and temples usually aren't the first places that come to mind. The majority of religions tend to be gloomy, somber affairs. In my experience, an atmosphere of heaviness and utmost gravity seems to surround them. Capturing this feeling, the great nineteenth century American orator Robert

Ingersoll once said, "When I was a boy, Sunday was considered altogether too holy to be happy in."[248]

We don't need to be familiar with a particular theology to understand that playfulness is typically not welcome among most religious traditions. Just take a peek at the faces of people participating in religious services, and they'll tell you everything you need to know. Most of the time, they look severely constipated. They communicate as much joy as those country or blues songs about someone cleaning out your bank account, running off with your spouse, killing your dog, and breaking your last bottle of beer.

The individuals who run many organized religions seem to believe sacredness and lightheartedness are mutually exclusive. Martin Luther's idea that "God can be found only in suffering and the Cross"[249] would certainly resonate with them. As cheerful as a kick in the groin, this penitential spirit shows up across plenty of different faiths. It almost makes you wonder if their rituals and worldviews were formed after one too many Chinese movie marathons. (For those of you who are unfamiliar with the joys of Chinese cinema, generally at least half of the characters end up killing themselves; and the rest either die a horrific death at the hands of a nasty villain with an evil laugh or spend the remainder of their existence in heartbreak and regret.)

To tell the truth, most of the world's religious scriptures are far from unanimous in explicitly condemning laughter. For example, here is what the Bible has to say on this topic: with its usual clarity, it tells us that joy and laughter are good, except for the fact that they are bad. Confused? Check it out for yourself. In Ecclesiastes 8:15 we read: "Then I commended mirth, because a man hath no better thing under the sun than to eat, and to drink, and to be merry."[250] Ready to pop the champagne and start the party then? Not so fast, for in an effort to prove that logical coherence is overrated just one section earlier Ecclesiastes 7:3–4 stated: "Sorrow is better than laughter; for by the sadness of the countenance the heart is made better. The heart of the wise is in the house of mourning; but the heart of fools is in the house of mirth."[251] As far as how Jesus himself dealt with these conflicting messages, the Gospels are silent. Did he value having a sense of humor or was he too engrossed in his being a Messiah and all to allow himself to smile? We don't know. But despite the ambiguity of the scriptures, much of Christianity has clearly chosen to emphasize the more severe, stern possibility.

When your religious authorities are constantly rapping about suffering, contrition, shame, fear, sin, and the fires of hell, it's kind of hard to have a good laugh. Drinking from these theological downers day after day, vast numbers of spiritual people have come to embrace the attitude that fun has no place in one's religious life. Fun—in their minds—is the opposite of serious. We have no time to play—we're talking about God here, and heaven and hell, and the meaning of life. This is serious business. If you want comedy, watch Jay Leno. Sacred stuff is no laughing matter. Unashamed joy, in their eyes, is a sin to be repressed.

What these people forget is that fun is not the opposite of serious. Fun is only the opposite of boring. I smell too much darkness and self-importance around them to want to join their crowd. I feel much more at home with Nietzsche when he advises, "we should call every truth false which was not accompanied by at least one laugh."[252]

Unlikely sources can sometimes deliver deep spiritual truths. Right after Nietzsche, it's time to quote the most famous big-boobed cartoon in Disney's history, Jessica Rabbit, the wife of the main character in *Who Framed Roger Rabbit*. At one point in the movie, she is asked why a hot woman like her (well, at least as hot as a cartoon can be . . .) is married to the extremely goofy-looking Roger Rabbit. The reason has nothing to do with the things that bunnies are famous for doing constantly. It's a Disney movie after all, not porn. "He makes me laugh," she answers. Many will dismiss it as a stupid Disney line, but I think the bunny's wife is on to something (I never thought I would get to write a sentence where the subject is "the bunny's wife" . . . I'm oddly pleased.) Whereas some religious authorities and stiff intellectuals like to dismiss playfulness as frivolous, I couldn't disagree more. In my own experience, playfulness is my lifeblood. It's what makes all the difference.

If I had to pick a single reason why I love the one and only Elizabeth Han, I would be hard-pressed. Is it because she is smart? No. The fact that she is smart is great, but that's not it. Is it because watching her unbelievably beautiful naked body go through a yoga sequence is one of the best things that human eyes have ever seen? That sure helps, but it's not it either. I know hundreds of smart people, but most of them bore me to death. I know hundreds of beautiful people who no longer look so beautiful once you see them for who they really are. There are plenty of reasons why I love her, but the main one is that she can laugh like no one else I know. Sometimes heaviness and mental bullshit weigh me down, and life feels like a math problem. But then I hear her laugh, and it's like a bomb of irrepressible joy tearing down all the walls that were keeping me prisoner. Her laughter is so damn contagious that you just can't resist it: it's a ceremony that frees me of any excessive mental baggage and makes me fall back in love with the beauty of it all. It chases away all the ghosts, for demons have power only as long as I take myself and my problems very seriously. Had Nietzsche heard her laugh, he would have never gone crazy.[253]

OK, man, so you love this woman whose laughter possesses demon-exorcising, love potion-dispensing, magical qualities. So what? What does this have to do with religion anyway? Whereas many traditions frown upon mixing humor and religion, some, like Zen, Taoism, Tantrism, and Sufism, just to name a few, embrace laughter and treasure it as their most prized possession. Ancient Egyptians believed that, following death, people would be judged by having their hearts weighed on a scale against a feather. Only if the hearts were lighter than the feather would they be deemed worthy of immortality. Lightheartedness to them was, quite literally, the key to heaven.

Among some American Indian tribes, humor is an integral component of the most sacred ceremonies. Once, during the Sun Dance, the most important ritual of the Plains tribes, I saw a group of little Lakota kids sitting in a circle singing "Barbie Girl" by Aqua. Hearing the refrain "I'm a blonde bimbo girl in a fantasy world" sung with gleeful satisfaction by a band of eight-year-olds in the midst of a pre-Columbian ceremony was shocking enough, but even more shocking was the fact that no one thought of chastising them for disrupting the ritual. The adults had a good laugh and carried on as if the song was part of the ritual itself. Maybe I shouldn't have been surprised. Lakota religion, after all, includes the role of the Heyoka, a sacred clown whose task is to behave in insanely bizarre ways making everyone crack up. For the Lakota, this is not just comedy but an extension of their spiritual life; as Lakota Elder Wallace Black Elk once told me, "The spirits like laughter. Spirits are funny."

Finding out that Lakota medicine men and Jessica Rabbit have much in common puts me in a good mood, and renews my conviction in the primary religious value of humor. Not only do I strongly feel that laughter and spiritual depth *can* go hand in hand, I would even venture to say that without laughter it is very likely religions will take a wrong turn. If you don't want to take my word for it, stay with me for the rest of this chapter as we explore why humor is more essential to the health of a religion than the most sophisticated theological arguments.

Laughter as Antidote to Dogma

Those experiences that we deem most sacred are always in danger of giving birth to dogmas. The more important something is to us, the more likely we are to want to preserve it, protect it, put it on a pedestal, and—continuing the alliteration of the deadly *p*'s—turn it into the exclusive Playground of Priests. Along the way, plenty of religious and political ideologies that began as vital, genuine sources of stimuli and liberation lost their flexibility and shifted into dark, sinister dogmas. The freshness of their messages dries up when their followers begin worrying about conserving the truths they've discovered. Proving that sometimes love can do as much damage as malice, followers embalm their favorite teachings in a protective layer of rigidity, mummify them, and ultimately kill them. Invariably, deadly seriousness and lack of humor plant the seeds of fanaticism, and fanaticism negates the very spirit that produced good ideas in the first place.

This is why, if we want to avoid falling into this trap, we should never neglect to feed our sense of humor. Any religion that can't laugh at itself is a scary religion. Precisely because something is sacred and important, we need to be able to laugh about it. Nietzsche had it right when he wrote, "I do not know any other way of associating with great tasks than play."[254] Laughter and playfulness, in fact, are the only antidotes to self-righteous dogmatism. They keep things loose. They save us from becoming too arrogant in our beliefs.

Any time I stumble into people who are too rigid to laugh at themselves, a warning bell goes off in my head. What are they scared of? Do they really have that little confidence in the power of their ideals as to believe they could be somehow weakened by a good joke? A lack of self-humor is a sure sign of pathological insecurity as much as macho posturing, defensiveness, and aggressiveness. It is the result of a very large but very fragile ego. As Tom Robbins writes, "People who are too self-important to laugh at their own frequently ridiculous behavior have a vested interest in gravity because it supports their illusions of grandiosity."[255]

Posers need to take themselves very seriously. They are extremely attached to the image they strive to project in public because deep down they know it's all they have—small dogs with a very big bark screaming "Look at me. I'm a bad, bad, big dog. You should be afraid of me and respect me. Can't you tell how important I am?" All their constant yapping is a desperate effort to convince everyone of their worth. But if they only possessed an ounce of real self-confidence, they could afford to lighten up. Big dogs don't need to make so much noise.

When I look at many self-described "spiritual" people, I feel the same way as when I see a Chihuahua acting tough. Their trying so hard to behave and talk "spiritually," their working so desperately to live up to an idealized image clearly tells me how far they are from that ideal. I was reminded of this when I witnessed an amusing interaction between two women at a Sun Dance ritual. After several, failed attempts at lighting a ceremonial pipe, a white woman in her thirties took a deep breath and with great gravity said, "Ah.

The spirits don't want us to smoke the pipe today." Next to her was a Lakota lady for whom the word "old" was a bland euphemism. Age, however, didn't prevent her from cracking up. In an effort to be polite, she subdued her laughter and advised the younger woman, "It's a windy day, that's all. Try putting your hands around the lighter and you won't have any problem." Right there was the difference between the real thing and a poor imitation. The old Lakota lady lived and breathed her religion, so she didn't need to overdo it: sometimes spirits are trying to tell you something; sometimes it's just a windy day. Her spirituality was concrete, tangible, grounded in day-to-day life. The other lady's spirituality, on the other hand, didn't flow naturally out of her being, but rather was all effort. It was full of *oooooh* and *aaaaaah*—it looked like a Hollywood production of what Lakota religion is supposed to be like.

The gravity that so many religious people cling to ends up spoiling whatever genuine insight they may have. Their lack of humor pushes them to idealize "spirituality" as something removed from honest-to-earth daily life. But real spirituality is not afraid to laugh and dance. Real spirituality revels in the miracle of ordinary experience. As a Zen poem recites, "How wondrous, how mysterious! I carry fuel, I draw water!"[256] When Zen breathes freely, humor is never far away.

Speaking of Zen, here is a tradition that doesn't shy away from making the most serious of points in the most hilarious of ways. One of my all-time-favorite Zen stories clarifies this perfectly. The hero of our tale is fifteenth century Japanese Zen master Ikkyū (a.k.a. "Crazy Cloud"), a Buddhist version of Bugs Bunny, a long-haired, sake-drinking, sex-hungry trickster who loved nothing better than to shake up powerful institutions and traditions. Some of his own

Zen brethren were terrified of his sharp wit. His approach to Zen was a little too raw, direct, and authentic for their taste.

The story tells us that, on a certain day, Ikkyū had an interesting encounter on a ferry with a *yamabushi*—an ascetic hermit who practiced a mix of Buddhism and Shinto. Feeling cocky, the yamabushi decided to play the old "my-religion-is-better-than-yours" game and boasted to Ikkyū about his ability to perform miracles. To prove his point, he began conducting an elaborate ritual until he conjured up the fiery image of one of his gods in the bow of the boat. "Can your Zen top this?" asked the yamabushi with smug satisfaction. Responding to the challenge, Ikkyū promptly pulled down his pants and pissed on top of the vision, putting the fire out. "Look!" exclaimed Ikkyū innocently. "Here's a miracle issuing out of my own body."[257] How can you not love this man?

But enough with the anecdotes and stories. The point is that by encouraging joy and mental flexibility, laughter and humor are the best weapons to avoid the fruits of religious dogma: conflict, violence, and "holy" wars. No one who can truly laugh and be relaxed about even their most important convictions would ever willingly kill or be killed in the name of religion. She wouldn't start deadly riots to protest cartoons poking fun at her faith; she wouldn't burn people at the stake because of spiritual differences; and she would never feel compelled to shove her beliefs down everyone else's throats.

Few things, in fact, can help bridge people with very different ideologies as much as humor. In my history of religion classes, I tell potentially offensive things to my students regularly. The only thing allowing us to chat about them pleasantly instead of murdering each other is a smile on our faces, reminding us that life is both deeper and more fun than attachment to any ideology. Whether someone can burst out in a spontaneous, deep belly laughter tells me more about our ability to get along than any similarities in our ideas. Far from being a secondary issue, laughter is what can save a religion from turning into a fanatical machine of violence and oppression.

When Reality Punches You in the Face, Laughter Helps You Roll with the Punches

Any way you slice it, life is tough. From sickness to death, old age to broken hearts, betrayals to failure, life has a whole menu of possibilities for dishing out pain. No matter who you are, how rich or poor, how lucky or not, the bottom line is that you'll get hurt—over and over again. Providing solace to this inevitable pain is one of religion's main functions. Religions try to minister to our injuries, nurse our wounds, console us with explanations, and promise us an escape from life's most unpleasant face.

I am sure that explanations and promises work well for some people, but they do nothing for me. They look too much like desperate attempts to exorcise misery with overly complicated rationalizations or delusional promises. In any case, most religions have a vested interest in perpetuating the notion that life is pain, and only they have the cure for it.

Personally, I prefer laughter. Yes, there are plenty of things in life to be bummed out about, but as long as I can find humor in the darkest of circumstances I can rise above it. I'm not overly fond of self-pity and depression—two of humanity's drugs of choice—and I find that laughter is the best weapon to keep them at bay. It's a natural antidote to anxiety, stress, and anger. Medical research indicates that even our immune systems are shaped into gear by laughing often. As Tom Robbins writes, "Armed with a playful attitude, a comic sensibility, we can deny suffering dominion over our lives."[258] Truly, words to live by.

This in no way means we should pretend that suffering doesn't exist. No, what we are talking about here is refusing to pay too much attention to it; refusing to take it too seriously, since suffering thrives on both attention and humorless gravity. Nothing annoys and disarms suffering more than acknowledging its existence but refusing it the power to rob us of our enthusiasm for life. Pain exists whether we like it or not—but how we choose to react to it is what makes the difference between becoming its hostage or not. Suffering doesn't cause depression; our reaction to suffering causes depression. If I may steal another line from Tom Robbins, "All depression has its roots in self-pity, and all self-pity is rooted in people taking themselves too seriously."[259]

Not at all disturbed by the threat of death—which, by the way, turned out to be very real when representatives of the US government successfully arranged to have him murdered—Lakota leader Sitting Bull, declared, "The whites may get me at last, but I will have good times till then."[260] In other words, events beyond our control can always take place, and there isn't much we can do about that. But, we *can* prevent them from draining the fun out of life. Admittedly, this is sometimes easier said than done but, like with any muscle, it's an ability that becomes stronger by exercising it. In my mind, the truly religious attitude needs to encourage an insistence on happiness in the midst of desperation; happiness regardless of all the pain and hurt that life may throw our way.

One of the reasons Ikkyū and Tom Robbins are two of my personal heroes is because they are masters of ceremonies in a religion that celebrates the sheer joy of being alive. So many very intelligent people allow misfortune to push them toward a gloom-and-doom vision of the world that it's refreshing to run into someone who doesn't let destiny boss them around. Whereas I have been prevented from hanging out with Ikkyū by the lack of a time machine and psychic powers, I had the honor of spending some time with Tom Robbins and consider it one of the most formative experiences of my life. I learned more by being around him for a little bit than in all the years I spent in school.

Neither Robbins nor Ikkyu are frivolous clowns who are blind to the misery and the suffering that stalk the world. What makes Robbins and Ikkyū unique is that they haven't allowed pain to rob them of their passion for life. They have consciously chosen playfulness as a way to keep finding beauty even when existence turns unkind. Robbins himself explains beautifully the paradox of being "cheerfully cynical":

> My view of the world is not that different from Kafka's, really. The difference is that Kafka let it make him miserable and I refuse. Life is too short. My personal motto has always been: Joy in spite of everything. Not just [mindless] joy, but joy in spite of everything. Recognizing the inequities and the suffering and the corruption and all that but refusing to let it rain on my parade. And I advocate this to other people.[261]

Anyone can whine about bad luck, and maybe they are right. Maybe their lives are truly terrible and painful. But endlessly lamenting never solved anything. My mother once delicately voiced this idea to my grandmother after listening to her complain for three days straight, "If you really don't think that you can be happy in life, and nothing can ever cheer you up, maybe you should just kill yourself and be done with it. If you want, I'll help you." We didn't hear a complaint out of my grandmother for weeks.

Being able to stare at tragedy in the face and still find the strength to laugh is an art, and I bow to anyone who can master it: this is what real spiritual depth is all about. Escaping from the clutches of melancholy is a sign of talent and courage. And as Nietzsche reminds us, "Courage wants to laugh. . . . Whoever climbs the highest mountains laughs at all tragic play and tragic seriousness."[262]

Laughter as an Aid to Sharpen Our Perceptions

Closing the door on dogma and defeating the ghosts of tragedy are the most fundamental ways laughter can help religion. But a third key function of laughter is its power to heighten our ability to feel and perceive the sacred.

Just mentioning the word "sacred" is enough to make many people stiffen up. The connection that exists in the minds of most people between "sacred" and "serious" chases away even the thought of a smile. Frowning brows and gloomy expressions stand in the way of getting the full experience out of rituals, prayers, or meditation. They limit our ability to feel and perceive things at a deeper level. A tense consciousness can only skim the surface; a relaxed one is more open to the experience of the sacred. This is why humor and laughter are so important; they help us unwind and relax. By making us take ourselves less seriously, and softening our nervous edges, they put us in a more receptive state of mind. And it's only in this state that we can have access to more profound sources of insight.

When we are facing a deeply spiritual event, gravity and somberness usually take over and run our consciousness. The problem with this is that suddenly turning overly serious can make us tense and rigid. And when we are not relaxed, our perceptions become dull. Instead, let's take a hint from Thoreau. He writes: "Not by constraint or severity shall you have access to true wisdom, but by abandonment and childlike mirthfulness."[263]

The same holds true for any other activity in life. Whenever we are in a state of relaxed awareness, we are able to think more clearly and get the job at hand done with less effort. Look at any athlete who is relaxed: their movements typically are sharper and more effective since tense muscles are not slowing them down. Look at a public speaker, or a masseuse, or whoever else you feel like looking at, and you'll see the same story repeating itself. In pretty much any human endeavor, physical or mental, relaxation aids fluidity. And fluid minds and bodies can think and act on their feet because they are not obstructed by any nervous energy.

This same idea is found in any tradition that embraces humor. From Black Elk to Zen master Hakuin, many insist that laughter has the power to unlock "the doors of perception" and make us ready to capture life's secrets.[264] Personally, I find this suggestion worth trying. In the best case scenario we gain access to greater wisdom than we ever thought possible, and in the worst we end up having a good time: not a bad deal.

Bad Humor

OK, I'll confess all the ugly truth. Although it's true that I'm passionately advocating the importance of laughter, even I have to admit that I am not always thrilled with humor, whether in a religious context or not. No rule is without exceptions, and humor is no different.

Mindful of what a turnoff painfully serious religions are, many pastors, priests, and other figures of authority have made the conscious choice to spice up their services with humor. They crack jokes, encourage laughter, and do their best to keep their audiences entertained. Just the same things I'm arguing for, right? Not really. If we are to tell it like it is, when certain people *try* to be funny but aren't, it's almost worse than when they are being rigid and somber. Trying to be funny and miserably failing is even sadder than being stiff and serious. Forced humor is worse than no humor at all.

The issue is not whether I like their jokes or not. Humor is not one size fits all, and it's not my business to be a censor. As long as someone finds it funny, good for them. No, the issue is in how unnatural and forced some efforts at humor are. Rather than flowing naturally, some people's humor is the result of having told themselves too many times that they are supposed to be funny. Rather than being spontaneous, inducing laughter turns into a choreographed performance and a duty—something that clearly defeats the very purpose of humor.

But I guess an effort toward laughter is better than no effort at all. And this is why, despite having had firsthand exposure to horrendously failed attempts at being funny, I still feel humor is one of the keys to a healthy religion.

The Paradox of a Deadly Serious, Funny Religion

In *Thus Spoke Zarathustra,* one of the most extraordinary books ever written, Friedrich Nietzsche asks a fundamental question: "Who among you can laugh and be elevated at the same time?"[265]

Typically, we are told laughter and wisdom don't go together. We are invited to choose between either path for—in the popular mind—we can't follow both. We can be superficial, happy, and outrageously funny *or* deep, wise, and deadly serious. Nietzsche addresses this suicidal dichotomy head-on. Why should we be satisfied with one or the other? Who is strong enough to take the best of both approaches and combine them in the same overabundant personality?

In my mind, if there ever was a challenge worth accepting, this is it. I'm not interested in gloomy religions created by and for depressed people. And I'm equally disinterested in the happy but stupid. What I want is to wed the greatest depth with the most intense enjoyment of life. It seems masochist and self-limiting to pursue one without the other. This is why I'm a paradox-hunter. The only religions fascinating me are those that can help me capture this beast.

Finding ways to keep happiness alive in the midst of a harsh world is far from a frivolous task. If my own religion has a mission, it's the expansion of joy. And laughter is its main ritual. When many things in our path will try to crush our spirit, laughter will be there to keep the flame burning. Like an orgasm, laughter erases all duality; it cleanses us from fear, dogma, and rigidity. It's a yes to life—all of life. It celebrates the unashamed enjoyment of being alive. It makes fun of "spirituality," heaviness, excess thought, rigid categories, unnecessarily complicated concepts, and all the sorry bullshit that chokes our souls. One good laugh does more for us than a thousand days locked up in churches or temples. It reminds us that life flows. It reminds us that after all is said and done, nothing, not even the most serious things in life—perhaps *especially* the most serious things in life—should be faced with gravity. The day when you stop laughing at yourself and the universe and everything else is the day you give some sad-looking priest power over your life. Laughter has no fear. Laughter is brave. Laughter defeats all the demons for me. Laughter refuses to bow on the altars of guilt, sin, and blame. The laughter I speak of is not only mindless amusement (even though mindless amusement is so much fun). The laughter I speak of doesn't back down from the most deadly serious challenges. It is precisely because of laughter that we can face our challenges better than an army of serious assholes too worried about the heaviness of it all to be able to ride the tallest waves. The laughter I speak of simply doesn't let staring at the deepest abyss ruin its good mood. This is the essence of my religion.

CHAPTER 13

HOW DO WE KNOW WHAT WE KNOW?

It's time to sharpen our weapons. It's time to choose which tools are the most appropriate for our journey. Without the right equipment, in fact, even the most well-intended and noble quest is doomed to fail before it even begins. Jump off a plane without a parachute and you quickly find out why preparations are important. Trust the wrong map, and rather than taking your kids to Disneyland, you'll find yourself vacationing among toothless rednecks and three-headed goats next to a nice nuclear dump site.

In venturing out to create our own religion, we need to first ask ourselves some basic epistemological questions. If I make it sound more complicated than it is, don't be alarmed. Epistemological questions are neither scary nor needlessly difficult. They are about figuring out how we know what we know. They are about deciding what instruments we will utilize in our search for answers. Philosophers, scientists, and religious leaders all praise the virtues of different methods to get to the truth. So let's roll up our sleeves and review our options.

Faith

"Faith" means not wanting to know what is true.
—Friedrich Nietzsche, *Thus Spoke Zarathustra*

"Blessed are those who have not seen and yet have believed," declares Jesus in the Gospel according to John.[266] As disturbing as the implications of this sentence are, they are child's play compared to the stories of the Old Testament addressing the same point. Genesis 22 tells a chilling tale that forms one of the theological pillars on which Judaism, Christianity, and Islam rest. Here we find God Himself calling on Abraham and giving him the pleasant order to sacrifice his own son. Incredibly enough, Abraham promptly agrees. It's only after Abraham has tied up his son, and raised the knife to drive it into his body that God sends an angel to cancel the order. It turns out that the whole sadistic drama was just a trick to test the depth of Abraham's faith. By obeying, Abraham passed the test with flying colors, and he is rewarded with a blessing from God and the promise that his descendants will prosper.[267]

I don't know about you, but I'm slightly puzzled by the notion that a parent willing to cut his kid's throat in an effort to obey the commands of a disembodied voice should be honored as a role model by all three main Western religions. Am I missing something here? Where I come from, whenever you start hearing voices telling you to murder your children, it's time to go have your head checked. Obeying it should earn you a one-way ticket to a criminal asylum, not God's blessing and the reverence of millions of believers.

This story, and Jesus' words quoted earlier, illustrates the importance of faith as an essential religious requirement. We are so used to hearing the word "faith" as being a desirable quality that it is easy to forget what faith actually means. If you are sure of your conclusions, you don't need faith. Faith has nothing to do with real knowledge (since knowledge depends on evidence) or rational thought (since rational thought depends on some logical basis). Faith comes into the picture when you don't know something, but you badly want to believe it anyway. Your need for reassuring certainties is strong enough not to let the total absence of supporting evidence stop you. When it comes to religious questions about the nature of life and the universe, even many people who depend on logic and reason in their day-to-day lives decide to forgo them in favor of faith. But as Sam Harris stated in his book *The End of Faith*, holding on to strong beliefs that lack any rational justification is a symptom of psychosis, not sainthood.[268] Its roots reach deep in the fertile ground of intellectual dishonesty.

How did faith get so popular then? How did a word that should be used as the name of a disease come to be so highly regarded by millions of people? It all goes back to the desire for answers when no logical answers are available. Remember the Big Two, God and the afterlife? The very annoying fact that we don't know anything about either of them is too much for most people to bear. For all their charms, logic and reason don't offer us any of the answers we crave. They don't tell us whether there is meaning in life or not. They don't tell us whether death is but a doorway to a more glorious world or it is the end of everything. They don't tell us whether our existence is supervised by an all-knowing, all-powerful, benign entity or a puppet in the hands of chaos. There are far too many key problems left unsolved by logic and reason.

This is why faith enters the picture: to substitute a cold silence with hope. When reason abandons you to face a grim reality, faith consoles you, enveloping you in a protective embrace. Faith has the power to rescue you from the demons of grief. It can infuse courage against the inevitability of death. It can give us a shot of optimism when there is no good reason to be optimistic. Faith is the logical (and yet illogical) consequence of having exhausted all rational options. If you can't accept uncertainty, made-up answers are more appealing than no answers. Some hope, however illusory it may be, is better than no hope. So it's no coincidence that the more a religion tries to reassure us about the existence of God and the afterlife, the more it will embrace faith. Proving that the reverse of this equation is also true, several religions that don't depend so heavily on the Big Two are much less interested in faith.

As much as I can sympathize with the very real needs addressed by faith, I can't help feeling that this is an acceptable solution only for people who are driven crazy by fear and desperation. Faith, after all, elevates delusion to the status of a legitimate tool to gain knowledge. It is the offspring of a one-night stand between superstition and dogmatism. It is what happens when religions fail to teach us to develop the courage to face life and death without any certainties.

So what, Bolelli? What's the harm in that? Yes, the emphasis on faith may betray a heavy load of anxiety, a strange relationship with logic, and a remarkable flexibility when it comes to stretching the truth, but is that so bad? As long as it makes us feel better and no one gets hurt, why fuss? Isn't life hard enough to go without faith?

I'm a firm supporter of whatever helps make us happy. So, in principle, faith shouldn't bother me. As long as faith can remain open-minded, I have nothing against it. But the problem is that faith can only rarely, and through the most difficult mental contortions, be open-minded. Most of the time, it is a medicine that comes with too many side effects. The reasons why I gladly leave faith out of my own religion are many. For the sake of simplicity, I'll focus on a couple of the main ones. After that, it's up to you to decide for yourself whether you agree with me in kicking faith to the curb, or if you find some redeeming qualities that make up for the problems faith creates.

The Dangers of Faith

The very premise of faith—its willingness to change the rules halfway through a game—has trouble written all over it. A healthy spirit of inquiry begins by looking at reality, examining evidence, and then drawing our conclusions. Faith does the exact opposite. It begins with a belief about the nature of things, and then goes looking for ways to make the evidence fit the belief. If it turns out that evidence supports our preconceived conclusion, great. If it doesn't, rather than revising the conclusion, faith conveniently decides that evidence doesn't matter. Since it accepts facts only as long as they confirm preexisting theories, faith is by definition the enemy of the essential requirement on which real knowledge depends: the willingness to change one's beliefs given the facts. This is not only embarrassingly dishonest, but downright dangerous.

By rejecting empirical evidence any time it challenges one's dogmas, faith is naturally at odds with science. Religion and science can dance cheek to cheek as long as religion doesn't stress the importance of a rigid faith. Whenever it does, however, problems arise. History records countless examples of religious fundamentalists coming after science with a vengeance. From the Catholic censure against the works of brilliant scientists such as Galileo and Copernicus to the

Scopes Trial of 1925 against the teaching of evolution in schools, fundamentalists have been consistently opposed to science, seeing it as a threat to faith.

Even today, plenty of believers still view scientific knowledge with suspicion. For example, in direct contradiction with archaeological findings, 48 percent of Americans like to hold on to the notion that humans were created within the last 10,000 years.[269] In 2007, in a failed effort not to appear like superstitious freaks straight out of the Middle Ages, a group of American fundamentalists inaugurated the Creation Museum near Petersburg, Kentucky, a sad attempt to reconcile a literal reading of the Bible with science. Among its highlights are exhibits showing dinosaurs and humans living side by side (nevermind the dinosaurs being extinct for a few million years before humans ever showed up in the neighborhood), and others subjecting math to strange tortures to "demonstrate" how the ancestors of all animal species on earth managed to fit in the 135-meter-long Noah's Ark.[270] If all of this is not weird enough, consider the case of Tom DeLay, a former Republican House Majority Leader, who blamed the epidemics of school shootings in the United States on the fact that schools teach evolution rather than Bible stories![271]

If some of these examples are laughable but innocuous, others are not. Still today the Catholic Church, along with many radical Muslim organizations, condemn contraception as sinful, thereby becoming unwitting accomplices in the spread of AIDS and other sexually transmitted diseases. In very real ways, when faith quarrels with science, the potential to cause tremendous suffering is extremely high.

This, however, is not the only way in which an uncompromising faith can hurt us. Since its claims are not subject to empirical tests, faith can easily turn into a tool for manipulation at the hands of religious authorities. Even if we rule out Machiavellian conspiracies, sincere faith is often at the roots of many conflicts. It is not surprising that faith-based religions, such as Christianity and Islam, are historically tied to a much greater amount of religious wars and bloodshed than religions that do not emphasize faith. The cause for this is simple. Reason allows us to compromise, but faith rarely does. Articles of faith are beyond rational discussions and negotiations. Because of its inflexible nature, faith will make it more difficult for people to soften or adapt the stances that brought them into conflict in the first place. If the Israeli-Palestinian conflict, for example, was only about land, compromises may have already solved the issue. But once you add to the dispute opposing faith-based claims to the land, and a history of bloodshed, ceding even one inch becomes complicated.

In a sense, faith, by its very nature, invites fanaticism since the strongest faith is the one for which you have the least evidence. The connection between faith and dogmatism is a close one, and the next link in the chain connects dogmatism to a propensity for "holy" wars and religiously motivated violence. This is not an automatic sequence; some people of great faith are sweet, lovable individuals who would never hurt anyone. But faith nonetheless gives us a push toward a dangerous direction. As disgustingly sick as the 9/11 hijackers were, they were perfect examples of the most extreme consequences of where faith may lead: these were people whose faith was so strong they were willing to kill and die for it.

For these reasons, in my own worldview I intend to make no space for faith. I think Dr. Charles Kimball nails it on the head when he writes, "Religion that requires adherents to disconnect their brain is often a big part of the problem."[272] And too often faith asks us to do exactly that.

Reason

After all the preceding words, we are back to square one. If faith is not a prime requirement for creating a healthy religion, then what is? Typically, those who are not particularly fond of faith exalt reason instead. And vice versa; the faith groupies equate reason with arrogance. In their minds, emphasizing the power of reason is a misguided human attempt to rely on oneself rather than accepting revealed dogma. This is what prompted Ignatius of Loyola, the founder of the Jesuit order, to state, "We sacrifice the intellect to God."[273] Despite the deep animosity that existed at that time between Catholics and Protestants, Martin Luther, the father of the Protestant movement, fully agreed with Loyola. "Reason," Martin Luther wrote, "is the devil's harlot, who can do naught but slander and harm whatever God says and does."[274] Proving that he was deeply insecure about his own beliefs, Luther was convinced that reason could only lead to atheism. So, instead of revising his beliefs, he rejected reason.

But this dichotomy between religion and reason is the product of the silly superstitions of disturbed men. Contrary to what some people think, I don't see a direct link between reason and atheism, since atheism—much like faith—claims to know precisely how the world works, and it further claims to be able to draw absolute conclusions about the nature of the universe on the basis of limited information.

If Loyola and Martin Luther are the bad guys on this issue, the good guys I want to root for in this tag team match are Galileo and Thomas Jefferson. Exposing the nearly blasphemous implications of the previous quotes, Galileo argued, "I do not feel obliged to believe that the same God who has endowed us with sense, reason, and intellect has intended us to forego their use."[275] Jefferson expands on the same idea by writing,

Shake off all the fears and servile prejudices under which weak minds are servilely crouched. Fix reason firmly in her seat, and call to her tribunal every fact, every opinion. Question with boldness even the existence of a god; because, if there be one, he must more approve the homage of reason, than that of blindfolded fear.[276]

Maybe Loyola and Martin Luther believe in a schizophrenic God who first gives human beings the ability to reason, but then wants them to sacrifice it on the altar of blind faith. Psycho, moody gods are not my thing, so I'll side with Galileo and Jefferson and gladly recruit reason as a valuable ally. Reason, after all, is the prerequisite for all sciences and the springboard of inquiry. It would hardly be possible to sail away on our quest for truth without its help.

Perhaps what I like most about reason is its revolutionary ability to put us in charge of our own destinies. It breaks us out of the jail of dogmatic ignorance, and sets us free to figure things out for ourselves. It kicks us in the ass when we get too complacent, and it forces us to take full responsibility for whatever answers we'll come up with. With great humility, it doesn't dictate the direction of our journey. It simply empowers us to use our minds as best we're able.

Yes, I'm definitely a fan of reason, but . . . c'mon, don't act surprised. You know this was coming. Just about every other time I praise something in glowing terms the "but" is not far away (my manly muscles are one of the few exceptions . . .) "But" is a three-letter stroke of genius. It keeps things in perspective. It prevents me from turning too rigid and self-righteous. It reminds me that hardly anything in life is black or white. Not even the best of things are immune from potential problems, and reason is no different. This is why as much as I appreciate reason and consider it an extremely valuable tool, I don't see it as the solution to all our problems.

Reason's Soft Underbelly

We do not speak to each other, because we know too much
. . . we smile our knowledge at each other.
—Friedrich Nietzsche, *Thus Spoke Zarathustra*

The first issue I have is with reason's little minions, the trusted allies reason depends on: words. In many ways, I love words. They fascinate me. They are my playmates, and I hardly ever tire toying with them. Ask anyone I know and they'll tell you that if talking were a competitive sport, I would be its heavyweight champ. But as much as I indulge in the very Italian habit of firing away never-ending streams of words, it doesn't mean I don't see their limits.

Remembering the vision that transformed his life forever, Lakota holy man Black Elk commented, "And while I stood there I saw more than I can tell and I understood more than I saw: for I was seeing in a sacred manner the shapes of all things in the spirit, and the shape of all shapes as they must live together like one being."[277] In similar fashion, when Thomas Aquinas penned the last word of his life's work, the *Summa Theologiæ,* he complained that what he had been able to write was but a fraction of what he had seen and knew in his heart.[278]

Anyone who has ever had a profoundly spiritual moment can understand what Aquinas and Black Elk are talking about. For that matter, anyone who has ever fallen in love can get it too. Somehow language doesn't seem to do justice to the intensity of certain feelings. If everything you have lived through can be easily summed up in words, you really haven't lived through much. Words are mental abstractions, feeble attempts to capture experiences that are much greater than any verbal formula. Trying to catch the totality of life through words is like going dinosaur-hunting with a mousetrap (not that I have ever tried, but I'm sure you get the picture.) The deepest things in life dwell in lands that words cannot reach.

This is why certain philosophies and religious traditions warn us over and over again not to get too attached to words. Zen Buddhists compare their own teachings to a finger pointed at the moon. Focusing too narrowly on the finger, we may miss what the finger is trying to show us all along: the living experience of a more enlightened state of being.

The very first line of the Tao Te Ching makes this point perfectly: "The Tao that can be told is not the universal Tao."[279] That first line could also be the last, because, after denying that words can capture the real Tao, how can you go on talking about it? But instead Lao Tzu goes on to write a whole book on the topic. Contradictory? No, just paradoxical. The opening sentence is the equivalent of a product's warning label reminding us not to get caught up on doctrine because the Tao is beyond words. Not a bad reminder considering that the history of many ideologies has been tinted with blood by people who were willing to kill and be killed in the name of doctrines. Once this is cleared, Lao Tzu has no problem discussing the Tao. As long as it's understood that words are vague approximations of reality, there's no harm in using them. As Chuang Tzu, another pillar of Taoism, once said in his typical tongue-in-cheek style, "Where can I find a man who has forgotten words so I can have a word with him?"[280]

It's easy to mistake a person's wisdom with their teachings. Sometimes different people will express the exact same concept, and I'll find myself agreeing with one and disagreeing with the other. Is it because I'm a moody bastard? Maybe. But maybe it's simply that while the content of the message may be the same, the experience, the emotion, and the intent behind it are not. Sometimes I even get along better with people I totally disagree with than with people who share my beliefs word for word. We are more than our words. Understanding somebody's words is obviously essential, but it's only the first step. If you get too attached to the letter of a message, you miss its spirit. And this is how all dogmas are born: from people who worship the letter and miss the spirit.

Anybody who has ever spent time in the halls of academia can see what happens when powerful ideas are reduced to useless chatter—a verbose game for nerds who seriously need to get out more often. By missing the spirit and focusing exclusively on the letter, most scholars become masters of empty philosophizing—pushers of useless knowledge for knowledge's sake. Rather than working to expand joy in our lives, the sterile, overly rational knowledge peddled in academic circles is rarely more than a way to fill our heads with too many notions. This type of knowledge is a heavy burden on the hunched shoulders of scholars. It does little more than inhibit creativity and age the soul.

The knowledge we are after is not to be found among the very rational but very boring intellectuals. But at the same time, I am certainly not preaching the anti-intellectualism popular among fundamentalists, who pride themselves on avoiding the "corrupting" influences of education. What we need is something entirely different. Zen and Taoism tell us that there are three stages to knowledge: The first stage is ignorance, which is where fundamentalism typically finds a home. The second stage is intellectual knowledge, which comes at the price of losing spontaneity and simplicity. Although it is certainly preferable to ignorance, this stage is often too dry, removed from reality, and overly analytical. It teaches us how to dissect and scrutinize existence, but not how to live it. Most people are stuck in one of these two stages. But it's at the third stage that things get interesting. Here, we let go of the excessive mental baggage accumulated during the second stage and retain only what we need to improve the quality of our lives. This is exactly what Thoreau meant when he wrote, "If you would be wise, learn science and then forget it."[281] Learn it all, let go of the superfluous, and retain the essential. By acquiring knowledge and moving beyond it, we transform knowledge into wisdom. Whereas knowledge is a heavy weight we carry in the head, wisdom is energy dancing in our muscles and keeping us warm at night.

Reason's Next Pitfall

Even though we are limited in what can be communicated through words, the problem with pure reason goes deeper than that. Those who reject the preeminence of faith can rarely do more than put reason on a pedestal. The cult of reason can often become its own faith, leading its followers to reject anything that is not logical, sober, and rationally explained. It buys into the advice given by one of reason's paladin, French philosopher René Descartes, who argued against our fascination with mystery and sense of wonder as primitive emotions to be rejected by a truly civilized man.[282]

Thanks for this pearl of stupidity, Descartes. Now you can crawl back to your grave. Banish mystery and sense of wonder?!? We may as well banish excitement and joy, and put a bullet in our very rational heads. Logic and reason are extremely valuable—and certainly preferable to most alternatives—but if we dismiss everything that is not perfectly rational, life would be horribly boring. If everyone followed logic, nobody would ever fall in love. Reason is too serious and restrained. It doesn't have a twinkle in its eye. Being unmoved by irrational impulses, it doesn't know how to dance, how to lighten up, how to roar with laughter. It thrives when it's time for examinations and careful explanations, but it is completely unfamiliar with ecstasy and wild abandon. Being dependent on words and concepts, reason too often stops at the letter of things but can never quite capture their spirit.

If earlier we had ringside seats to the tag team match between Loyola and Luther versus Jefferson and Galileo, we now get to see the championship bout between two of the giants of Greek philosophy. In the blue corner, wearing striped trunks, we have "The father of Western thought," the reigning champ, the one and only *Aaariiistoootleeeee!* And in the red corner, wearing Yin-Yang trunks, here is "The Riddling," "The Dark," "The Paradox Assassin," our challenger, *Heeeraaaacliiitussss!* Aristotle, being the strict rationalist that he was, viewed Heraclitus with disdain. Heraclitus, in fact, was a Greek version of Lao Tzu. His writings are the most Taoist ever produced outside of China. Heraclitus' love for paradoxes drove Aristotle crazy. Paradoxes—in Aristotle's very logical mind—are nothing but contradictions. The notion that opposites can go hand in hand makes no sense to him. In Aristotle's thinking, opposites are opposites, and that's the end of it. His philosophy, being perfectly rational, has become the foundation of Western science for over two thousand years. And yet, the discoveries of modern physics demonstrate that Heraclitus was onto something that Aristotle's rigid logic was unable to grasp. Physics tells us that everything, including apparently unchanging solid matter, is in constant movement. Even science today is beginning to see that the essence of life is paradoxical. It turns out that mystics have sometimes gained insights about the nature of the universe that have escaped scientists until now.

This, in my book, is reason's greatest limitation: the inability to deal with life's paradoxical character.

Ultimately, the human soul craves much more than reason alone can deliver. Life's mysteries are too deep and too many for reason to solve them all. This does not mean I'm advocating getting rid of science in favor of trying to fix our problems by meditating under a tree. The scientific method and rational thought can be some of our best allies in discovering how to live in harmony with the world. But like all methods, they can turn into dogmatic perversions if taken too rigidly. When science and reason begin advocating that they are the *only* true, reliable way to gain knowledge, they turn into what Huston Smith calls scientism: an arrogant form of secular fundamentalism that—much like religious fundamentalism—seeks to squash any alternative way of looking at things. As Paul Feyerabend beautifully explained, once a method begins to lose its flexibility and becomes unwilling to admit the possibility of insight coming from other modes of knowledge, it turns into an obstacle to true science. This is true even for the best of methods.

When Europeans first met members of the Iroquois Confederacy, they heard a legend about three sisters who during a time of famine volunteered to shapeshift into plants (namely, corn, squash, and beans) to provide food for the people. In exchange, the tribe would always have to plant the sisters together. At the time, no European thought this story carried any deep scientific meaning. Sisters who shapeshift into plants to feed humans?!? These weird Indians sure do believe in the strangest superstitions! And so Europeans continued planting corn, squash, and beans separately, as they had always done, thereby exhausting the soil very quickly. It was only at a much later date that Western scientists began to understand the nitrogen cycle, and learned that corn, squash, and beans have a symbiotic relationship helping each plant grow without overtaxing the soil. Just because an insight is not expressed in the language of science does not mean it lacks value.

True science needs to be smarter than this. It needs to be open-minded and employ a variety of methodologies, occasionally even choosing to embrace those that don't obey the dictates of reason. True science should be confident enough to not be afraid of appearing unscientific at times.

Beyond the Reason Versus Faith Dichotomy

Most people are addicted to binary oppositions: good or bad, black or white, masculine or feminine. Driven by this mentality, anyone who rejects faith as a mode of knowledge usually jumps on the reason bandwagon, and vice versa. Even though I take reason over faith any day, I don't like being confined to a single path. What I'm advocating here is an approach to life that transcends all dualisms.

Lao Tzu refers to the Tao, the essence of everything that exists, as a "cosmic mystery," and I couldn't agree more. Everywhere we turn, mystery surrounds us. For all our flaunted technological achievements, what we understand about the universe is still a drop in the ocean compared to what we don't understand. Our logic and our theoretical models only go so far. So it seems only natural, when faced with mysteries greater than us, that we should be open to any method that can potentially help us.

In ancient Greece, it was said that the Delphic oracle proclaimed Socrates the wisest of men. What made him so wise? Paradoxically, it was the fact that he didn't consider himself wise and was painfully aware of the limits of his knowledge. Lacking the arrogance of those who believe they know everything there's to know, Socrates had to remain constantly open-minded, ready to experiment with many different paths, and willing to question everything—including his own conclusions.

The Tao Te Ching is in perfect agreement with the Delphic oracle: "Who knows that he does not know is the highest."[283] Doubt, according to them, is the root of all curiosity, all inquiry; and for this reason it is a precious source of wisdom. Dogma works against this. Dogma fears that if it doesn't make bold assertions of having monopoly over the truth, it will appear weak and indecisive. This applies to irrational, faith-based claims to knowing God's will as well as the scientific refusal to even acknowledge anything that can't be proven through the limited confines of a particular methodology. But being so quick to dismiss possible alternatives is not a sign of strength. It is a symptom of insecurity and fear. The truly strong don't have to hide behind a façade of absolute certainty in their ideas, and so are able to stay flexible.

We need to combine the strengths of as many paths to wisdom as possible, without depending on any one of them exclusively. Too often we divide knowledge into tiny compartments, believing that the more we narrow our focus, the better results we'll achieve. In order to reach this goal, we end up devoting all our time and energy to perfecting one particular trade at the expense of all others. This is how the expert is born, and the complete human being dies.

Now, clearly a level of expertise is necessary in any activity. If I am to have heart surgery, I don't care whether my surgeon is also a good poet. As much as I appreciate multitalented people, I want my surgeon to be the most capable expert I can find. But at the same time, some of the greatest advances in any field are often made by outsiders able to look at issues from many different angles. Einstein did some of his best scientific work when he wasn't yet a professional scientist. Jimi Hendrix couldn't even read music since he had never formally studied it. This kind of genius had not been domesticated by too many rules. And this allowed these two men to experiment in daring ways—something that experts in any one field, being over-specialized, are usually unable to do.

The target of our quest is life, and nothing less. The point is not to dedicate our lives to one particular field of knowledge, but to utilize multiple fields to create better lives. One of the most important skills we can develop is the ability to draw connections between seemingly unrelated ideas, activities, and methodologies. Give me science *and* spirituality. I gladly enlist reason, but not without strong emotions. I want a vibrant mind along with a healthy, powerful body. The pinnacle of refinement needs to go hand in hand with sharp instincts and barbaric passion.

The reason I insist on taking the best from many different paths is because life itself doesn't speak a single language. Interconnectedness is the name of the game. Things are always much more intertwined than a simplistic, linear logic would have us think. Just look at nature and you'll see there are no sharp lines dividing it up into separate compartments. A linear logic, for example, would tell us that wolves have no impact on the fish population in a river. Wolves, after all, don't interact with fish. But they do hunt elk. Elk, in turn, eat shrubs and the bark of trees. In an ecosystem in which their jugulars are the constant targets of wolves, elk are not going to stop for a meal by a river crossing, where it is easier for wolves to attack. This means that the trees there will remain undisturbed, thereby reducing erosion, and helping to regulate the water temperature in ways that will favor fish reproduction and survival. But anyone looking at fish too narrowly would miss this chain of events, and fail to see the connections that are central to the fish's very existence.

This is why I don't reject anything if it holds even modest hopes of turning out useful. As Shakespeare put it, "There are more things in heaven and earth, Horatio, than are dreamt of in your philosophy."[284] In a similar vein, science tells us that we use only a tiny fraction of our brains. Who knows what possibilities are left to be explored? Intuition and dreams, for example, are typically not considered the most scientific approaches to problem solving, and yet in many cases they have helped where logic could not.

Despite my distrust for the fanaticism that often accompanies faith, prayer doesn't bother me a bit. Maybe there are gods or spirits who listen. Maybe there aren't, but prayer can affect reality anyway by helping someone focus their energy on a particular outcome. In the worst case, it serves as a placebo comforting the person praying and the one the prayer is for. None of these scenarios present a problem for me.

Ultimately, I'm not interested in anything but in what produces results. Even though I'm not a big fan of faith, if by any chance it can help somebody's life without causing harm to others, I have nothing against it.

I have no quarrel with whatever doesn't seek to restrict my range of choices. Actions mean much more to me than stated beliefs. As Thomas Paine wrote, "I believe that religious duties consist in doing justice, loving mercy, and endeavoring to make our fellow creatures happy."[285] And this is why I bow to any method, any idea, any philosophy, any religion that encourages human beings to be kinder to each other and to all other living things.

CHAPTER 14

ON A TIGHTROPE STRETCHED BETWEEN GOOD AND EVIL: MORALITY WITHOUT FASCISM; MORE HEART AND FEWER LAWS

No Relativism, But No Dogmatic Absolutes Either

Good and Evil are the lead stars in religion's drama. Scriptures obsess about them as much as tabloids obsess about Hollywood celebrities. Ignoring them is simply not an option. Their central importance forces every living human being to pay them proper consideration.

Every religion, without exception, has to tackle good and evil. This is no idle philosophical game—mind you. How we end up defining them determines the range of what we view as acceptable choices. Ultimately, it determines how we intend to live. What a given religion decides to call good or evil will encourage or prohibit certain activities accordingly. Providing guidelines—and in some cases strict rules—for how people should behave is one of the central functions of most religions.

But this is where the similarities end, for different religions offer radically different answers about the nature of good and evil as well as about the specific steps human beings should take, from the moral absolutes, literally written in stone, of the Ten Commandments to the Taoist libertarianism best expressed in the maxim "The more prohibitions there are, the poorer the people become."[286] With so many options at our disposal, it is wise—before coming up with our own answers—to examine what pushes different traditions toward certain conclusions.

On one end of the spectrum we have the idea of a divinely ordained morality. This concept is the bedrock of Western religions and is present in branches of other world religions as well. These traditions assume that God is the ultimate arbiter of good and evil. In his infinite wisdom, he creates rules of behavior that human beings should follow. According to this view, ethics and morality are rooted in how closely we adhere to God's laws. Followers of this theology are more likely to be suspicious of separation between church and state because man-made laws should not allow what God prohibits, or vice versa. The freedom to live one's own life the way they see fit should not extend to what God deems evil.

The obvious problem with this very popular idea rests on a basic question: how does anyone know what God wants us to do? How do we know what God considers good or evil? Clearly, something must be getting lost in translation since various people, equally committed to obeying God's dictates, hear very different messages. So either God is a trickster who loves messing with people, or somebody is getting it wrong. When separate religions give you very different rules to live by, and they all claim the rules come straight from God, who should you listen to? George W. Bush and Osama bin Laden both claim to be doing God's will and fighting against evil. How do we know which one (if either) is right?

All these major disagreements seem to indicate that good and evil are not self-evident, purely objective categories. Distinguishing between man-made laws and God's laws is a bad joke because without a shred of objective evidence no one can realistically claim that any set of rules enjoys God's stamp of approval.

Even though it defies logic, the enduring appeal of a divinely revealed morality is easy to understand. Wouldn't it be nice—as the Beach Boys ask—if we knew precisely what is good and what is evil, and we could behave accordingly embracing the former and avoiding the latter? Wouldn't life be easier if we only knew exactly what a benevolent God wants us to do? Things would be simple and straightforward, then. No nagging moral ambiguities. No struggling with complicated choices. Just execute God's game plan, and that's it. No wonder most human beings badly want to believe. Otherwise, the burden to make difficult decisions and live with the consequences would fall entirely on their shoulders.

Unfortunately, since no one has the number to God's private line, life is not so simple. As Jared Diamond writes, "History, as well as life itself, is complicated; neither life nor history is an enterprise for those who seek simplicity and consistency."[287]

Drawing a sharp line between good and evil, we end up painting the whole world black and white, without leaving any room for greater complexity. "The enemy of my enemy is my friend" is the logical, albeit suicidal, political consequence of this dualistic mentality. The support given by the US government to Islamic fundamentalists in Afghanistan during the 1980s is a perfect example of the failure of this idea. We are in the middle of the Cold War, the US government reasoned, so anyone fighting against those Communist Russian bastards is our ally. The Soviet Union invaded Afghanistan? Let's not waste time, then, and send plenty of weapons and military training to anyone willing to fight them—including the most extremist Islamic fanatics.

Sounds reasonable, right? Too bad this seemingly coherent rationale leads the US government to offering a terrorist finishing school for Osama bin Laden and friends—the very same people who just a few years later will kill more Americans than the Soviet Union was ever able to do. This is precisely the kind of thing that can be expected when we want to oversimplify reality into a game of good guys versus bad guys.

Wanting to divide all phenomena between these two opposite categories is a violation of the complexity of existence. Even the scriptures of religions declaiming an uncompromising good versus evil rhetoric indicate that the demand for moral absolutes is more bark than bite. In the Bible, sometimes God comes across as a moral relativist since one moment he proclaims the sanctity of human life and categorically prohibits murder, and the next he either praises murdering entire populations (the native inhabitants of Canaan, for example), or takes matters in his own hands (such as when he kills all of the first-born children among the Egyptians—an event still gleefully celebrated in the religious holiday of Passover). It seems like killing can either be a horrible sin or an honorable activity, depending entirely on the context. This is hardly an example of moral absolutism. Similarly, plenty of Old Testament laws requiring grievous punishments for violators are amended or altogether eliminated by God at a later date.[288] These instances of moral relativism raise the obvious questions: Did God change his mind? How can something be evil one day but acceptable the next? If we are going to allow for so many exceptions, why have absolute laws written in stone to begin with?

Despite these flagrant violations, some religions still find it appealing to praise (at least in theory) moral absolutism. The reason for this is simple: they believe any moral flexibility will be abused by human beings out to find justifications for their selfishness. Giving people some leeway, they fear, will open the door to chaos and immorality. Even though this worry is very legitimate, the heavy dose of rigid, moral laws they prescribe as a cure does nothing to solve the problem.

Unfortunately, dogmatic, unchanging rules are drunken elephants in the house of crystal that is life. Rules without exceptions do more damage than good, for they don't possess the necessary delicate touch to be able to adjust the game plan to the present. By inviting us to follow the same recipe in all contexts at all times, they force us to apply a static model to a dynamic situation. But everything in life is in flux, as Heraclitus famously indicated. Very few things always hold true regardless of the specific context. Change and movement never fail to keep the world spinning. So, trusting an unchanging strategy to work in a reality that is always changing is plain delusional.

Paradoxically, the essence of morality seems to be found in timing. Nothing good comes from following the right rule at the wrong time. Telling the truth is a great policy, but not always. If during World War II, a person hiding Jewish refugees was asked by an SS soldier whether he had seen any Jews, answering truthfully wouldn't be virtuous—just stupid. Similarly, in a more ordinary context, it wouldn't be wise to offer a brutal truth to someone who is not ready to handle it. The only result of not telling a white lie would be to needlessly hurt them. The rule against killing people is obviously legitimate. But breaking it is the only morally good choice when it's done in order to stop someone from inflicting horrendous cruelties against the innocent and the defenseless.

More Heart, Less Laws

What I'm endorsing here is not some wishy-washy form of moral relativism. The moral relativists who tell us that good and evil are only a matter of opinion must live in a much nicer world than the one I wake up in everyday. Evil has stared into my eyes too many times for me to pretend it's not there. When you see it, you can't mistake it for the simple carelessness and stupidity that are at the roots of many horrible, evil actions. Straight up, old-fashioned evil is something else.

Out of many encounters with evil, one instance stands out for me. When you hang out in the visiting room of San Quentin's death row, you expect to run into a few unsavory characters. These were the good old days when the inmates there still visited in a large communal room rather than behind a glass, so I was smack in the middle of a couple dozen convicted killers awaiting lethal injection. Some seemed to be polite, warm, caring. (Yeah . . . I know . . . not exactly what you would expect.) Others struck me as selfish little bastards who wouldn't think twice about putting a bullet in your head if you stood in their way. No big deal, though. Nothing I hadn't seen before. One guy, however, was in a whole different category. When he fixed his gaze on me, I literally felt chills running down my spine. This was no trigger-happy robber killing people for money, or some random, violent guy getting carried away in the heat of the moment. The man was pure evil—no doubt about it. His eyes were of someone whose favorite hobby was torturing people. Drawing blood, inflicting pain, and rejoicing in the screams of his victims were the guy's idea of a good time. When I asked who he was, I was told he was none other than Richard Ramirez, a.k.a. The Night Stalker, one of California's most infamous serial killers. If you haven't run into someone like him, take my word for it, if you did, you wouldn't think there's anything relativistic about evil.

Evil is much more real and concrete than what moral relativists claim, but so is good. To act as a counterbalance to people like Richard Ramirez are many individuals in my life whose hearts overflow with kindness, empathy, and a love that keeps giving until it hurts and beyond—nothing relativistic about these qualities either.

Similarly, just like people, certain actions contain no shades of gray, and their moral standing doesn't change depending on the context. Unlike the delicate souls who believe in rehabilitating rapists, my moral flexibility doesn't stretch that far. Whereas even killing could be justified, there is never such a thing as self-defense rape. Rape is indefensible no matter what the surrounding circumstances are. No possible scenario exists under which it could ever be considered a good thing. Any intentional act of cruelty toward a sentient being is evil—period. I make no exceptions about this.

But this doesn't mean all of life, or even the majority of it, is so clear-cut. Most people and most actions are not so one-sided. Even though it may sound like a hyperbolic paradox, I firmly believe reality is made with more exceptions than rules. Too often, we are blackmailed into thinking that if we reject dogmatic absolutism, then we should promote absolute relativism, and the notion that there is no such a thing as "good" or "evil." The first approach is the cousin of Fascism, while the latter is a symptom of the spinelessness (did I make up this word or does it really exist?) of postmodernism. Neither one offers us a healthy solution; so let's explore some alternatives.

No rigid moral laws can ever replace the one thing we need most: the awareness and the talent to choose wisely case by case. The greatest balance is not to be found in the adherence to a static rule, but in the dynamic ability to read the present situation and be able to make the right call. In violation of Mosaic laws, Jesus went toe to toe with the political and religious traditions of his times by healing the sick during the Sabbath and preventing a mob from legally executing a woman for adultery. Through these radical actions (which were punishable by death), "outlaw" Jesus demonstrated real morality is greater than any legislation, and true virtue is not afraid to break "virtuous" dogmas. The goody-goody morality of those who would never dream of departing from the rules is a very distant second best to the ability to think and act on one's feet. Laws and theoretical models, in fact, should be treated as little more than guidelines in an ever-changing universe. Guidelines help us navigate through life, but fixed precepts are for people too stupid to live without them. As Thoreau writes, "I do not mean to prescribe rules to strong and valiant natures, who will mind their own affairs . . ."[289]

This is, clearly, easier said than done. Living unbound by rigid rules without inventing justifications for all kinds of self-serving behaviors requires tremendous skill, self-awareness, and sensitivity. As Bob Dylan sang in his song "Absolutely Sweet Marie," "To live outside the law, you must be honest." Only a crystal clear consciousness will not abuse this freedom.

But for someone who does indeed possess equal measures of integrity and intelligence, a blind obedience to the laws is a cage. Forcing them to stick to a pre-set ideology inevitably means restricting their ability to make choices moment by moment. When someone hits you, sometimes it is wise to turn the other cheek. Other times, it's better to knock their head into tomorrow. There's nothing wrong with keeping our options open.

One of the tasks of a vital religion consists in instilling good judgment and self-confidence. It's about helping us develop the tools to forge a powerful, yet flexible character. Shoving down our throats a myriad of specific rules is a poor substitute for creating a balanced personality. Rules and absolute laws are necessary only for people whose internal guidance system is broken, and who would be lost without dogmas to lean on. But as Thoreau again warns us, "No method nor discipline can supersede the necessity of being forever on the alert."[290] At best, absolute laws can only limit the damage certain individuals can be capable of—nothing more. But real character is greater than this petty morality. Expecting talented individuals to always bow to the rules is like telling great explorers they should always remain on the beaten trail, or telling master chefs they should always stick to a recipe.

From Confucianism to Islam, the majority of organized religions would recoil in horror at this idea. Without absolute laws, they believe there can be no morality. For them, suggesting that human beings should follow their internal sensibility rather than rules is blasphemy. Taoism, on the other hand, is one of the very few traditions believing no number of rules can fix the lack of good instincts. As the Tao Te Ching tells, "The mighty Way declined among the folk and then came kindness and morality."[291] In other words, the external trappings of outer morality are for those who lack inner morality. Just as Jesus repeatedly broke the traditional codes of accepted behavior of his times in the name of this deeper, inner call, Taoism tells us we need more heart and fewer laws.

Some People Need Rules

That's nice and all, Bolelli, but what about the millions of people who don't have what it takes to regularly make good choices? Would you have child molesters follow their instincts over laws? Should we leave fairness up to the goodness of the hearts of people obsessed with greed?

The quick answer is: no. Even Taoism doesn't preach the elimination of all rules for everybody. What separates Taoism from most branches of Confucianism, Christianity, Islam, Judaism, and all other religions emphasizing absolute laws of behavior is the fact that Taoism is speaking to a different audience. Taoists downplay the importance of rigid codes because they focus only on individuals of superior heart, mind, and talent. Since it plays with a very refined, aware audience, philosophical Taoism (which is different from the more mainstream, popular version of religious Taoism) can afford the luxury to invite them to take a step forward, and move beyond an obsessive attachment to the letter of the law. This is why Taoism dismisses Confucian doctrines, with their insistence on etiquette and rules of conduct, as a crash course in morality for idiots.

But even if they are right, so what? There are plenty of people in the world who are too weak to handle life without the crutch of absolute laws. Just telling them they should be smarter is not going to raise their IQ. They don't know how to choose wisely, or when to stop. Unable to find a healthy balance, they badly need guidelines and directives spelling for them how to behave.

Taoism is the first to recognize this, and makes no mystery that its message is not for everybody. "If you don't have what it takes," Taoism seems to say, "don't even bother playing with us. You would only get confused and hurt yourself. It's better for you to follow Confucianism. There, they'll give you a simple system of ethics to guide you and prevent you from screwing up your life too badly." If this sounds more than a little elitist, it's because it is. But so is life. Talent is not a democratic virtue. Taoism has no patience for the fairy tale telling us everybody is the same. Too much evidence indicates otherwise. Recognizing this fact prompted William Blake to write, "One law for the lion and ox is oppression"—a very Taoist sentiment indeed.[292]

Unlike Taoism, most religions take upon themselves the responsibility for directing people who are selfish, shortsighted, and only too happy to hurt someone else to gratify their own desires. In an effort to set some boundaries for them, these traditions impose tough laws and try to instill a fear of supernatural punishments (hell or karma) as an incentive to comply. There's nothing wrong with this mission: most people simply need these rules. The only problem with this is assuming that *all* people need them. Many individuals, being insensitive to anything but selfish considerations, can't fathom behaving ethically without some hope for reward or fear of punishment; but decent human beings can. Offering a safety net to those likely to fall is a key task for any healthy religion, but even more important is teaching people to refine their instincts and giving them the tools to trust themselves.

Morality Without Fascism

The game is a tricky one—no doubt about it. Our dance with good and evil takes place on a rope stretched across the abyss. Tilt too much one way, and we fall on the side of a self-righteous fascism willing to trample freedom in order to impose its ideas on everyone. A step too far in the opposite direction, and we end up lost in a jungle of relativism and weak values. It truly takes good feet to maintain the delicate balance of this dance.

When it comes to morality, the safest, most basic step is to guarantee people the full freedom to make their own choices *as long as* they don't infringe on someone else's freedom. The desire to promote any other value should never violate this essential premise. There's absolutely nothing wrong in wanting to share cherished ideas with others. If we feel they can help multitudes of people, it only makes sense to want to spread our ideological treasures. But too often many religions can't accept the fact that some people may want to live by different values. As the Tao Te Ching indicates, the spirit of moral crusaders offers their medicine to others but "when no one responds to it, then it angrily rolls up its sleeves and forces people to comply."[293] Like psychotic spurned lovers who can't take no for an answer, they fall for the temptation to impose their own ideas by force. Rather than trusting the power of their message to conquer people by fascinating them, they take the shortcut of wanting to dictate it by law. This denotes a deep lack of confidence in the beauty of their ideas, for if they were more secure, they would trust persuasion without ever feeling the need to resort to coercion.

Many religions portray God as the guardian of morality. Breaking social rules undetected is not too hard, so some religions like to emphasize how no one can escape the never-distracted eyes of God, who acts simultaneously as the super-cop of the sky, as well as judge and jury. Accordingly, heaven and hell are seen as essential tools to coax people into behaving decently. Morality through fear is the name of the game. But even though it may occasionally act as an effective deterrent, fear doesn't work nearly as well as its supporters claim.

Too often, a stern, fear-based morality is a tough façade hiding a tremendous hypocrisy. The number of very religious people who, on a regular basis, preach one thing and do another never fails to surprise me. A strong belief in heaven and hell is obviously not enough of an incentive to actually practice the same morality they preach. When they are exposed, the list of excuses is always the same . . .

"The devil made me do it; I'm a sinner, but Jesus will forgive me." Borrowing a page from Martin Luther, rather than taking responsibility, they never stop whining about the sinfulness of the human condition and the weakness of the flesh. Somehow, however, they usually emphasize how through faith they'll be forgiven for their shortcomings.

This sorry spectacle irks me to no end (in case you don't have a dictionary handy, "irks me" is a fancy way of saying it pisses me off). Rather than wasting so many words condemning "immorality," just save your energy to grow a damned spine, and be able to walk your talk. People so ready to make excuses for their actions shouldn't be so aggressive about wanting to enforce a code of ethics they are too weak to follow. Clearly, strict rules of behavior and the fear of supernatural punishments don't have such a good record when it comes to spreading high standards of morality.

A recent study analyzing the correlation between adherence to organized religions and the rate of social dysfunctions underscores this irony very well. Contrary to popular expectations, the places with the highest participation in organized religion are also the leaders in the rates of murder, abortion, divorce, teen pregnancy, sexually transmitted diseases, etc.—something that holds true both worldwide and within the United States. This doesn't necessarily mean organized religion causes a spike in the very illnesses it attacks, but it does mean that *(a)* it is not particularly effective at stopping them, and *(b)* the lack of a belief in supernatural rewards and punishments (i.e., heaven and hell or karma) doesn't drive people toward moral anarchy.[294]

A fear-based morality is like hoping to prevent a flood by sticking a finger in the crack of a dam. OK, maybe it's slightly more effective—superglue on the cracks rather than a finger. But like any strategy that's only aimed at containing massive damage, it's not going to work by itself. Religions and ethical philosophies shouldn't be satisfied with such an elementary approach.

Fear, guilt, shame, the threat of punishment, and the lure of rewards do absolutely nothing to spur me toward moral behavior. Maybe they work for some people, but definitely not for me. If anything, I take these tactics as a challenge. Feeling that I'm being tricked into being "good," my first instinct is to rebel against these manipulative efforts to direct my choices. I agree 100 percent with Albert Einstein when he writes, "I am convinced that a vivid consciousness of the primary importance of moral principles for the betterment and ennoblement of life does not need the idea of a law-giver, especially a law-giver who works on the basis of reward and punishment."[295]

Luckily, my parents felt the same way. They never yelled at me, prodding me to take certain actions, or prohibited me from taking others. They taught me good judgment by example, and left the rest up to me. Knowing I had their full trust did more to shape my sense of morality than a million lectures on proper behavior. Being entrusted with the freedom to make my own choices injected me with a dose of self-confidence and implicitly gave me the message there was nothing wrong with my instincts. I was no evil sinner whose innate essence was fundamentally flawed and in need of redemption. I didn't need to be ashamed of who I was. Through the occasional, gentle advice I was encouraged to hone and refine my natural instincts, but never to repress them. Even when I made poor choices, I was pushed to see them as learning experiences—not as reasons to start second-guessing myself. Just learn from your mistakes and move on.

This feeling of not having anything to hide gave me a sense of great freedom, and yet paradoxically also instilled in me a great sense of responsibility. Precisely because I haven't been burdened with millions of rules, I am dead serious about always living in a way as to be deserving of so much trust.

Just to set the record straight, I'll freely admit that, in more ways than one, my morality is extremely flexible. Many of my choices fly in the face of most rules cherished by moral crusaders. I routinely break laws—both religious and secular alike—for I only obey the laws I agree with. Robin Hood always seemed much cooler to me than the Sheriff of Nottingham. My ethics are flexible, sure, but in some ways I'm far more demanding of myself than even the most severe fans of moral absolutism. Those who peddle a strict, inflexible morality often appear to me too ready to make excuses for whenever their actions fall short of their ideals. Their bark is loud, but their bite is soft. Their loud speech is a cover for their inability to live up to their values. By contrast, I don't blab so much about morality, I violate traditional moral codes every other step I take, and yet I never, ever violate my own ethical code—whether I can get away with it or not.

Every second of my existence, I make it a point not to cause unnecessary pain to any living being, and I'm almost paranoid about not wanting to inconvenience people around me. Unlike the staunch defenders of monogamy, I don't see it as something particularly desirable, but if I decide to be in a monogamous relationship, there's not a chance in hell I'll break my word. Betraying somebody's trust in me is simply not an option. My word is sacred, and I don't break it for anything or anybody—ever. What motivates me is not the fear of punishment and the hope for rewards in this life, or another. It's simply that this is how I want to live. If people who love me couldn't trust me, if I couldn't trust myself, nothing else would matter.

In my religion, morality is both super-flexible and super-strict. The goal is not simply to keep a sad, shallow humanity from doing too much damage, but to shape a better humanity altogether. What I am interested in is forging human beings who don't need laws to remind them how to act.

CHAPTER 15

TOWARD A PARADOX-FLAVORED CONSCIOUSNESS

Only the obtuse are unappreciative of paradox.
—Tom Robbins, *Fierce Invalids Home from Hot Climates*

At the Root of It All

This work is haunted—no doubt about it. An invisible presence keeps poking its head in every chapter, but every time you turn to catch it, it's already gone. You are not imagining things. It's true. A little, literary ninja has been stalking the pages of this book. For too long now, it has been toying with us as it hides between the words. But don't worry. The little bastard hasn't been as careful as it should have been. I woke up before dawn to follow the tracks it left behind, and laid in wait. It was only a matter of time until it fell into my trap. I've got a hold of it now, and I'm not letting go. No more hide-and-seek games. It's time to bring our elusive guest forward—into the spotlight.

If there is a single, recurring theme that shows up in every section of this book, it's paradox. Over and over, regardless of which topic we are playing with, we end up bringing together ideas and values that most people keep separate. And mixing together the most unlikely ingredients in such a way as to make conventional wisdom blush is precisely the game paradox loves best.

I swear I'm not doing this just for the sake of being the proverbial pain in the equally proverbial ass, or because I like flirting with apparent contradictions. Paradox only seems contradictory in the eyes of people who worship a narrow-minded logic, and divide existence into tiny compartments. But the essence of life itself defies rigid schemes, and prefers dwelling in the harmonious play of opposite qualities. As Tom Robbins tells it, "Reality *is* contradictory. And it's paradoxical. If . . . there's any one word—if you had to pick one word to describe the nature of the universe . . . I think that word would be paradox. That's true at the subatomic level, right through sociological, psychological, philosophical levels on up to cosmic levels."[296]

Being kissed by a paradox-flavored consciousness, however, is not for everybody. More than 2,000 years ago, a master of paradox named Lao Tzu wrote, "My teachings are very easy to understand and very easy to practice, but no one can understand them and no one can practice them."[297] In a similar spirit, the Friedrich Nietzsche masterpiece *Thus Spoke Zarathustra* is subtitled "A Book for All and None." What these sly old foxes were trying to tell us, in their typical tongue-in-cheek style, is that the deepest secrets of life are theoretically accessible to everyone, but most people will never be able to grasp them since they are hopelessly addicted to a dualistic mentality. And this leaves them ill equipped to be able to embrace the paradoxical nature of the universe.

Being too afraid of ambiguity and disorder, and too confused by a messy, constantly changing reality, the majority of human beings find solace in breaking things down into neatly divided, easily understood categories: God or the Devil, reason or faith, earthly or heavenly, feminine or masculine, good or evil, physical or spiritual, mind or matter, natural or man-made. These binary opposites comfort them and help them make order out of chaos. They simplify existence and make it predictable. Too bad the result is not simple as much as simplistic. The natural order of things is infinitely more intricate, more dynamic, and more alive than some people would like to think. It can't be made to fit into a black-and-white theoretical model.

As Gregory Bateson indicated, the combination of powerful technologies and the dependence on a dualistic worldview is a recipe for disaster.[298] The inflexible lines we draw between binary opposites reinforce a way of thinking built on separation. Trusting the reassuring lies of dualism, we end up truly believing our souls to be at war with our bodies, or strength to be incompatible with flexibility and tenderness. Worse yet, we forget how everything is interconnected; and this illusion to exist apart from nature leads to the destruction of the very things that make life possible. From quantum physics to ecology, modern sciences are showing us with increasing clarity how dangerously misguided the illusion of separation is. Many of the problems we face today find their roots here.

Paradox, then, is not just a rebellious act of provocation, or a middle finger raised toward common sense. Rather, our little ninja is the philosophical stance most in tune with the process of life itself. It moves to the beat of the universe. It's the key to the deepest and most advanced form of consciousness. Paradox is the perfect antidote against the artificial, "common sense" categories of a world where everything is segregated. This is why I wield paradox as a weapon, administer it as medicine, and place it at the center of my own religion. It is a way to free us from the shackles of dualism and awaken us to more enlightened modes of perception.

Yin and Yang Go on a Date

No symbol captures the spirit of paradox as well as the Taoist Yin-Yang. Every time I look at it, I gain new insight into how this seemingly silly circle applies to everything that exists, and I never fail to be amazed by the genius of the Chinese man or woman—whose name is now lost in history—who first came up with it.

At first, the stark contrast between the black and white halves of the circle may make us think we are staring at a dualistic image. Like many other religions and philosophies, it seems to divide the world in warring camps between cosmically opposing forces: mutually incompatible energies fighting for supremacy. This would actually be true if the circle were divided by a straight line, forcing Yin and Yang to stare at each other across a symbolic Berlin Wall. But rather than standing on opposite sides of a battle line, Yin and Yang get to make out thanks to the soft, sensual curve marking their very flexible borders. By substituting the straight line with a curve, Yin and Yang see encounters and possibilities where others see potential conflict—interconnectedness rather than separation. To further underscore this idea, a dot of white plays in the black field, and a dot of black enjoys similar hospitality in the white field.

The Union of the Opposites

Life, Yin and Yang are trying to tell us, is just a lot more fun when we give opposite energies a chance to dance together. This may sound scandalous and counterintuitive to a rigid, linear logic, but paradox is not so stiff. "Do you want this *or* that?" linear logic asks us, trying to blackmail us into picking between mutually exclusive choices. "Both," answers paradox. "The answer is always both."

The either/or approach restricts our options and forces us to stick to a fixed formula. The both approach reveals that so-called mutually exclusive choices are not so exclusive after all, but rather they complement each other. As my father writes, once we substitute "or" with "and" our mental horizons will widen, and nothing will ever be the same.[299] Anytime we are asked to choose between a healthy body or a healthy mind, creativity or logic, laughter or single-minded seriousness, happiness or success, the ability to see the big picture or specialized knowledge, our answer should always be "both." The only thing we gain by picking one at the expense of the other is turning into a stereotype. This is what gives birth to the suicidal dichotomies we witness everyday: the trashy, spectacular pop vulgarity of reality shows pit against the gray, boring stuff that makes up "high" intellectual culture; spineless liberals against fascist conservatives; the paralyzing futility of relativism against the freedom-squashing power of dogma; Britney Spears against the Pope. Always two sides of the same sad coin.

The original meaning of the Sanskrit term "yoga" is "to join together," and this is exactly what paradox invites us to do. The door to a richer, brighter world is opened by a talent for uniting what most people keep divided. Every page of this book is an arrow aimed at this target. The human being my religion wishes to cultivate is physical, spiritual, and intellectual at the same time. A child born from the union of heaven and earth, he or she is optimistic and realistic, visionary and pragmatic, scientific and mystical, sweet and tough. Imperturbable calmness goes hand in hand with adrenaline, delicate sensitivity with an iron will. Speaking of this human being,

Nietzsche wrote, "in him [or her] all opposites are fused together into a new unity." [300] And then again, "Sharp and mild, rough and fine, strange and familiar, impure and clean, a place where fool and sage convene: all this I am and wish to mean."[301]

Once we finally kick the addiction to a worldview built on binary opposites, we are free to forge a richer, more complete personality. A healthy religion should constantly encourage us to develop the ability to embody talents that seemingly don't go together.

This is what I try to do in my own life. By nature, I'm extremely sensitive, nonconfrontational, relaxed, and somewhat nerdy. So when I first picked up martial arts, I was immediately attracted to styles emphasizing these qualities, such as Tai Chi or Aikido. But I quickly realized that dedicating myself to these arts would be overkill. They would only help me become more of what I already was. Training felt comfortable and familiar but didn't really push me to grow beyond my natural boundaries. What I needed was to add an edge to my personality. What I needed was to put it all on the line confronting fear and danger. What I needed was assertiveness and toughness. My Yin nature needed to be enriched with a Yang practice: less aesthetic beauty and philosophy, and more muscle and sweat. Accordingly, I traded gentle, soft, internal arts for the hyperaggressive, competitive, testosterone-laden world of combat sports—anything from boxing to wrestling, from submission grappling to mixed martial arts. All-out combat became my spiritual practice. Had I possessed these qualities to begin with, I would have followed the opposite path, and balanced natural toughness with styles teaching me to be flexible and yielding. No two people should follow the exact same formula. The only rule is to find whichever path can make *you* more complete and well-rounded.

The Problem with Sweet, Spiritual People

Fairly often, I run into people I should theoretically feel a bond with—people who seem to share many of my ideas. Instead, my first instinct is to take off in the opposite direction, to run for my life. My reaction usually strikes me as being horribly unfair. After all, these are people who strive to be kind to others rather than kill them over ideological differences. They try to develop a healthy relationship with their bodies rather than eating crap all day long. They protect nature rather than destroying it. And for the most part, they wouldn't dream of restricting my freedom of choice. So, why do they bug me so much then? I'm afraid my taste for paradox is to blame.

Too often, plenty of people try far too hard to live up to an idealized image of what being "spiritual" is supposed to be about. When I listen to them speak, even when I agree with the content, I still smell too much effort in their words. Their actions and demeanor always strike me as a bit contrived. Rather than being something that they learned naturally along with how to wipe their ass and play in the mud, spirituality to them is a mystical discovery, a special, sacred state of consciousness entirely distinguished from everyday life. But as Gary Snyder says, "I don't know that I like the idea of distinguishing between the sacred and the non-sacred."[302]

Actually, now that I think about it, Gary Snyder is too polite. Unlike his somewhat tentative answer, I am totally and completely turned off by the division between sacred and mundane. It seems unnatural and perverse. Real spirituality is not some esoteric state, high up in the clouds, removed from worldly concerns. Real spirituality is found in how you get up in the morning, how you walk, talk, breathe, smile, fight, and burp. Real spirituality doesn't require a special sacred lingo, and it most certainly doesn't need all this self-importance. The real thing doesn't even bother considering itself "spiritual." "Spiritual . . . as opposed to what?" it asks innocently. Paradox frowns on separating spirituality from every other aspect of life.

This division opens the door to a whole set of other problems. By cultivating soft, yielding, flexible, nurturing qualities while neglecting to feed fighting spirit, fearlessness, and an indomitable will, most of these people usually end up being too one-sided. Their energy is all Yin and no Yang. They are typically nice, gentle, good-natured individuals, and even though this is highly preferable to mean, rude, obnoxious jerks, it still lacks something. No fire burns in their eyes. Not enough intensity shaking them to the core. No overwhelming passion threatening to tear them apart if it doesn't find an outlet. This is why many women find bad boys more attractive than sweet, mellow ones. It's as if their peaceful disposition came at the price of losing strength and power. Their emotions are too tame for my taste—too domesticated. I simply can't quite relate to people who have never felt the need to drive their fist through a glass door (yeah, about that . . . I'm still sorry about your door, mom . . .). I would appreciate them a whole lot more if a raw, barbaric streak rounded out their spirituality. The day these delicate souls are able to talk about "positive energy" while singing an Eminem song is when I'll gain a new level of respect for them.

And so here we are, stuck with the inevitable dichotomy that's bound to happen wherever paradox is not welcome. Some of the nicest and most sensitive people around are too soft to manage our collective reality, too lost in their own inner world to have any meaningful impact, whereas typically the most effective and driven have the discipline and the lucidity to get things done, but little empathy or vision. What we need instead is a paradoxical recipe mixing heart and muscle, sweetness and toughness, flexibility and strong values. Paradox is the magic potion necessary to heal ourselves and the world around us.

Complete, Not Perfect

As an added bonus to its many practical advantages, paradox rescues us from a lifetime of staleness and dullness. Even the greatest qualities, in fact, become painfully boring if they are not spiced up with a touch of unpredictability. As much good press as it gets, perfection makes us yawn. You always know what to expect from it. No surprises, no mystery, no excitement. Paradox, on the other hand, keeps stirring the pot. No one can guess what it will come up with. Like Shiva, it has many arms so as to be able to touch all aspects of life. It is not perfect, but it's complete. It is not consistent, but it's whole. It is not the best in a single field of knowledge, but it can play in all fields. Drawing from the totality of experience, it balances within the same individual radically different qualities.

This balance I speak of is not some middle-of-the-road, moderate compromise between opposites. Too often, moderation turns out to be a fancy name for mediocrity. No, what we are talking about here is the ability to experience both extremes (and everything in between) without ever losing our balance. Have you ever watched a surfer riding the waves or an acrobat walking on a tightrope? If they always tried to stay in the middle, they would inevitably fall. Real balance is more dynamic than that. Surfers and acrobats are constantly off balance, in one direction or another, but they always know how to adjust with a move in the opposite direction. Knowing the exact moment to make the adjustment is what separates a great surfer from someone who will scrape the bottom of the ocean and turn into food for the fish.

This ability to read the present situation and adapt accordingly is what can allow us to flow through the complexities of life without ever falling prey to dogma. Dogma, in fact, thrives on a rigid, inflexible commitment to a fixed formula. Fear of losing perspective and being unprepared when Destiny throws us a curveball makes the apparent solidity of dogma appealing. Paradox, instead, gives us no such reassurance, for it knows that no unchanging rule can prepare us to face a world that's constantly changing. But it does offer us the confidence to know that no matter how the universe will push us around, we can use the vast range of choices at our disposal to find a way to keep riding the wave. Whereas dogma can only be rigid, paradox is so flexible that it can even afford to be rigid at times, but only when the present situation calls for it. With no allegiance to any doctrine or method, paradox is free to tackle reality as it sees fit.

So let's be brave and give it a try. Our new, global world deserves the creation of improbable, multifaceted personalities who can handle a future where interconnectedness will be the name of the game. Many challenges lie ahead. And if we are to avoid self-destruction, it's time to plant the seeds of worldviews richer and weirder than anyone ever imagined; it's time to start celebrating paradoxical marriages of opposites. What we need from the religions of the future is the ability to unite what so far has been kept separate.

Ah . . . the hour is late and it's time for me to finally shut up. My typing fingers are tired, and the smell of pasta sauce heating on the stove is drawing my stomach away from this page. I can tell you this: creating your own religion can sure make you hungry.

But before I dive headfirst into the biggest plate of spaghetti ever cooked, I have one last thing to say. As much as I stand behind every syllable I have written, my goal here is not to sell you a set of ideas. If you can gain anything useful from these pages, great: my job is done and I can go on to enjoy my well-deserved pasta. If not, I don't take it personally. Whether you agree with me or not is not the point. The only truly important thing is that—either here or elsewhere—you find the answers you need to bring greater happiness to your life and to everyone around you. Finding ways to multiply joy is what it's all about. So if you don't like these answers (and perhaps even if you do), just go ahead and create your own.

ACKNOWLEDGMENTS

To Isabella Han Bolelli:

You're my three-year-old hero. You're the reason why I smiled my way through hell. I can't possibly love anyone more than I love you—even though you made me listen to Bob Marley's "Buffalo Soldier" more times than should be legally allowed.

To Gloria and Franco:

Since my very first day on this planet . . . my best allies, accomplices, and friends.

To Pete McCormack, Matt Staggs, Chris Stiles, Liezel Legaspi, Jeff Hendricks, Thaddeus Russell, and Mike Vallely:

A universe that has allowed me to cross paths with you can't be all bad. Thank you for being my friends.

To Savannah Em:

I never wanted another relationship again. I had already tasted more love, more intensity, more passion than any mortal could hope to experience. It was clear to me there was no way I'd run into someone able to match that. That door had closed for me. I had made my peace with it. And then I met you . . . and you kicked the door down. When your lips are pressed to mine, all evil in the world disappears.

To Zina Bolelli:

Ti amo—e non solo per avermi cucinato i cibi piu' buoni che abbia mai mangiato.

To Duncan Trussell and Joe Rogan:

There aren't enough words to thank you. You have helped me more than you know. If you need help burying a body, I'm your man.

To the memory of Marina Mattioni, Stelio Bolelli, Liliana Germani, Sidney Keith, Shannon Richardson, and Ray Allen.

And, of course, to Elizabeth Han:

I miss you, sweetie . . . so fuckin' much.

I love you—now and forever.

Thank you to my partners in crime: Marlon Mercado; Tatianna Em; Cody and Monique; Chris and Tania Reid; Manuela Mantegazza; Ben Harper; Shannon Lee; José Camacho; Junella Chin; Federico Giordano; Julio Perez; Rick Tucci; Gary Baddeley; Jan Johnson; Giancarlo Serafino; Tom and Alexa Robbins; Amy and Wes Tang; Rich Evirs; Evan Culver; Ale Rossi; Rocco Attisani; Anthony Formoso; Roberto Bonomelli and Lory; Roberto Banchini and his tribe; James Weddell; Viva Guerrero; Emilie Nguyen; Heming Gu;

Genevieve Dezso; John Evans; Will Ford; Jane Dabel; Brenda De River; Adonis Puentes; Alex Rueda; Lynn Cavallaro; Shawn Brennan; Maria Ramas; Bruno Dorella; Aronne dell'Oro; Michele Dalai; John Torres; Li Schroeder; Lorenzo Cherubini; Tatiana Molinar; Jason Yaselli; Joseph and Elizabeth Morales; Joey Calmer; Luciano Palermi; Rachael Pugh; Melinda Martinez and Jorge Ojeda; Kriszanne Napalan; Scott Czerniak; Giorgio Presca; Shannon Seta; Cavan Cox; Daniel Guedea; Jack Clark; Jack Carter; Litty Mathew and Melkon Khosrovian; Emily and Jamie Ludovise; Axel Hernandez and Adriana Yanez; Annie and Mike and Michaela Esposito; Diana and Jeff Gordon; Troy Johnson; Nancy Quam-Wickham; Harvey Stromberg; Tim Lopez, Brian Carr, Eddie Martinez, and everyone at CSULB BJJ; Tim Cartmell; Sharon Wikel; Dennis Jelinek; Al Herrera; Kolja Fuchs; Felicia Federico; Leo Hirai; Alessandra Chiricosta; Paul Bowman; Adam Scorgie; Alan Predolin; Igor Neyman; Jason Corliss; Joey Varner; Manolo Macchetta; Angela Morado; Sif Goodale; Eugene and Margaret Carpenter; Paul Klawiter; Robert Subiaga; Sam Sheridan; Sumati Bonsai; and Bryan Kest.

NOTES

1. The full quote reads, "The world we have made as a result of the level of thinking we have done thus far creates problems we cannot solve at the same level at which we created them. . . . We shall require a substantial new manner of thinking if humanity is to survive." In James Christian, *Philosophy: An Introduction to the Art of Wondering,* 9th edition (Stamford: Wadsworth, 2006), 40.

2. Huston Smith, *Why Religion Matters: The Fate of the Human Spirit in an Age of Disbelief* (New York: HarperOne, 2001), 191.

3. Huston Smith, *A Seat at the Table: Huston Smith in Conversation with Native Americans on Religious Freedom* (Berkeley: University of California Press, 2007), 31.

4. Ibid., 12.

5. Ibid., xvi.

6. Susan Jacoby, *Freethinkers: A History of American Secularism* (New York: Metropolitan Books, 2004), 120.

7. Giangiorgio Pasqualotto, *Il Tao della Filosofia: Corrispondenza tra Pensieri d'Oriente e d'Occidente* (Milan, Italy: Nuova Pratica Editrice, 1997 [1989]), 120.

8. Friedrich Nietzsche as quoted in Daniele Bolelli, *On the Warrior's Path: Philosophy, Figthing and Martial Arts Mythology* (Berkeley: Frog, Ltd. 2003).

9. Thomas Paine, *The Age of Reason* (London: G. P. Putnam's Sons, 1896), 31.

10. William Blake quoted in Tom Robbins, *Another Roadside Attraction* (New York: Bantam, 2003 [1972]), 213.

11. Walt Whitman quoted in Jacoby, *Freethinkers*, 214–5.

12. Alan Watts, *The Spirit of Zen: A Way of Life, Work, and Art in the Far East* (New York: Grove Press, 1994 [1936]), 49.

13. John Stevens, *Three Zen Masters: Ikkyū, Hakuin, and Ryōkan* (New York: Kodansha International, 1993), 46.

14. E. A. Burtt, ed., *Teachings of the Compassionate Buddha* (New York: Signet, 1955).

15. Chuang Tzu, *Chuang Tzu: Basic Writings,* trans. Burton Watson (New York: Columbia University Press, 1964), 37.

16. Bruce Lee, *The Tao of Jeet Kune Do* (Santa Clarita: Ohara Publications, 1975).

17. Ibid.

18. Bruce Lee, *The Warrior Within,* trans. John Little (Chicago: Contemporary Books, 1996), 114.

19. Lee, *The Tao of Jeet Kune Do.*

20. Thomas Merton, *The Way of Chuang Tzu* (New York: New Directions Publishing Corporation, 1969), 104.

21. Friedrich Nietzsche, *Thus Spoke Zarathustra* (New York: The Modern Library, 1995 [1885]), 105.

22. Hermann Hesse, *Steppenwolf: A Novel* (New York: Picador, 2002 [1927]), 32.

23. If you think this title sounds familiar, you are probably right. I have been watching a CSI marathon, and Grissom's immortal words are stuck in my head.

24. Rosa Brooks, "The Dark Side of Faith," *Los Angeles Times* (Oct. 1, 2005). Brooks refers to a study by Gregory Paul of Creighton University's Center for the Study of Religion. The study was published in the *Journal of Religion and Society*

under the title "Cross-National Correlations of Quantifiable Societal Health with Popular Religiosity and Secularism in the Prosperous Democracies."

25. Paine, *The Age of Reason*, 196.

26. A. H. Shaw and I. H. Harper, *Life and Work of Susan B. Anthony* vol 4, chapter 16 (1902).

27. Christopher Hitchens, *God Is Not Great: How Religion Poisons Everything* (New York: Twelve Books, 2007), 167.

28. Ibn Warraq, *Why I Am Not a Muslim* (New York: Prometheus Books, 2003 [1995]), 100.

29. Paine, *The Age of Reason,* 48.

30. Helen Dukas and Banesh Hoffman, eds., *Albert Einstein, The Human Side* (Princeton, NJ: Princeton University Press, 1981), 43.

31. Lao Tzu, *The Sayings of Lao Tzu,* trans. Lin Yutang (Taipei: Confucius Publishing Company).

32. Ibid., 245.

33. Lao Tzu, *Tao Te Ching,* trans. Ralph Alan Dale (New York: Barnes & Noble Books, 2005), 9.

34. Huston Smith, *A Seat at the Table,* 148.

35. Lao Tzu, *The Sayings of Lao Tzu,* trans. Lin Yutang, 167.

36. Bruce Bawer, *Stealing Jesus: How Fundamentalism Betrays Christianity* (New York: Three Rivers Press, 1998), 125.

37. Karl Marx, *The Portable Karl Marx* (New York: Penguin Books, 1983), 115.

38. Hitchens, *God Is Not Great,* 247.

39. Ibid., 57.

40. Lewis M. Hopfe, *Religions of the World,* 7th edition, ed. Mark R. Woodward, (Upper Saddle River, NJ: Prentice Hall, 1998), 247.

41. Leviticus 18:19, 15:19–24, 18:29.

42. Matthew 24:34

43. John 18:36.

44. "New bin Laden Video Shows 9/11 Hijacker," *The Independent UK* (Sept. 11, 2007), *www.independent.co.uk*

45. 1 John 2:15–16.

46. Koran, Sura 29:64.

47. Koran, Sura 57:20. See also Sura 3:185.

48. Jacoby, *Freethinkers,* 358.

49. Robert Spencer, "Sharon's Stroke," *Front Page Magazine* (December 19, 2005). *FrontPageMagazine.com.* See also Steven Stalinsky "Dealing in Death," *National Review* (May 24, 2004), online version.

50. Peter C. Myers, *Frederick Douglass: Race and the Rebirth of American Liberalism* (Lawrence: University Press of Kansas, 2008), 63.

51. David Miller, *Custer's Fall: The Native American Side of the Story* (New York: Penguin Group, 1992 [1957]), 131.

52. Kathryn Sparling, trans., *The Way of the Samurai: Yukio Mishima on Hagakure in Modern Life* (New York: Basic Books, 1977), 128.

53. Daniele Bolelli, *On the Warrior's Path: Philosophy, Fighting, and Martial Arts Mythology* (Berkeley, CA: Blue Snake Books, 2008 [2003]), 197.

54. Paul Reps and Nyogen Senzaki, comps., *Zen Flesh, Zen Bones: A Collection of Zen and Pre-Zen Writings* (North Clarendon, VT: Charles E. Tuttle Company, 1998 [1957]), 39.

55. Exodus 32:26–27

56. Numbers 25

57. 1 Kings 18

58. 2 Kings 9: 30–37

59. Jonathan Kirsch, *God Against the Gods: The History of the War Between Monotheism and Polytheism.* (New York: Viking Adult, 2004), 7.

60. Paine, *The Age of Reason,* 208.

61. Gary B. Nash, *Red, White and Black: The Peoples of Early North America,* 4th edition (Upper Saddle River, NJ: Prentice Hall, 2000 [1974]), 66–7.

62. John 14:6. Plenty of other passages reinforce the same idea in the Bible, both in the Old and New Testament. Consider for example Acts 4:12: "Salvation is found in no one else," or John 3:18: "Whoever believes in him is not condemned, but whoever does not believe stands condemned already because he has not believed in the name of God's one and only Son."

63. Matthew 12:30, Luke 11:23. In other parts of the Gospels, Jesus states the exact opposite. In Mark 9:40, Jesus says, ". . . for whoever is not against us is for us." This logical contradiction has allowed both inclusive and exclusive Christians to make a case for Jesus saying what they want him to say. They can conveniently cite the passage that supports their position and ignore the others.

64. Transcript of President Bush's address to a joint session of Congress on Thursday night, September 20, 2001. CNN, *edition.cnn.com/2001/US/09/20/gen.bush.transcript.*

65. Helen Ellerbe, *The Dark Side of Christian History* (Orlando, FL: Morningstar and Lark, 1999), 183.

66. Bruce Bawer, *While Europe Slept: How Radical Islam Is Destroying the West from Within* (New York: Broadway Books, 2006), 16.

67. Charles Kimball, *When Religion Becomes Evil: Five Warning Signs* (San Francisco: HarperOne, 2008), 249.

68. Chris Hedges, *American Fascists: The Christian Right and the War on America* (New York: Free Press, 2006), 109.

69. While we would be hard-pressed to discover alliances between Communism and organized religion, Fascism was often openly allied to the Catholic Church. In the infamous 1929 Lateran Pacts, the Pope encouraged Catholics to support Mussolini's Fascist regime in exchange for Mussolini naming Catholicism the only official religion of the state, giving them a monopoly over issues of birth, death, marriage, and education. Pressured to justify the use of poisonous gas against the Ethiopians, Mussolini painted himself as a paladin of Catholic dogma by saying the Ethiopians deserved it since they practiced a heretical form of Christianity. The Church also supported Fascist movements in Spain, Portugal, and Croatia.

In regards to Nazism, even though the Church was not too enthusiastic about the occasional pagan references in Nazi ideology, it nonetheless ended up legitimizing the Nazi movement. In the 1933 Concordat between the Catholic Church and the Nazi regime, the Vatican agreed to dissolve a Catholic party in Germany in order to avoid competition for Hitler. Furthermore, it never threatened to excommunicate the thousands of SS soldiers who were practicing Catholics. The Church ordered celebrations for Hitler's birthday and he was officially blessed by a German Archbishop—I think you get the picture. Not to be outdone, several Protestant denominations set up their own deals with Hitler. The Holocaust itself would hardly have been possible without centuries of anti-Semitism promoted by Catholics and Protestants alike. Hitler himself declared "I am now as before a Catholic and will always remain so" (from John Toland's *Adolf Hitler,* New York: Anchor Publishing, 1992, 507). What emerges from this picture is that Christian institutions actively supported Fascism and refrained from opposing Nazism.

70. Paine, *The Age of Reason*, 85.

71. Repeated references to this are found in Christopher Hitchens' *God Is Not Great* and Ibn Warraq's *Why I Am Not a Muslim.*

72. Tim Rutten, "Drawn into a Religious Conflict," *Los Angeles Times* (February 4, 2006). Bill Clinton also condemned the cartoons, calling them "outrageous" in Anthony Browne's

"Denmark Faces International Boycott Over Muslim Cartoons," *The Times* (January 31, 2006).

73. Syed Saleem Shahzad, "Losing Faith in Afghanistan," *Asia Times* (March 25, 2006), *www.atimes.com/atimes/South_Asia/HC25Df02.html*.

74. Sanjoy Majumder, "Mood Hardens Against Afghan Convert," BBC News (March 24, 2006), *news.bbc.co.uk/2/hi/south_asia/4841334.stm*.

75. Leviticus 24:16

76. Deuteronomy 13:7–11. Other passages confirming the same penalty are found in Deuteronomy 17:2–7 and Deuteronomy 13:12–16.

77. Deuteronomy 17:11–13

78. Jonathan Kirsch, *God Against the Gods: The History of the War Between Monotheism and Polytheism* (New York: Viking Adult, 2004), 274.

79. Peter Nabokov, *Where the Lightning Strikes: The Lives of American Indian Sacred Places* (New York: Penguin, 2007), 284. See also Smith, *A Seat at the Table,* 30.

80. John Toland, *Adolf Hitler: The Definitive Biography* (New York: Anchor Books, 1992 [1976]), 310.

81. Lao Tzu, *The Sayings of Lao Tzu*, trans. Lin Yutang, 208–9.

82. Matthew 26:52

83. Numbers 31:17

84. Numbers 31:18. Another book of the Bible, Deuteronomy 21:10–14, explains the proper rules for raping a captive. You need to give her a full month to mourn her relatives whom you killed, and only then are you allowed to rape her.

85. Deuteronomy 7:16

86. 1 Samuel 15:2–3

87. Deuteronomy 20:16–17. Jewish soldiers report following this advice to the letter in Deuteronomy 2:34: "And we utterly destroyed every city, the men, and the women, and the little ones. We left none remaining."

88. Hear, for example, the gleeful description of the conquest of Jerusalem during the Crusades left by the chronicler Raymond of Agiles: "Some of our men . . . cut off the heads of their enemies; others shot them with arrows, so that they fell from the towers; others tortured them longer by casting them into flames. Piles of heads, hands and feet were to be seen in the streets of the city. It was necessary to pick one's way over the bodies of men and horses. But these were small matters compared to what happened at the temple of Solomon . . . What happened there? If I tell the truth, it will exceed your

powers of belief. So let it suffice to say this much at least, that in the temple and portico of Solomon, men rode in blood up to their knees and the bridle reins. Indeed, it was a just and splendid judgment of God that this place should be filled with the blood of unbelievers, when it had suffered so long from their blasphemies. Now that the city was taken it was worth all our previous labors and hardships to see the devotion of the pilgrims at the Holy Sepulcher. How they rejoiced and exulted and sang the ninth chant to the Lord." (Kimball, *When Religion Becomes Evil,* 175–6).

89. In this regard, consider the following quote: "The object of colonization, one colonial promoter wrote in 1584, was 'enlarging the glorious Gospel of Christ, and leading the infinite multitudes of these simple people that are in error into the right and perfect way of salvation.' Although these are the words of the English imperialist Richard Hakluyt, they could as easily have come from the Spanish padres Kino or Serra or the Jesuit missionaries at Kahnawake" [John Mack Faragher, et al., *Out of Many: A History of the American People,* 3rd edition (Upper Saddle River, NJ: Prentice Hall, 2000 [1994], 111)].

Similarly, the Puritan minister Cotton Mather viewed America as a promised land, and said Indians were "devils in our way" and as such they needed to be eliminated (Nabokov, *Where the Lightning Strikes,* 12). Mather also declared that the Devil "generally resembles an Indian." The Puritans, in fact, believed Satan ruled the wilderness surrounding their settlements, and God had called them to defeat Satan in order to create a promised land.

Not to be outdone, the Anglican Robert Gray used the Old Testament account of the genocidal war waged by the Jewish tribes against the inhabitants of Canaan to justify the conquest of the Indians: "Because of their godless ignorance and blasphemous idolatry they are worse than those beasts which are of the most wild and savage nature." [John D. Loftin, *The Big Picture: A Short World History of Religions* (Jefferson, NC: McFarland and Company, 2000)].

For a discussion of how the conquest of the Americas was justified through Christianity, see Smith, *A Seat at the Table*, 171.

90. Anthony Browne, "Muslim Radical Confesses to Van Gogh Killing in Court Tirade," *The Times* (London) (July 12, 2005), online.

A slightly different translation of Bouyeri's declaration is also found in Bruce Bawer's *While Europe Slept: How Radical Islam Is Destroying the West from Within*, 226.

91. See Sura 8:61: "If your enemy inclines toward peace then you too should seek peace and put your trust in God." See also Sura 50:45: "We well know what the infidels say: but you are not to compel them." See also Sura 43:88–89: "And [Muhammad says,] 'O Lord, these are people who do not believe'. Bear with them and wish them 'Peace.' In the end they shall know their folly." And Sura 2:256: "There is no compulsion in religion."

92. Sura 47:4

93. Jeremiah 48:10

94. Sura 9:39

95. Lao Tzu, *The Sayings of Lao Tzu,* trans. Lin Yutang, 239.

96. Hedges, *American Fascists,* 14.

97. Kevin Phillips, *American Theocracy: The Peril and Politics of Radical Religion, Oil, and Borrowed Money in the 21st Century* (New York: Viking Penguin, 2006), 203, 375. See also Hedges, *American Fascists,* 46.

98. Warraq, *Why I Am Not a Muslim,* 135.

99. Genesis 1:28

100. Ron Wolf, "God, James Watt, and the Public Land." *Audubon* 83 (3):65, 1981.

101. Sam Harris, *The End of Faith: Religion, Terror, and the Future of Reason* (New York: W.W. Norton & Company, 2004), 174.

102. Lao Tzu, *The Sayings of Lao Tzu,* trans. Lin Yutang, 29.

103. Nabokov, *Where the Lightning Strikes.*

104. Ibid.

105. John Stevens, trans., *Wild Ways: Zen Poems of Ikkyū* (Buffalo NY: White Pine Press, 2007).

106. William Blake, *The Poems of William Blake* (Whitefish, MT: Kessinger Publishing, 2006), 90.

107. Rex Weyler, *Blood of the Land: The Government and Corporate War Against First Nations* (Philadelphia: New Society Publishers, 1992), 28.

108. Peter Matthiessen, *The Snow Leopard* (New York: Penguin Books, 1996 [1978]), 35.

109. Alan Watts, *Nature, Man and Woman* (New York: Vintage Books, 1991 [1958]), 26.

110. Adriano Gaspani, *La Civilta' dei Camuni: Cielo, Luna, Stelle nell' Antica Valcamonica* (Aosta, Italy: Keltia Editrice, 2001), 31.

111. Genesis 3:17–18

112. Phillips, *American Theocracy,* 3.

113. Weyler, *Blood of the Land,* 55.

114. See the concluding chapters of Jared Diamond, *Collapse: How Societies Choose to Fail or Succeed* (New York: Penguin, 2005).

115. Ibid., passim. Interestingly, the Bush administration, which was very much tied to the oil industry, decided to simply ignore the report.

116. Here is a perfect example of the suicidal economic creed that we urgently need to free ourselves from, courtesy of logging baron and former president of Louisiana-Pacific Harry Merlo: "You know it always annoys me to leave anything on the ground when we log our own land. There shouldn't be anything left on the ground. We need everything that's out there. . . . We log to infinity. Because it's out there, it's ours and we need it all, now." Judi Bari, *Timber Wars* (Monroe ME: Common Courage Press, 1994), 21.

117. Vine Deloria Jr., *God Is Red: A Native View of Religion* (Golden, CO: Fulcrum Publishing, 2003 [1973]), 288.

118. Genesis 1:28

119. Despite the ideal mentioned here, Buddhism does not have a spotless record when it comes to environmental ethics. Movement in a more pro-environmentalist direction, however, is underway. For example, an article in the January 2010 issue of the *Shambala Sun* about the 17th Karmapa, one of the highest authorities on Tibetan Buddhism, clarifies how a new generation of Buddhists is embracing environmental issues as a key part of their message.

120. Revelation 11:18

121. 2 Corinthians 5:6–8

122. Ibid., 155–156.

123. René Descartes, *Discourse on Method and Meditations on First Philosophy* (BN Publishing, 2008 [1637]), 31.

124. Friedrich Nietzsche, *The Gay Science,* trans. Walter Kaufmann (New York: Vintage Books, 1974 [1887]), 322.

125. Henry David Thoreau, *Walden* (Cambridge, MA: The Riverside Press, 1960 [1854]), 51, 74.

126. Friedrich Nietzsche, *Basic Writings of Nietzsche,* trans. Walter Kaufmann (New York: Modern Library, 1992 [Ecce Homo 1908]), 695–6.

127. Nils Johan Ringdal, *Love for Sale: A World History of Prostitution* (New York: Grove Press, 2004).

128. Eva Wong, *The Shambhala Guide to Taoism* (Boston: Shambhala Publications, 1997), and Geoffrey Parrinder, *Sex in World Religions* (New York: Oxford University Press, 1980).

129. The god Shiva and his wife Parvati, for example, are often portrayed engaged in wild, passionate lovemaking. Not to be outdone, in the Puranas, Krishna seduces thousands of women, leads them into the forest, and clones his own body multiple times in order to have sex with all of them at the same time. See Parrinder, *Sex in World Religions.*

130. See Ringdal, *Love for Sale* and Parrinder, *Sex in World Religions*.

131. John Stevens, *Lust for Enlightenment: Buddhism and Sex* (Boston: Shambhala Publications, 1990), 23. This puritan streak within Buddhism attributes to Buddha the following quote, "The one thing that enslaves a man above all else is a woman . . . Stay away from them at all costs."

132. Parrinder, *Sex in World Religions*, 41.

133. Stevens, *Lust for Enlightenment*, 50.

134. Deuteronomy 22:22

135. Leviticus 20:13

136. Deuteronomy 21:11–14

137. Genesis 19:30–38

138. Judges 19:22–30

139. 2 Samuel 13:1–22

140. 2 Samuel 16:21–22

141. This lovely episode is narrated in Ezekiel 23:1–49. Several books pick up similar themes. In particular, this is among the main subjects in the books of Jeremiah and Ezekiel.

142. See Sura 4:16 in regards to homosexuality and Sura 24:2 for adultery. However, perhaps out of a desire to appear as tough as ancient Judaism, even in the present day, some Muslim countries ignore the Koran and impose stoning as punishment for adultery.

143. See Sura 4:34 for the Koran's approval of wife-beating. In regards to honor killings, family members who kill female relatives for their "scandalous" behavior are often not charged at all or, if convicted, are given very light sentences because their motive for murder was "honorable." See Bruce Bawer, *While Europe Slept: How Radical Islam Is Destroying the West from Within*, 24.

144. Sura 78:31–33 as quoted in Warraq, *Why I Am Not a Muslim*, 307.

145. See Sura 37, 44, 52, 55, and 56.

146. Saint Augustine, one of the most important theologians in Christianity, had a field day with this idea. In his work *On Concupiscence* (Book I, Chapter 13), he writes that the virgin birth is the way in which Jesus teaches "that every one who is born of sexual intercourse is in fact sinful flesh, since that alone which was not born of such intercourse was not sinful flesh."

147. Matthew 5:27–30

148. One piece of evidence indicating Jesus is probably playing an elaborate joke is in Matthew 5:21–27. Jesus states that anyone hurling hurtful insults may end up in hell just as a murderer would. But in Matthew 23:17, Jesus freely insults some of his opponents, which means that either he is a hypocrite or he was joking in the earlier passage.

149. Kirsch, *God Against the Gods*.

150. 1 Corinthians 7:29–31

151. David Stannard, *American Holocaust: The Conquest of the New World* (New York: Oxford University Press, 1992), 156. On this same page, Stannard draws the logical conclusion that "such fanatically aggressive opposition to sex can only occur among people who are fanatically obsessed *with* sex."

152. For the masochists among you, here are some quotes from Augustine spelling out his views:

"Then follows the connexion of fellowship in children, which is the one alone worthy fruit. . . of the sexual intercourse" (*On Marriage, Section 1*).

"Intercourse of marriage for the sake of begetting hath not fault; but for the satisfying of lust, but yet with husband or wife, by reason of the faith of the bed, it hath venial fault: but adultery or fornication hath deadly fault, and, through this, continence from all intercourse is indeed better even than the intercourse of marriage itself, which takes place for the sake of begetting" (*On Marriage, Section 6*).

"For necessary sexual intercourse for begetting is free from blame, and itself is alone worthy of marriage. But that which goes beyond this necessity, no longer follows reason, but lust" (*On Marriage, Section 11*).

Curiously enough, however, Augustine was instrumental in keeping legalized brothels in the Western world until the 1500s, since he argued that without access to prostitutes sinful men would try to seduce good Christian women. Turning necessity into a virtue, quite a few Popes taxed prostitutes and used part of the money to build Saint Peter's Cathedral. For an extended discussion of this, see Ringdal, *Love for Sale*.

153. This fanatical obsession reached at times some very funny and telling points. In Victorian England, for example, some proper British Christians would wrap the legs of their tables with cloth. Why? Because they were legs, and if they were bare they may give you ideas . . . I took a break to check out the legs of my table, and I regret to inform you that the verdict is: no, they don't do it for me.

154. Ringdal, *Love for Sale,* 158.

155. Karen Armstrong, *The Battle for God* (New York: Ballantine Books, 2000), 240.

156. Eric Schlosser, *Reefer Madness: Sex, Drugs, and Cheap Labor in the American Black Market* (New York: Houghton Mifflin, 2003), 117.

157. Whitman defined himself in one of his poems as "liberal and lusty as Nature," so it's little surprise that Comstock hated his

guts. See Jacoby's *Freethinkers* and Schlosser's *Reefer Madness* for some great narratives of Comstock's career.

158. The United States government's Commission on Pornography and Obscenity, created in 1968, argued that all obscenity laws should be eliminated since after much research it had found no evidence that sexually explicit materials caused criminal behavior. Actually, what the Commission discovered was that sex offenders were less likely to have used porn than the average man and more likely to have been raised in conservative households (Schlosser, *Reefer Madness*).

159. Consider, for example, how religious authorities have banned something as innocent as dancing. In a campaign against the tango, the Vatican thundered against "this animal dance of irresponsible languor and high-breathing passion," with the vicar of Rome in 1914 writing, "Whoever persists in dancing the tango commits a sin!"

In the early 1900s, women performing dances such as the turkey trot and bunny hug in the United States could be fined and even jailed. The Charleston was accused of being partially responsible for the "moral downfall" of the United States. And even the introduction of something as rigid and composed as the waltz induced *The Times* of London to fire off an indignant editorial that read, "So long as this obscene display was confined to prostitutes and adulteresses, we did not think it deserving of notice; but now that it is attempted to be forced on the respectable classes of society . . . we feel it a duty to warn every parent against exposing his daughter to so fatal a contagion" *Los Angeles Times* (October 17, 2006).

160. Lisa McGirr, *Suburban Warriors: The Origins of the New American Right* (Princeton, NJ: Princeton University Press, 2001), 31.

161. For a comprehensive discussion of the Mann Act, see David J. Langum, *Crossing Over the Line: Legislating Morality and the Mann Act* (Chicago: The University of Chicago Press, 1994).

162. See Ringdal, *Love for Sale* in passim.

163. Good books in the English language about Ikkyū are hard to come by. Among them are:
John Stevens, *Three Zen Masters: Ikkyū, Hakuin, and Ryōkan* (New York: Kodansha International, 1993).
John Stevens, trans., *Wild Ways: Zen Poems of Ikkyū* (Buffalo, NY: White Pine Press, 2007).
Stephen Berg, *Crow With No Mouth* (Port Townsend, WA: Copper Canyon Press, 2000).
Sonja Arntzen, *Ikkyū and the Crazy Cloud Anthology* (Tokyo: University of Tokyo Press, 1987).
For the definitive biography of Ikkyū's life, see Jon Carter Covell and Sobin Yamada, *Unraveling Zen's Red Thread: Ikkyū's Controversial Way* (Elizabeth, NJ: HollyM International, 1980).

164. Stevens, *Lust for Enlightenment,* 98. Interestingly enough, Jesus, much like Ikkyū, positively compared prostitutes to priests.

165. Stevens, *Wild Ways.*

166. This is my own reworking of a translation by Berg, *Crow With No Mouth*, 54.

167. Stevens, *Lust for Enlightenment*, 103. In this same book, Stevens tells stories indicating that as puritanical as Buddhism could sometimes be, it also made room for wild, unorthodox people like Ikkyū. For example, the crazy Tibetan saint Drukpa Kunley was renowned for his sexual adventures. Apparently, his standard question wherever he went was, "Where can I find the best Tibetan beer and the prettiest women?" (75). Women flocked to him, sometimes making love with him even in public places. And legend has it some of them achieved enlightenment while having sex with him.

    Another character that would have gotten along with Ikkyū was Ch'an master Tao-chi. When the emperor heard of his reputation as a brilliant master, he sent for him—but no one could find him. After the imperial delegation departed, Tao-chi returned to his monastery, telling his friends that he had been "Drinking in the wine shops and sleeping in the brothels—that is where I practice best, not in the palace" (92).

168. William Blake, *Libri Profetici* (Milano, Italy: Tascabili Bompiani, 1986 [1793]), 19.

169. Song of Songs (a.k.a. Song of Solomon) 1:6

170. Song of Songs 8:12

171. Song of Songs 5:4–5

172. Song of Songs 1:13

173. Song of Songs 4:5

174. Song of Songs 2:3

175. Nietzsche, trans. Kaufmann, *Basic Writings of Nietzsche*, 714.

176. See Riane Eisler, *The Chalice and the Blade: Our History, Our Future* (New York: HarperOne, 1988). Even though I enjoy the ideals behind these conclusions, I just don't see enough historical evidence to support them.

177. Ringdal's *Love for Sale* examines this theme masterfully.

178. Genesis 3:16

179. Ecclesiasticus 25:24. The book of Ecclesiasticus is accepted as part of the biblical canon by Jews, Catholics, and the Eastern Orthodox, but not by Protestant denominations.

180. Arvind Sharma, ed. *Women in World Religions* (Albany: State University of New York Press, 1987), 221.

181. The Song of Songs is a notable exception to this pattern.

182. Exodus 20:17

183. This story is told in various parts of 2 Samuel, in particular 12:11–12, 16:21, and 20:3.

184. Leviticus 12:1–5

185. Deuteronomy 22:21

186. 1 Corinthians 11:3 spells out a hierarchical vision of the world with God at the top, males next, and females at the bottom of the pyramid.

   1 Corinthians 11:7–9 reads, "For a man indeed ought not to cover his head, forasmuch as he is the image and glory of God: but the woman is the glory of the man. For the man is not of the woman: but the woman of the man. Neither was the man created for the woman; but the woman for the man."

   1 Corinthians 14:34–5 adds, "Let women keep silent in the churches . . . and if they wish to learn anything, let them ask their husbands at home: for it is shameful for a woman to speak in the church."

   And to round things up, Ephesians 5:22–25 orders, "Wives, submit yourself unto your own husbands, as unto the Lord. For the husband is the head of the wife, even as Christ is the head of the church . . . Therefore as the church is subject unto Christ, so let the wives be to their own in every thing. Husbands, love your wives, even as Christ also loved the church, and gave himself for it."

   A lonely exception, instead, is provided by Galatians

3:28, "There is neither Jew nor Greek, slave nor free, male nor female, for you are all one in Christ Jesus," which openly attacks ethnocentrism, classism, and sexism in an effort to establish the equality of all human beings in front of God. Had Saint Paul actually stuck with this idea, the history of Christianity may have turned very different.

187. Julia Hughes Jones, *The Secret History of Weeds: What Women Need to Know About Their History* (Booklocker.com, Inc., 2009).

188. Sharma, *Women in World Religions*, 24.

189. June Sochen, *Herstory: A Woman's View of American History* (New York: Alfred Publishing, 1974), 19.

190. Karen Armstrong, *A History of God: The 4000-Year Quest of Judaism, Christianity and Islam* (New York: Ballantine Books, 1993), 124.

191. Saint Thomas Aquinas: "Woman was created to be man's helpmate, but her unique role is in conception . . . since for other purposes men would be better assisted by other men" (Sochen, *Herstory*, 19).

The Abbot of the Premonstratensian Order, Conrad of Marchtal: "We . . . , recognizing that the wickedness of women is greater than all the other wickedness of the world, and that there is no anger like that of women, and that the poison of asps and dragons is more curable and less dangerous to men than the familiarity of women, have unanimously decreed for the safety of our souls, no less than for that of our bodies and goods, that we will on no account receive any more sisters to the increase of our perdition, but will avoid them like poisonous animals" [Karen Anderson, *Chain Her by One Foot: The Subjugation of Native Women in Seventeenth-Century New France* (New York: Routledge, 1993), 58].

Saint Augustine: "What can be worse than a house where the woman has the mastery over the man? But that house is rightly ordered where the man commands and the woman obeys" (*On John, Tractate 2, Section 14*).

One of the early Church Fathers, Tertullian: "Do you not know that you are each an Eve? The sentence of God on this sex of yours lives in this age: the guilt must of necessity live too. You are the devil's gateway; you are the unsealer of that forbidden tree, you are the first deserter of the divine law; you are she who persuaded him whom the devil was not valiant enough to attack. You so carelessly destroyed man, God's image. On account of your desert, even the Son of God had to die" (Armstrong, *A History of God,* 124).

Again Saint Augustine, who, puzzled by the fact that God even bothered to create women, mused, "If it was good company and conversation that Adam needed, it would have been much better arranged to have two men together as friends, not a man and a woman" (Ibid.).

And to wrap things up, the always sweet and compassionate Martin Luther: "Even though they grow weary and wear themselves out with child-bearing, it does not matter; let them go on bearing children till they die, that is what they are there for" (Works 20.84).

192. Desmond Butler, "U.S. Astonished by Saudi Rape Sentence," *Los Angeles Times* (November 20, 2007).

193. Here are few precious examples of post-Koranic misogyny among leading figures within the history of Islam, as quoted in Ibn Warraq, *Why I Am Not a Muslim,* 299–300:

Omar, the second Caliph declared, "Prevent the women from learning to write! Say no to their capricious ways." Ali, the fourth caliph said, "The entire woman is an evil and what is worse is that it is a necessary evil! You should never ask a woman her advice because her advice is worthless. Hide them so that they cannot see other men! . . . Do not spend too much time in their company for they will lead you to your downfall!" The renowned Muslim philosopher Al-Ghazali had this to say about women, "She should stay at home and get on with her spinning, she should not go out often, she must not be well-informed . . . she should take care of her husband and respect him in his presence and his absence and seek to satisfy him in everything. . . She should be clean and ready to satisfy her husband's sexual needs at any moment."

194. Sura 4:11

195. Sura 2:228

196. Sura 2:282

197. Sura 4:98

198. Sura 4:15

199. Sura 37:22–23

200. Sura 4:34

201. To those who argued that widows may starve without a provider if they were not allowed to remarry, the neo-Confucian Ch'eng I responded by saying ". . . to starve to death is a very small matter. To lose one's integrity, however, is a very serious matter" (Sharma, *Women in World Religions*, 155–6).

202. As one Buddhist wrote, "Woman is not worthy even of being forgotten" [Jon Covell and Yamada Sobin, *Zen at Daitoku-Ji* (Tokyo: Kodansha International Ltd., 1974), 185].

203. Zen master Dogen is an example of this more progressive brand of Buddhism, since he argued that any man who couldn't accept a woman as his teacher had not really understood much about Buddhism (see Sharma, *Women in World Religions,* 126).

204. The misogynist Buddhist team attributes this highly questionable sentence to Buddha, "The one thing that enslaves a man above all else is a woman . . . Stay away from them at all costs" (Stevens, *Lust for Enlightenment,* 23).

205. It is not a coincidence that Elizabeth Stanton, one of the early leaders of the women's rights movement in the 1800s, identified organized religion as one of the main obstacles to change (Jacoby, *Freethinkers*).

206. For example, the 17th Karmapa, one of the leading figures of Tibetan Buddhism, argues that those Buddhists who promoted patriarchy over the centuries misunderstood Buddha's teachings. Whereas many Buddhists don't like to discuss this dark stain on their historical record, the 17th Karmapa is very outspoken about the need to eliminate patriarchy from Asian culture. See an interview with him in the January 2010 issue of *Shambala Sun*.

Another famous example is offered by the Indian reformer Gandhi, who insisted on including women's rights as part of the Indian constitution (Sharma, *Women in World Religions*, 95).

207. I am always amazed by ultraconservative women attacking the liberal politics and religious interpretations that are responsible for giving them rights in the first place. The Sarah Palins of the world, in fact, would never have had the opportunities they enjoy if not for those very ideologies that they despise.

208. Consider a resolution adopted in 1984 by the Southern Baptist Convention, in which they reasserted their belief in female submission to male authority (Phillips, *American Theocracy*, 241).

209. John Micklethwait and Adrian Wooldridge, *The Right Nation: Conservative Power in America* (New York: Penguin, 2004), 122.

210. Kimball, *When Religion Becomes Evil*, 219.

211. The title of this section and much of its vision owes inspiration to a book written by my father. If you can read Italian, check it out. Franco Bolelli, *Con Il Cuore e Con Le Palle* (Garzanti Libri: Milano, 2005).

212. Examples of this neo-patriarchy can be seen everywhere. The worldview advocated by evangelical leaders like Tim LaHaye and James Dobson, or organizations like Promise Keepers, are perfect examples.

213. For anyone who may be wondering, the lady was Sharon Wikel, an 8th degree black belt in Tsoi Li Ho Fut Hung (a.k.a. San Soo).

214. Deuteronomy 26:10, Leviticus 19:910

215. Matthew 6:24

216. Matthew 6:19–21

217. Luke 6:24

218. 1 Timothy 6:7–10

219. Matthew 19:23–24

220. Matthew 6:24–34 and Luke 12: 24–27

221. Lao Tzu, *The Sayings of Lao Tzu,* trans. Lin Yutang, 227.

222. Ibid., 176.

223. Ibid., poems 53 and 75.

224. Ibid., 262.

225. Stevens, *Three Zen Masters,* 120.

226. Paul Reps and Nyogen Senzaki, *Zen Flesh, Zen Bones: A Collection of Zen and Pre-Zen Writings* (Boston: Tuttle Publishing, 1998 [1957]), 27.

227. Guy Davenport, trans., *Herakleitos & Diogenes* (Bolinas, CA: Grey Fox Press, 1976), fragment 97 of Diogenes.

228. Philip Wheelwright, trans., *Heraclitus* (Oxford, UK: Oxford University Press, 1999 [1959]), fragment 96.

229. Thoreau, *Walden,* 6, 10.

230. As the missionaries preached to the Lakota Indians, "Believe that property and wealth are signs of divine approval." [Richard Erdoes and Mary Crow Dog, *Lakota Woman* (New York: Harper Perennial, 1991), 31].

231. David Stannard, *American Holocaust* (New York: Oxford University Press, 1992), 233.

232. Hedges, *American Fascists,* 166.

233. McGirr, *Suburban Warriors*, 106.

234. Weyler, *Blood of the Land*, 64.

235. Loftin, *The Big Picture*, 247.

236. See Phillips' *American Theocracy* for a good exploration of this topic.

237. In "Einstein's Letter: God and Superstition—What He Wrote," *The Guardian*, May 12, 2008. Translated from the German by Joan Stambaugh.

238. Matthew 10:5–6

239. Matthew 15:22–28

240. Kirsch, *God Against the Gods*.

241. Romans 13:1–4

242. Kirsch, *God Against the Gods*, 172.

243. Charles T. Wood, *Joan of Arc and Richard III: Sex, Saints, and Government in the Middle Ages* (Oxford: Oxford University Press, 1991), 146.

244. Kirsch, *God Against the Gods*, 282.

245. Lewis Mumford, *The Culture of Cities* (Mariner Books, 1970 [1938]), 273.

246. On the concept of a nation Lewis Mumford writes, "a term inherently so vague and so contradictory that it must always be taken in a mystic sense, as meaning whatever the ruling classes hold it convenient to mean at the moment" (Mumford, *The Culture of Cities*, 349). Similarly, historian Howard Zinn writes, "Nations are not communities and never have been" [Howard Zinn, *A People's History of the United States: 1492– Present* (New York: Harper Perennial, 2003), 10]. And in a beautiful quote (that, however, I'm beginning to hate since I can't find the source despite much searching . . .) George Bernard Shaw had this to say, "Patriotism is your conviction that this country is superior to all others because you were born in it."

247. Just to give you an idea of how wild this man was, when Alexander the Great, impressed by the philosopher's reputation, accosted Diogenes while he was sunbathing and offered to give him anything he wished, Diogenes's only request was for Alexander to move out of the way so that his shadow would stop blocking the sun. [Luis E. Navia, *Diogenes the Cynic: The War Against the World* (New York: Humanity Books, 2005)].

248. Jacoby, *Freethinkers*.

249. Armstrong, *A History of God*, 277.

250. Ecclesiastes 8:15

251. Ecclesiastes 7:3-4

252. Nietzsche, *Thus Spoke Zarathustra*, 210.

253. Even though she died in 2011, this entire paragraph is in the present tense because I can't quite bring myself to writing about my wife using the past tense.

254. Nietzsche, trans. Kaufmann, *Basic Writings of Nietzsche,* 714.

255. Tom Robbins, *Wild Ducks Flying Backwards* (New York: Bantam, 2006), 184.

256. Matthiessen, *The Snow Leopard*, 35.

257. Stevens, *Three Zen Masters,* 33–34.

258. Tom Robbins, *Wild Ducks Flying Backwards,* 186.

259. Tom Robbins, *Fierce Invalids Home from Hot Climates,* 44.

260. Joe Starita, *The Dull Knifes of Pine Ridge: A Lakota Odyssey* (Berkley Books, 1996), 107.

261. Linda Richards, *January Magazine* Interview of Tom Robbins (June, 2000), *januarymagazine.com/profiles/robbins.html.*

262. Nietzsche, *Thus Spoke Zarathustra*, 40–41.

263. Henry David Thoreau, *Uncommon Learning: Thoreau on Education* (New York: Mariner Books, 1999 [1840]), 53.

264. Black Elk says, "people shall be made to feel jolly and happy first, so that it may be easier for the power to come to them" [John Neihardt, *Black Elk Speaks: Being the Life Story of a Holy Man of the Oglala Sioux* (Lincoln, NE: University of Nebraska Press, 1979 [1932]). 188]. Similarly, Hakuin insisted that laughter was the key to Zen. In his mind, the deeper one's enlightenment is, the deeper the laughter (Stevens, *Three Zen Masters*, 79).

265. Friedrich Nietzsche, *Thus Spoke Zarathustra*, 40–41.

266. John 20:29. New International Version.

267. Genesis 22; Koran 37:101–113

268. Harris, *The End of Faith*, 72.

269. "In God's Name: A Special Report on Religion and Public Life," *The Economist.* (November 3, 2007), 20.

270. Ibid.

271. Jacoby, *Freethinkers*, 360.

272. Kimball, *When Religion Becomes Evil*, 29.

273. Hitchens, *God Is Not Great*, 63.

274. Ibid.

275. James Reichley, *Faith in Politics* (Washington, DC: Brookings Institution Press, 2002), 44.

276. Thomas Jefferson, *The Portable Thomas Jefferson* (New York: Penguin Books, 1977), 425. This quote comes from a letter Jefferson wrote to his nephew in 1787.

277. Neihardt, *Black Elk Speaks.*

278. Armstrong, *A History of God,* 205.

279. Lao Tzu, *Tao Te Ching,* trans. Ralph Alan Dale.

280. Burton Watson, trans., *Chuang Tzu: Basic Writings* (New York: Columbia University Press, 1964), 140.

281. Thoreau, *Uncommon Learning,* 3.

282. Kirsch, *God Against the Gods,* 301.

283. Lao Tzu, *The Sayings of Lao Tzu,* trans. Lin Yutang.

284. William Shakespeare, "Hamlet" (New York: Washington Square Press, 2003), 67.

285. Paine, *The Age of Reason,* 21.

286. Lao Tzu, *The Sayings of Lao Tzu,* trans. Lin Yutang, 239.

287. Diamond, *Collapse*, 373.

288. Most of the more than 600 laws listed in the Old Testament were abandoned just a few generations later. See Leviticus to find many examples of such laws.

289. Thoreau, *Walden*, 10.

290. Ibid., 77.

291. Lao Tzu, *The Sayings of Lao Tzu*, trans. Lin Yutang, 86.

292. Blake, *Libri Profetici*, 38.

293. Lao Tzu, *Tao Te Ching*, trans. Robert G. Henricks (New York: Modern Library, 1993), 101.

294. Brooks, "The Dark Side of Faith," *Los Angeles Times*. Brooks quotes a study by Creighton University's Center for the Study of Religion by Gregory Paul originally published in the *Journal of Religion and Society*. The title of the original report is "Cross-National Correlations of Quantifiable Societal Health with Popular Religiosity and Secularism in the Prosperous Democracies."

295. Alice Calaprice, ed., *The Expanded Quotable Einstein* (Princeton, NJ: Princeton University Press, 2000), 216.

296. Richards, *January Magazine* Interview of Tom Robbins.

297. Lao Tzu, *The Sayings of Lao Tzu,* trans. Lin Yutang, 255.

298. Gregory Bateson, *Steps to an Ecology of Mind: Collected Essays in Anthropology, Psychiatry, Evolution, and Epistemology* (Chicago: University of Chicago Press, 2000).

299. Franco Bolelli, *Cartesio Non Balla: Definitiva Superiorita' della Cultura Pop (Quella Piu' Avanzata)* (Milano, Italy: Garzanti Libri, 2007), 54.

300. Friedrich Nietzsche, *Ecce Homo: How One Becomes What Is,* trans. Duncan Large (New York: Oxford University Press, 2007 [1888]), 103.

301. Nietzsche, *The Gay Science,* 45.

302. Nabokov, *Where the Lightning Strikes,* 15.

ABOUT THE AUTHOR

 Daniele Bolelli (M.A.) is a writer, a college professor and a martial artist. He is the author of *On the Warrior's Path*, which has quickly become one of the modern cult books on the philosophy of martial arts, and of *50 Things You Are Not Supposed to Know: Religion*. He teaches at many top universities in Southern California and has competed professionally in Mixed Martial Arts. He is also the host of *The Drunken Taoist Podcast*. Visit him online at *www.danielebolelli.com*.